Growth

By **JOHN R. CLARK**

CHARLOTTE W. JUNGE

HAROLD E. MOSER

ILLUSTRATED BY

JANET SMALLEY

in Arithmetic

GRADE THREE

World Book Company

YONKERS · ON · HUDSON · NEW YORK

Contents

Using arithmetic

The children in Miss Bell's class have been talking about ways to use arithmetic. Look at the picture. Read what they have been saying.

The children told Miss Bell other ways they use arithmetic. They said they use it most often when they tell time and when they use money.

Tom said, "I think we can learn more about telling time and using money."

"That's a good idea, Tom," said Miss Bell. "We'll start our arithmetic by studying about clocks and coins."

1. Do you use arithmetic in the ways Miss Bell's class uses it?

2. In what other ways have you used arithmetic today?

3. Do you often need to tell time? Tell when.

4. What time is it by the clock in Miss Bell's room?

5. Do you often need to use coins? Tell when.

6. On pages 2 to 4 are some lessons on telling time and using money. Miss Bell's children can answer all the questions. Can you?

Telling time

1. Ding-a-ling goes Billy's alarm clock. At what time does Billy get up? At what time do you get up?

2. At 7 o'clock the short hand points to _?_; the long hand points to _?_.

3. What time does each of the clocks below say?

4. Which clock shows about what time Billy's school starts in the morning? about when Billy goes home to lunch? when his school closes in the afternoon? when he eats his supper?

5. To what number does the short hand point at 10 o'clock? 5 o'clock? 6 o'clock? 11 o'clock? 4 o'clock? 2 o'clock?

6. To what number does the long hand point at each hour in Example 5?

7. What time does each of these toy clocks say?

2

Ann said, "The long hand makes me think of a clown. At 1, 2, 3, 4, 5, 6, 7, 8, 9, 10, 11, 12 o'clock he stands up straight.

"At half past any hour he stands on his head.

"At quarter of or quarter past any hour he lies down."

1. Look at the toy clocks at the bottom of page 2. Does Ann's rule for the long hand work?

2. Make a toy clock. Does Ann's rule work when it says:
● 1 o'clock, 2 o'clock, and so on up to 12 o'clock?
● Half past 1, half past 2, and so on up to half past 12?
● 15 minutes past 1, 15 minutes past 2, and so on up to 15 minutes past 12? (Another way of saying "15 minutes past 12" is "quarter past 12.")
● 15 minutes of 1, 15 minutes of 2, and so on up to 15 minutes of 12? ("15 minutes of 12" is the same as "quarter of 12.")

3. Show how the clock looks and tell the time every 5 minutes from 10 o'clock until 11 o'clock.

4. At 8 o'clock the long hand points to _?_. What time will it be the next time the long hand points to 12?

5. How long does it take the long hand to go from 12 around to 12?

6. Use the alarm clock on page 2 to prove that there are 60 minutes in an hour. Count the minute marks by 5's.

7. From 7 o'clock until 8 o'clock is how many minutes?

8. Tell things you might do at 8 A.M.; at 7 P.M.

LEARN THIS

12 o'clock in the daytime is *noon*.
6 A.M. is 6 o'clock in the *morning*.
6 P.M. is 6 o'clock in the *evening*.
There are 60 minutes in an hour.

1. Tell some things you could buy if you had a cent; a nickel; a dime; a quarter.

CENT	NICKEL	DIME	QUARTER
1¢	5¢	10¢	25¢

2. A 5-cent piece is called a __?__ .

3. A 10-cent piece is called a __?__ .

4. A 25-cent piece is called a __?__ .

5. The sign ¢ means __?__ ; 8¢ means __?__ cents.

Tell the missing numbers. Be sure to make fair trades.

6. John traded a nickel for __?__ cents.

7. He traded a dime for __?__ cents.

8. He traded a dime for __?__ nickels.

9. He traded a quarter for __?__ cents.

10. He traded a quarter for __?__ nickels.

11. He traded a quarter for 2 dimes and __?__ cents.

12. Can you tell 6 other ways to change a quarter?

13. Read these prices: 8¢, 3¢, 10¢, 15¢, 20¢, 25¢.

14. What coins could you give to pay for a 23-cent toy? a 17-cent ball? a 6-cent candy bar? a 25-cent ticket?

15. Mary has two dimes and a nickel. Does she have enough money to buy a ball that costs a quarter?

Discoveries about numbers to 10

1. Tom had 6 pebbles. He used them to discover everything he could about the number 6. Look at his paper. What discoveries did he make?

Tom Barton

● ● ● ● ●   ●   ● ● ● ●   ● ●

5 and 1 are 6	4 and 2 are 6
1 and 5 are 6	2 and 4 are 6
1 from 6 is 5	2 from 6 is 4
5 from 6 is 1	4 from 6 is 2

● ● ●   ● ● ●   ● ●   ● ●   ● ●

3 and 3 are 6	3 twos are 6
3 from 6 is 3	
2 threes are 6	

2. Use 8 pebbles to discover what you can about the number 8. Write down what you discover. Draw dot pictures of your discoveries.

3. In the same way make all the discoveries you can about the number 7; the number 9; the number 10.

4. 6 and 1 are as many as 5 and ___?___.

5. 4 and 4 are as many as 5 and ___?___.

6. Tell all the pairs of numbers that make:

      5   6   7   8   9   10

Learning about 2
1. ● ●

Learning abo
2. ● ●

Learning abo
3. ● ● ● ●

Miss Bell showed the boys and girls the chart on page 7.

She said, "Little children say this chart tells number stories.

"Older children, like you, say it shows *number facts*.

"What number facts does Row 1 show?"

Ben said, "Row 1 shows that
    1 and 1 are 2."

Then he walked up to the chart and covered 1 of the dots to show that
    1 from 2 is 1.

1. Look at the chart on page 7. Use Row 2 to show these facts:

2 and 1 are 3	2 from 3 is 1
1 and 2 are 3	1 from 3 is 2

2. What 4 facts can you learn from Row 3?

3. What 2 facts can you learn from Row 4?

4. What facts can you learn from each of the other rows?

5. Tell how you might need to use the facts in each row. For example, Row 1 answers either of these questions:

● Dick had 1 cent. He found another cent. How many cents did he have then?

● Molly has 2 apples. If she eats 1 apple, how many apples will she have left?

Number Chart

Learning about 2

1. ● ●

Learning about 3

2. ● ● ●

Learning about 4

3. ● ● ● ●
4. ● ● ● ●

Learning about 5

5. ● ● ● ● ●
6. ● ● ● ● ●

Learning about 6

7. ● ● ● ● ● ●
8. ● ● ● ● ● ●
9. ● ● ● ● ● ●
10. ● ● ● ● ● ●

Learning about 7

11. ● ● ● ● ● ● ●
12. ● ● ● ● ● ● ●
13. ● ● ● ● ● ● ●

Learning about 8

14. ● ● ● ● ● ● ● ●
15. ● ● ● ● ● ● ● ●
16. ● ● ● ● ● ● ● ●
17. ● ● ● ● ● ● ● ●
18. ● ● ● ● ● ● ● ●

Learning about 9

19. ● ● ● ● ● ● ● ● ●
20. ● ● ● ● ● ● ● ● ●
21. ● ● ● ● ● ● ● ● ●
22. ● ● ● ● ● ● ● ● ●
23. ● ● ● ● ● ● ● ● ●

Learning about 10

24. ● ● ● ● ● ● ● ● ● ●
25. ● ● ● ● ● ● ● ● ● ●
26. ● ● ● ● ● ● ● ● ● ●
27. ● ● ● ● ● ● ● ● ● ●
28. ● ● ● ● ● ● ● ● ● ●
29. ● ● ● ● ● ● ● ● ● ●

▶ Facts that coins teach you

Coins help you learn arithmetic. Picture 1 teaches that:

5 and 1 are 6	1 from 6 is 5
1 and 5 are 6	5 from 6 is 1

Tell four facts you can learn from Picture 2; Picture 3; Picture 4.

1.    **2.**

3.    **4.**

Tell two things you can learn from each of these pictures:

5.    **6.**

7. Do Pictures 5 and 6 teach that 2 fives are 10?

8. Tell how you might use the arithmetic you learn from each picture on this page. For example, Picture 1 helps to answer these questions:

● Bob had 1¢. He found a nickel. Then he had __?__ cents.

● Tom had 6¢. He lost a nickel. Then he had __?__ cent.

● Mary had 5 paper dolls. She made 1 more. Then she had __?__ paper dolls.

● Joe had 6 toy planes. He broke 1. Then he had __?__.

▶ Facts that counting teaches you

1. Counting by 1's to 10 teaches you that 1 and 1 are 2; 2 and 1 are 3; 3 and 1 are 4. Name 6 other facts that counting to 10 teaches you.

2. Count backward from 10. That teaches that 1 from 10 is 9; 1 from 9 is 8; 1 from 8 is 7. Name 6 other facts that counting backward teaches you.

3. Counting by 2's to 10 teaches you what facts?

4. Counting by 3's to 9 teaches what facts?

5. What facts do you learn by counting backward by 2's from 10? by 3's from 9?

▶ Facts that doubles teach you

1 and 1 are 2	3 and 3 are 6	4 and 4 are 8
2 and 2 are 4		5 and 5 are 10

1. If you know that 3 and 3 are 6, then you know that 3 and 4 are _?_; that 3 and 2 are _?_.

2. What facts can you learn from 2 and 2 are 4? from 4 and 4 are 8? from 5 and 5 are 10?

▶ Facts that number families teach you

1. Why are these four facts called a Number Family?

3 and 4 are 7	3 from 7 is 4
4 and 3 are 7	4 from 7 is 3

Name the 3 other members in the family of each fact below:

2. 4 and 5 are 9	3 from 8 is 5	2 from 9 is 7
3. 2 and 5 are 7	9 and 1 are 10	2 from 5 is 3
4. 4 from 10 is 6	3 and 6 are 9	3 from 10 is 7

Shapes have names

1. Bob is studying about Indians. He learned that the Indians used the shapes below in their writing. Read the names of these shapes. How many of these shapes can you see in your classroom?

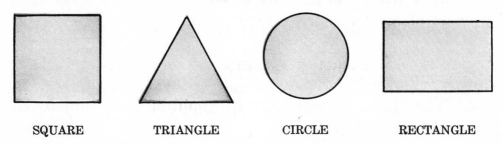

SQUARE   TRIANGLE   CIRCLE   RECTANGLE

2. Bob made a drum from a round oatmeal box. He used Indian writing to decorate his drum. Below is some of the writing he used.

Can you find any squares in the Indian writing? any triangles? any circles? any rectangles?

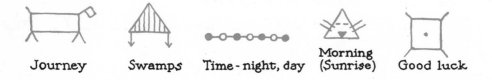

Journey   Swamps   Time - night, day   Morning (Sunrise)   Good luck

3. You will soon start an Arithmetic Folder. You will want to write figures well in your folder. Look carefully at the figures below. Then practice writing them until you make them look right.

1 2 3 4 5 6 7 8 9 10

Halves — fourths — thirds

▶Jane cut a candy bar into 2 pieces the same size. She gave one piece to Mary and kept one piece. Each girl has *one half* of the candy bar.

$\frac{1}{2}$ **means one half.**

In a whole candy bar there are __?__ halves.

▶There are 4 equal pieces in a waffle. Mother, Father, Jane, and Joe each ate one part of the waffle. Each one ate *one fourth* of the waffle.

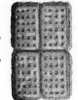

$\frac{1}{4}$ **means one fourth.**

In a whole waffle there are __?__ fourths.

▶Tom broke a candy stick into 3 pieces the same size. He gave one piece to Billy and one to Jim. He kept one piece. Each boy got *one third* of the candy stick. $\frac{1}{3}$ **means one third.**

In a whole candy stick there are __?__ thirds.

1. Tell what part of each picture is red.

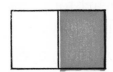 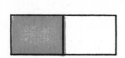 

2. Which cup is $\frac{1}{2}$ full? $\frac{1}{4}$ full? $\frac{1}{3}$ full?

3. A whole equals __?__ halves; __?__ thirds; __?__ fourths.

The next page shows a paper in Molly's Arithmetic Folder. Study it. Make an Arithmetic Folder to keep your best work in this year.

Make a page now for your folder, showing halves, thirds, and fourths. Exs. 1 to 4 will help you.

1. Draw and cut out a circle. A paper milk-bottle top makes a good pattern. Fold the circle into 2 equal parts. Write one half in figures on each half. Paste the circle on the page for your folder.

2. Make a square for your folder. What will you use for a pattern? Fold the square into 3 equal parts. Write one third in figures on each third of the square.

3. Make a rectangle for your folder. Fold the rectangle into 2 equal parts. Fold it again to make 4 equal parts. Write one fourth in figures on each fourth of the rectangle.

Which is larger, $\frac{1}{2}$ of the rectangle or $\frac{1}{4}$ of it? Does 1 half of the rectangle equal 2 fourths of it?

4. Would you like to cut out a red paper heart for your folder? Do it this way:

● Fold a piece of red paper into halves.

● Draw a half heart against the fold in the paper, as Nancy has done in the picture.

● Fold the paper and cut along the line you drew.

Molly Turner

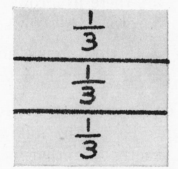

This cookie is divided into halves

This cookie is divided into fourths

This is a cake. It is cut into 2 pieces. The 2 pieces are not the same size, so the cake is not cut in half.

Ten-Tens Counter

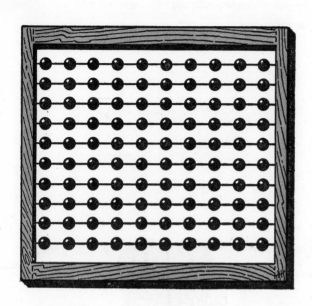

1. How many beads are there in each row?

2. Count all the beads by 10's. How many are there? Why is this called a Ten-Tens Counter?

3. How many beads are there in 2 rows? in 3 rows? in 4 rows?

4. How many are 2 tens? 3 tens? 4 tens?

On the next page is another Ten-Tens Counter. It is partly covered by a piece of paper. To do the following examples, you will need a paper exactly like that piece. Your teacher will tell you how to make it.

5. Look at the counter on page 15. You can see 10 beads and 3 more. That is _?_ beads. Take the piece of paper you cut out. Place it on the bead counter on this page so that you can see 10 beads and 3 more.

6. Show 10 beads and 1 more. How many beads is that?

7. Show 10 beads and 2 more. How many beads is that?

8. Show 10 beads and 5 more. How many beads is that?

Show on the bead counter:

9. 10 and 6 are _?_
10 and 8 are _?_

10. 10 and 4 are _?_
10 and 9 are _?_

To the Teacher: See Note 1 on page 311.

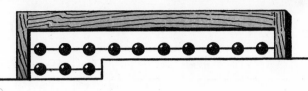

I use this piece of paper on the Ten-Tens Counter.

Mary Jane Miller

Show on the bead counter on page 14:

1. 2 tens are __?__
2 tens and 5 are __?__
2 tens and 2 are __?__

2. 2 tens and 1 are __?__
2 tens and 7 are __?__
2 tens and 9 are __?__

3. How many beads are there in 3 rows? in 4 rows? 6 rows? 8 rows? 5 rows? 9? 7? 10?

4. How many are 3 tens? 4 tens? 6 tens? 8 tens? 5 tens? 9 tens? 7 tens? 10 tens?

Show on the bead counter:

5. 3 tens and 5 are __?__
3 tens and 7 are __?__

7. 6 tens and 6 are __?__
7 tens and 5 are __?__

6. 4 tens and 6 are __?__
5 tens and 7 are __?__

8. 8 tens and 1 are __?__
9 tens and 5 are __?__

9. Which is more: 3 tens and 7, or 7 tens and 3?

10. Which is more: 8 tens and 4, or 4 tens and 8?

1	2	3	4	5	6	7	8	9	10
11	12	13	14	15	16	17	18	19	20
21	22	23	24	25	26	27	28	29	30
31	32	33	34	35	36	37	38	39	40
41	42	43	44	45	46	47	48	49	50
51	52	53	54	55	56	57	58	59	60
61	62	63	64	65	66	67	68	69	70
71	72	73	74	75	76	77	78	79	80
81	82	83	84	85	86	87	88	89	90
91	92	93	94	95	96	97	98	99	100

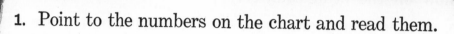

1. Point to the numbers on the chart and read them.

2. Point to the chart and count the squares by 10's; by 5's; by 2's.

3. Read the number that tells how many squares there are in 1 row; 2 rows; 4; 3; 5; 8; 9; 6; 7; 10.

4. Read the number that means 2 tens; 4 tens; 3 tens; 5 tens; 8 tens; 9 tens; 6 tens; 7 tens; 10 tens.

16

On the chart find and read the number that means:

1. 10 and 4   20 and 3   30 and 6   40 and 2

2. 50 and 5   60 and 9   70 and 1   90 and 7

3. 1 ten and 6   5 tens and 6   3 tens and 2   4 tens and 7

4. 6 tens and 7   2 tens and 1   9 tens and 5   7 tens and 2

5. 37 means __?__ tens and __?__   11 means __?__ ten and __?__

6. 48 means __?__ tens and __?__   54 means __?__ tens and __?__

7. 65 means __?__ tens and __?__   72 means __?__ tens and __?__

8. What number comes just after 19? just after 29? just after 39? 69? 89? 99? 49? 79? 59?

9. What number comes just before 20? just before 30? just before 40? 50? 100? 60? 90? 80? 70?

10. Use a "quick trick" for finding these numbers on the chart: 7   18   38   59   40   52   75   23   84   97

11. Beginning with 5, count by 10's to 95.   Say: "5, 15, 25, . . ."   Point to the chart as you count.

12. Beginning with 7, count by 10's to 97.

13. Beginning with 2, count by 10's to 92.

14. What number is 10 more than 6? 10 more than 26? 10 more than 35? 10 more than 54? 10 more than 78?

15. What number is 10 less than 16? 10 less than 47? 10 less than 53? 10 less than 77? 10 less than 98?

16. Which is larger, 64 or 46?   35 or 53?   27 or 72? 56 or 35?   52 or 28?   74 or 69?   28 or 82?
Prove your answers on the Ten-Tens Chart.

Dick asked, "Miss Bell, may I show the class an easy way to understand numbers larger than 10?"

"Of course," said Miss Bell. "What is your way?"

"Well, I use dimes and pennies. A dime is worth 10 cents. I look at 2 dimes and 3 pennies, and count: '10 cents, 20 cents, and 3 more cents make 23 cents.' That helps me see that 2 tens and 3 are 23."

Then Dick gave the class these examples to do:

1. 4 dimes and 2 cents are __?__ ¢   4 tens and 2 are __?__

2. 1 dime and 5 cents are __?__ ¢   1 ten and 5 are __?__

3. 3 dimes and 6 cents are __?__ ¢   3 tens and 6 are __?__

4. 5 dimes and 7 cents are __?__ ¢   5 tens and 7 are __?__

5. 2 dimes and 4 cents are __?__ ¢   2 tens and 4 are __?__

6. 4 dimes and 4 cents are __?__ ¢   4 tens and 4 are __?__

7. 1 dime and 9 cents are __?__ ¢   1 ten and 9 are __?__

8. 6 dimes and 8 cents are __?__ ¢   6 tens and 8 are __?__

9. 8 dimes and 6 cents are __?__ ¢   8 tens and 6 are __?__

10. A quarter is worth __?__ dimes and __?__ cents.

11. Count to 100 by 10's. Write the numbers.

12. Write the numbers from 28 to 32; from 37 to 41.

13. Write the number that means 10 more than 14; 10 more than 37; 10 less than 50; 10 less than 62.

14. Ask your teacher to say numbers for you to write.

Sums to 10

The picture shows that Ann needed 6 paper hats for the girls and 4 for the boys at her party. 6 hats and 4 hats are 10 hats. 6 and 4 are 10.

▶ When you say *"6 and 4 are 10,"* you *add* 6 and 4. You are doing an *addition* example.

$$\begin{array}{r} 6 \\ 4 \\ \hline 10 \end{array}$$

▶ An addition may be written like this: ⟶ It is read "6 and 4 are 10."

▶ Another way to write this addition is *6 + 4 = 10.*
The sign **+** is a *plus sign.* The sign **=** is an *equal sign.*
6 + 4 = 10 is read *"6 plus 4 equals 10."*

1. Read this picture-writing: •• and ••• are •••••

2. Here are 3 other ways to write the fact shown in Ex. 1. Read them. Which ways seem shortest and easiest?

$$2 \text{ and } 3 \text{ are } 5 \qquad \begin{array}{r} 2 \\ +3 \\ \hline 5 \end{array}$$

$$2 + 3 = 5$$

Write each fact in this picture-writing in 3 other ways.

3. ☆ ☆ ☆ and ☆ ☆ ☆ ☆ are ☆ ☆ ☆ ☆ ☆ ☆ ☆

4. ✕ ✕ ✕ ✕ ✕ and ✕ ✕ ✕ are ✕ ✕ ✕ ✕ ✕ ✕ ✕ ✕

▶ In the addition example 3 + 6 = 9, we say the *sum* is 9. "Sum" is the name of the answer to an addition example.

19

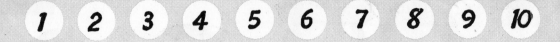

Read the additions below and tell the sums. Practice until you can tell every sum without the help of the circles.

1. $6 + 3 = \underline{?}$ $5 + 4 = \underline{?}$
    $3 + 6 = \underline{?}$ $4 + 5 = \underline{?}$

2. $3 + 4 = \underline{?}$ $2 + 5 = \underline{?}$
    $4 + 3 = \underline{?}$ $5 + 2 = \underline{?}$

3. | 7 | 3 | 6 | 5 | 2 | 7 |
    |---|---|---|---|---|---|
    | 1 | 5 | 2 | 3 | 8 | 3 |

4. | 4 | 2 | 1 | 2 | 8 | 3 |
    |---|---|---|---|---|---|
    | 2 | 4 | 7 | 6 | 2 | 7 |

5. | 3 | 7 | 6 | 1 | 2 | 4 |
    |---|---|---|---|---|---|
    | 5 | 2 | 1 | 9 | 3 | 6 |

6. | 5 | 2 | 1 | 9 | 2 | 6 |
    |---|---|---|---|---|---|
    | 3 | 7 | 6 | 1 | 3 | 4 |

7. $2 + 2 = \underline{?}$ $4 + 4 = \underline{?}$
    $3 + 3 = \underline{?}$ $5 + 5 = \underline{?}$

8. Copy Exs. 3 to 7 and write the sums.

What addition fact do you use to find each missing number below? Write each fact in 2 ways.

9. John has 2 nickels; so he has $\underline{?}$ ¢.

10. Tom had 4¢. He earned a nickel. He then had $\underline{?}$ ¢.

11. Jack spent 3¢ and 7¢. In all he spent $\underline{?}$ ¢.

12. Joan has 3 kittens and 2 rabbits. She has $\underline{?}$ pets.

13. Ted has 4 marbles in 1 pocket. He has 3 marbles in another pocket. All together he has $\underline{?}$ marbles.

14. Joe is in school 3 hours in the morning and 2 hours in the afternoon. He is in school $\underline{?}$ hours each day.

15. Ann has a nickel. She says she needs 3¢ more to buy a ball. The ball costs $\underline{?}$ ¢.

To the Teacher: See Note 2 on page 311.

Using addition to 10

1. Jane has 10 jacks. When she is "for 5's," she picks up 5 jacks. Then she picks up 5 more. Do her jacks show that $5 + 5 = 10$?

2. When Jane is "for 6's," she picks up 6 jacks and then 4 more. Draw jacks to show that $6+4=10$.

3. What additions do Jane's jacks show when she is "for 7's"? "for 8's"? "for 9's"?

What additions do you use to find the missing numbers in the problems below? Write each fact in 2 ways.

4. Jack has 2 pencils at school. He has 7 pencils at home. In all, he has __?__ pencils.

5. Peter has a nickel in one pocket. He has 4 cents in another pocket. In the two pockets he has __?__ cents.

6. Two pairs of mittens are __?__ mittens.

Practice until you can say all these sums. Then write the sums on folded paper without copying the examples. The picture shows you how to do it. Number each row and put a dash between answers. Do not write in your book.

7.	4	2	7	5
	6	8	2	3
8.	9	8	6	8
	1	2	4	1
9.	5	1	4	7
	5	9	5	3

> Ann Taylor
>
> 7. 10 - 10 - 9 - 8
>
> 8.
>
> 9.

1. Tell what each addition in Ex. 2 below could stand for. For example, $\frac{9}{1}$ could mean, "Tommy had 9 cents. He found another cent. Then he had __?__ cents."

2. Practice until you can say every sum. Then write the sums on folded paper.

3	4	4	7	1	6	2	1	7
7	5	4	2	9	2	5	2	1

3. Did you make mistakes in writing any sums in Ex. 2? If so, you need practice in remembering those additions.

On the next page you will learn how to make and use Help-Yourself Cards for the facts you need to practice.

Study the cards. Then do Ex. 2 again. Keep studying the cards and doing Ex. 2 until you can write all the answers correctly.

Now do Exs. 4 to 7 in the same way.

4.
3	7	3	6	1	6	1	6	1
6	3	4	4	5	3	3	1	6

5.
5	3	4	5	2	5	2	1	8
4	3	3	1	6	5	3	1	1

6.
4	3	4	4	2	8	1	1	2
4	2	6	2	8	2	4	7	1

7.
3	1	2	2	3	2	5	3	4
1	8	2	4	5	7	2	7	1

Help-Yourself Cards

Betsy has made herself a pack of Help-Yourself Cards for the facts she needs to practice. On the front of each card is an addition example. On the back of the card the example is written with the answer.

Betsy looks at the front of each card and says the answer as quickly as she can. Then she looks at the back of the card to see if she said it correctly. If she did, she puts it in her "Know" pile. If she didn't, she puts it in her "Don't Know" pile.

After Betsy has finished, she studies all the examples in her "Don't Know" pile very carefully. When she thinks she knows them, she mixes them with the cards in her "Know" pile. The next day she tests herself again to see if she can give every answer correctly.

When you make your cards, you can find the correct answers to write on the backs of them on page 309.

To the Teacher: See Note 3 on page 311.

How wide? How long? How deep?

Miss Bell's pupils want to bring a table from the library to their room. They are not sure it will go through their door.

▶Tom said, "Let's bring the table to the door and see if the door is wide enough."

▶ Jim said, "I have a better idea. I'll cut off a piece of string to show how wide the table is. Then I'll carry only the string to see if the door is wide enough."

▶ John said, "We can use a foot ruler to find how wide the table and door are."

▶ Joe said, "Yes, we could use a foot ruler, but it will be easier if we use a yardstick to measure the door and table."

1. Will the boys' ideas help? Whose idea is best? Why?

2. Jane is going to buy a new pair of curtains for her room. Can she take the window to the store, so that she can buy curtains just long enough? What should she do?

3. If two things cannot be placed side by side, what is the best way to find which is wider, or longer, or taller, or deeper?

4. Hold your hands about an inch apart; a foot apart; a yard apart.

5. Which would you measure in inches? in feet? in yards?

pencil   window   blackboard   ribbon   rug

1. Have you ever needed to measure? Tell when.

2. On the blackboard draw a line you think is 1 foot long. Draw another 1 yard long. Check by measuring.

3. Ask your teacher to draw 12 lines on the board. First guess how long each line is. Then measure it.

4. Measure a yardstick with a foot ruler. How many feet are in a yard?

5. How many inches long is a foot ruler? a yardstick?

LEARN THESE FACTS

12 inches (in.) = 1 foot (ft.)
3 feet (ft.) = 1 yard (yd.)
36 inches = 1 yard

6. Notice that *in.* is a short way of writing *inch* or *inches*. What is a short way of writing *foot* or *feet*? a short way of writing *yard* or *yards*?

7. Make these holding-hands paper dolls to keep in your Arithmetic Folder.

● Cut a paper 5 inches wide and 16 inches long.
● Fold the paper into fourths *exactly* the way Martha is doing in the picture.
● Draw a picture of a doll on ¼ of the strip, as Martha did. Be sure the doll's arms reach from side to side of the paper.
● Fold the paper together. Cut around the pattern of the doll through 4 thicknesses of paper.

"Today is my birthday," said Ann. "It is the tenth of September. I am eight years old."

The children sang "Happy Birthday" to Ann.

Then Miss Bell said, "Let's make a birthday chart. It will show when each one of you has a birthday. Maybe we can plan a surprise for each birthday.

"We must know the names of the months before we make our chart. You name the months. I will write them."

Read what Miss Bell wrote:

1. January	4. April	7. July	10. October
2. February	5. May	8. August	11. November
3. March	6. June	9. September	12. December

Miss Bell said, "January is the first month of the year. So the January birthdays go first on our chart. Raise your hand if your birthday comes in January."

Two children raised their hands.

Jean said, "My birthday comes on January 21."

Sally said, "My birthday comes on January 4."

1. Look at the birthday chart on the next page. Why did Miss Bell write Sally's name before Jean's?

2. Miss Bell wrote January on the chart in a short way. How did she write it?

3. What month comes after January? How do you write February in a short way?

4. Look at the chart and tell whose birthday comes in February; in March.

5. Read the whole birthday chart.

6. Betsy and Jack are twins. How does the chart show that?

7. How many months (mo.) are there in a year (yr.)? Name them in order.

8. Write the names of the months the long way. Then write them the short way.

9. Do you know what month comes after December?

10. Find the date of your birthday on a calendar.

11. On what day of the week is your birthday this year?

12. Perhaps your class would like to make a birthday chart.

13. Make a small birthday chart for your Arithmetic Folder. Show on your chart the birthdays of the people you like best.

	Name	Birthday	Name	Birthday	
		Mo. Da.		Mo. Da.	
	Sally	Jan. 4	Paul	July 8	
	Jean	Jan. 21	Teddy	July 30	
	Eddy	Feb. 6	Janet	Aug. 5	
	Linda	Mar. 10	Ann	Sept. 10	
	Kitty	Mar. 28	Betsy	Sept. 12	
			Jack	Sept. 12	
	Fred	Apr. 2			
	Mona	Apr. 17	Kent	Oct. 14	
	Larry	Apr. 22			
			Cathy	Nov. 5	
	Marie	May 14	Tom	Nov. 18	
	Roger	June 1	Gerry	Dec. 29	

Measuring liquids

1. Rita wants to make pudding. The directions call for 2 cups of milk. Rita does not have a measuring cup. She has a pint bottle of milk. Has she enough milk?

2. To find out if Rita has enough milk, fill a pint bottle with water. Pour the water into drinking glasses. A measuring cup and a regular-size drinking glass hold the same amount. How many glasses can you fill?

LEARN THIS

2 glasses = 1 pint

3. Tom carefully poured one pint of water into a quart bottle. Then he poured another pint of water into the quart bottle. The two pints just filled the quart bottle.

Tom said, "There are two pints in a quart."
Is he right?

LEARN THIS

2 pints (pt.) = 1 quart (qt.)

4. Tony says he can fill 4 glasses with 1 quart of milk. Do you think he can? Prove it.

5. Edith mixed 1 pint of grape juice with 1 pint of water. How much liquid did she have? Did she have enough to give a glass to Ann, Jane, Jean, and herself?

6. Judy wants to fill 8 glasses with apple juice. How many glasses can she fill from 1 pint bottle? 2 pint bottles? 3? 4?

7. Jim's mother is canning plums. She asked Jim to go to the cellar for 4 quart jars. Jim can find only 3 quart jars, but there are some pint jars. What will Jim do?

8. Sally is serving ice cream to 6 girls. A pint serves 3 girls. Will a quart serve 6? Why?

9. Carl and Dick need a quart of paint for their hut. They have a pint. Dick says, "Buy another pint." Do you agree?

10. A quart bottle of lemon drink costs 18¢. A pint bottle costs 10¢. Bobby says, "It's cheaper to buy lemon drink in quart bottles." What does he mean?

11. Lee had a quart carton of milk. She filled 2 glasses with milk. How much was left in the carton?

12. How many things can you name that are sold by the pint and by the quart?

13. How much does a quart of milk cost at your store? How much does a pint cost?

14. A committee may bring to class some bottles, jars, and cans. Try to guess how much water each will hold. How can you find out who made the best guesses?

Subtracting from 10

John has 10¢. He plans to spend 4¢ for a top. He wonders how many cents he will have left.

To find out, look at the 10 cents he has. Cover the 4¢ he will spend. Then you see that he will have __?__¢ left. John said, "4 from 10 is 6."

▶ When John says *"4 from 10 is 6,"* he is *subtracting* 4 from 10. He is doing a *subtraction* example. To *subtract* means to *take away* one number from another.

▶ A subtraction may be written this way: ⟶

$$\begin{array}{r} 10 \\ -\ 4 \\ \hline 6 \end{array}$$

▶ Here are three ways to read it: ⟶

4 from 10 is 6
10 take away 4 is 6
10 minus 4 is 6

▶ The sign − is a *minus sign.* It tells you to subtract.

▶ Another way to write the subtraction is *10 − 4 = 6.*

1. Use the picture above to find these answers:

$$\begin{array}{r} 10 \\ -\ 9 \\ \hline \end{array} \qquad \begin{array}{r} 10 \\ -\ 8 \\ \hline \end{array} \qquad \begin{array}{r} 10 \\ -\ 3 \\ \hline \end{array} \qquad \begin{array}{r} 10 \\ -\ 7 \\ \hline \end{array}$$

$$\begin{array}{r} 10 \\ -\ 2 \\ \hline \end{array} \qquad \begin{array}{r} 10 \\ -\ 6 \\ \hline \end{array} \qquad \begin{array}{r} 10 \\ -\ 4 \\ \hline \end{array} \qquad \begin{array}{r} 10 \\ -\ 5 \\ \hline \end{array}$$

2. Read each subtraction in Ex. 1 in 3 ways.

3. Make up a problem for each example in Ex. 1.

4. Billy has 7¢. He is going to buy a 4-cent pencil. Here are 6 ways to show how much he will have left. Which way do you like best? least?

- $\begin{array}{r} 7 \\ -\ 4 \\ \hline 3 \end{array}$
- 7 *take away* 4 is 3
- 7 *minus* 4 is 3
- 4 *from* 7 is 3
- 7 − 4 = 3

Practice until you can say every answer in Exs. 1 to 7 without the help of the dot pictures.

● ● ● ● ● ● ● ● ●   ● ● ● ● ● ● ●

1. $\begin{array}{r} 9 \\ -4 \end{array}$ $\begin{array}{r} 9 \\ -6 \end{array}$ $\begin{array}{r} 9 \\ -2 \end{array}$ $\begin{array}{r} 9 \\ -1 \end{array}$

5. $7 - 6 = \underline{\ ?\ }$ $7 - 1 = \underline{\ ?\ }$
6. $7 - 4 = \underline{\ ?\ }$ $7 - 3 = \underline{\ ?\ }$
7. $7 - 2 = \underline{\ ?\ }$ $7 - 5 = \underline{\ ?\ }$

2. $\begin{array}{r} 9 \\ -7 \end{array}$ $\begin{array}{r} 9 \\ -5 \end{array}$ $\begin{array}{r} 9 \\ -3 \end{array}$ $\begin{array}{r} 9 \\ -8 \end{array}$

Draw dot pictures if you need help on these subtractions:

● ● ● ● ● ● ● ●

8. $6 - 4 = \underline{\ ?\ }$ $6 - 3 = \underline{\ ?\ }$

3. $\begin{array}{r} 8 \\ -4 \end{array}$ $\begin{array}{r} 8 \\ -3 \end{array}$ $\begin{array}{r} 8 \\ -7 \end{array}$ $\begin{array}{r} 8 \\ -1 \end{array}$

9. $5 - 3 = \underline{\ ?\ }$ $4 - 3 = \underline{\ ?\ }$
10. $3 - 2 = \underline{\ ?\ }$ $5 - 2 = \underline{\ ?\ }$

4. $\begin{array}{r} 8 \\ -6 \end{array}$ $\begin{array}{r} 8 \\ -5 \end{array}$ $\begin{array}{r} 8 \\ -2 \end{array}$ $\begin{array}{r} 8 \\ -3 \end{array}$

11. $4 - 2 = \underline{\ ?\ }$ $3 - 1 = \underline{\ ?\ }$
12. $6 - 5 = \underline{\ ?\ }$ $6 - 2 = \underline{\ ?\ }$

13. Tom had 5 pebbles. He put them down in a row like this: ● ● ● ●   ● He says they show these 2 additions and 2 subtractions:

$4 + 1 = 5$ $1 + 4 = 5$ $5 - 4 = 1$ $5 - 1 = 4$

Tell 2 additions and 2 subtractions that Tom's 5 pebbles show when he puts them this way: ● ● ●   ● ●

14. Write all the additions and subtractions you can learn from 6 pebbles; from 7; 8; 9; 10.

15. If $7 + 3 = 10$, then $10 - 3 = \underline{\ ?\ }$, and $10 - 7 = \underline{\ ?\ }$.

16. If $6 + 2 = 8$, then $8 - 6 = \underline{\ ?\ }$, and $8 - 2 = \underline{\ ?\ }$.

Tell 3 other members of the family of each fact below:

17. $6 + 3 = \underline{\ ?\ }$ $8 - 3 = \underline{\ ?\ }$ $9 - 5 = \underline{\ ?\ }$ $2 + 3 = \underline{\ ?\ }$

18. $4 + 6 = \underline{\ ?\ }$ $10 - 7 = \underline{\ ?\ }$ $6 + 2 = \underline{\ ?\ }$ $7 - 3 = \underline{\ ?\ }$

What is the missing number in each of these examples?

1.
$$\begin{cases} 10 - 2 = ? \\ 10 - 8 = ? \\ \\ 8 + 2 = ? \\ 2 + 8 = ? \end{cases}$$

2.
$$\begin{cases} 10 - 6 = ? \\ 10 - 4 = ? \\ \\ 6 + 4 = ? \\ 4 + 6 = ? \end{cases}$$

3.
$$\begin{cases} 10 - 7 = ? \\ 10 - 3 = ? \\ \\ 7 + 3 = ? \\ 3 + 7 = ? \end{cases}$$

4.
$$\begin{cases} 9 - 5 = ? \\ 9 - 4 = ? \\ \\ 5 + 4 = ? \\ 4 + 5 = ? \end{cases}$$

5.
$$\begin{cases} 9 - 6 = ? \\ 9 - 3 = ? \\ \\ 6 + 3 = ? \\ 3 + 6 = ? \end{cases}$$

6.
$$\begin{cases} 9 - 7 = ? \\ 9 - 2 = ? \\ \\ 7 + 2 = ? \\ 2 + 7 = ? \end{cases}$$

7.
$$\begin{cases} 8 - 5 = ? \\ 8 - 3 = ? \\ \\ 5 + 3 = ? \\ 3 + 5 = ? \end{cases}$$

8.
$$\begin{cases} 7 - 4 = ? \\ 7 - 3 = ? \\ \\ 4 + 3 = ? \\ 3 + 4 = ? \end{cases}$$

Find the answers to Exs. 9–13. What fact do you use to find each answer? Write each fact in 2 ways. Make drawings to prove your answers are right.

9. Ken found 8 walnuts. He ate 5. How many did he have left?

10. Dan made 9 paper airplanes. He threw away 3 that wouldn't fly. How many did he have then?

11. Ann had a dime. She spent 6¢. How much did she have left?

12. Roy had 9 toy trucks. He broke 2 trucks. How many did he have then?

13. Peter had 7 cookies. He gave Bill 3 cookies. How many did he have left?

To find the number left, you subtract.

14. Example 13 uses one of the facts in Ex. 8. Which one? Make up problems to show how you might need to use the other facts in Ex. 8.

Look at the pennies across the top of the picture. How many pennies are there?

Use the picture of 10 pennies to find each answer in Ex. 1. Cover the number of pennies you have. Then look to see how many more cents you need.

1. How many more pennies will you need to buy a 10-cent toy if you have 8¢? a nickel? 3¢? 9¢? 6¢? 7¢? 4¢? 2¢? 5¢? 1¢?

To find how many more you need, you subtract.

Use the picture of 10 pennies to do Exs. 2 to 6 if you need to.

2. 5 and _?_ are 10	5 from 10 = _?_	10 − 5 = _?_
3. 7 and _?_ are 10	7 from 10 = _?_	10 − 7 = _?_
4. 4 and _?_ are 10	4 from 10 = _?_	10 − 4 = _?_
5. 2 and _?_ are 10	2 from 10 = _?_	10 − 2 = _?_
6. 3 and _?_ are 10	3 from 10 = _?_	10 − 3 = _?_

Larger or smaller — more or less

1. Whose fish is longer, Sue's or John's? Can you tell from the picture exactly how many inches longer John's fish is than Sue's?

2. To find out how many inches longer John's fish is than Sue's, what would you need to know about John's fish? about Sue's fish?

3. John's fish is 10 inches long. Sue's is 7 inches long. Do you add or subtract to find how many inches longer John's fish is than Sue's?

4. Is the missing number the same in each of these?
John's fish is _?_ inches longer than Sue's.
Sue's fish is _?_ inches shorter than John's.

5. What do you need *to know* and *to do*:
- to find how many more cents John has than Sue?
- to find how many years younger Sue is than John?
- to find how many inches shorter Sue is than John?
- to find how many pounds heavier John is than Sue?

34

● ● ● ● ● ● ●

1. If you cover 3 of these 7 dots, you can see that 7 is _?_ more than 3. $7 - 3 = $ _?_

2. If you cover 5 dots, you can see that 7 is _?_ more than 5. $7 - 5 = $ _?_

3. Use the dots to find how much larger 7 is than 1; than 2; than 4; than 6.

4. Cover 3 dots to find how much less 3 is than 7.
$7 - 3 = $ _?_

5. Cover 5 dots to find how much less 5 is than 7.
$7 - 5 = $ _?_

6. John has 7¢. Sue has 4¢. John has _?_¢ more than Sue. Sue has _?_¢ less than John. $7 - 4 = $ _?_

7. 7 is _?_ larger than 5.
$7 - 5 = $ _?_

8. 7 is _?_ more than 1.
$7 - 1 = $ _?_

9. 4 is _?_ smaller than 7.
$7 - 4 = $ _?_

To find how much larger or smaller one number is than another, you subtract.

10. To find how much more 9 is than 6, Tom wrote this subtraction. What is wrong? Tell a rule to keep Tom from making that mistake again.

$$\begin{array}{r} 6 \\ - 9 \\ \hline \end{array} \textit{wrong}$$

11. Polly says she can find the answer to each of the problems below by covering 5 of these 8 circles. Is Polly right?   ○ ○ ○ ○ ○ ○ ○ ○

● Peter had 8¢. He spent a nickel. He had _?_¢ left.
● Sue has a nickel. She wants to buy an 8-cent ball. She needs _?_¢ more.
● Ann has 8¢. Joe has 5¢. Ann has _?_¢ more than Joe.

12. Write the subtraction fact you used in Ex. 11.

13. Make up a problem for each of these subtractions:

$$\begin{array}{r} 10 \\ - 5 \\ \hline \end{array} \qquad \begin{array}{r} 9 \\ - 6 \\ \hline \end{array} \qquad \begin{array}{r} 8 \\ - 4 \\ \hline \end{array} \qquad \begin{array}{r} 7 \\ - 5 \\ \hline \end{array}$$

Everyday problems

What number fact do you use to find each answer? Write each fact in 2 ways.

1. Joan wants to make a bottle-top necklace like this for herself and one for Sue. How many bottle tops will she need for her necklace? for Sue's? for both necklaces?

2. Dick sold 10 tickets for the class show. Jerry sold 7. How many more did Dick sell than Jerry?

3. There are 5 girls and 5 boys on Alice's team. How many children are on her team?

4. Don had 3 pencils. His grandfather gave him 2 more. How many pencils had he then?

5. Jack had 8¢ in his bank. He shook out a nickel for Sunday school. How many pennies were left in his bank?

6. Billy needs 9 wickets for a game of croquet. He can find only 7. He must hunt for the other _?_ wickets.

7. George is 9 years old. Tom is 6. George is how many years older than Tom?

8. Dick had 4¢. Then he found 6¢. He said, "I'll trade all my money for a dime." Would that be a fair trade?

9. There were 6 children playing in the yard. One had to go home. How many were left playing in the yard?

36

Learning to remember subtraction facts

▶ Tell what each subtraction fact in Ex. 1 could stand for. For example, $\frac{6}{-4}$ could mean: "Molly has 6¢. If she spends 4¢, how much will she have left?"

1.
$$\begin{array}{cccccccc} 6 & 5 & 3 & 8 & 10 & 4 & 6 & 10 & 9 \\ -4 & -1 & -2 & -1 & -7 & -1 & -5 & -3 & -2 \end{array}$$

▶ Now subtract. Practice until you can say every answer in Ex. 1. Then write the answers on folded paper.

▶ Did you make any mistakes in writing the answers in Ex. 1? If so, make Help-Yourself Cards for any facts you do not know. Study the cards. Then do Ex. 1 again.

▶ Now do Exs. 2 to 5 in the same way.

2.
$$\begin{array}{ccccccccc} 10 & 5 & 4 & 8 & 7 & 10 & 2 & 6 & 7 \\ -5 & -3 & -3 & -6 & -2 & -9 & -1 & -2 & -4 \end{array}$$

3.
$$\begin{array}{ccccccccc} 8 & 7 & 6 & 8 & 7 & 5 & 6 & 9 & 4 \\ -3 & -1 & -3 & -2 & -6 & -2 & -1 & -4 & -2 \end{array}$$

4.
$$\begin{array}{ccccccccc} 7 & 9 & 10 & 9 & 5 & 3 & 9 & 8 & 10 \\ -5 & -3 & -1 & -5 & -4 & -1 & -7 & -4 & -4 \end{array}$$

5.
$$\begin{array}{ccccccccc} 10 & 8 & 9 & 7 & 10 & 9 & 9 & 8 & 10 \\ -2 & -5 & -6 & -3 & -8 & -1 & -8 & -7 & -6 \end{array}$$

▶ Do the additions on page 22 again today.

Just for fun

POS $+\dfrac{4}{3}$

Name this animal.

F ⊞ 1

Name this bird.

1. To pay for a 17-cent loaf of bread, you could give a dime, a nickel, and _?_ pennies.

2. Molly has a nickel and 4 pennies. Has she enough to buy a 10-cent bag of popcorn?

3. If 4 boys share a watermelon equally, what part of the melon will each get? Write your answer in figures.

4. At half past 3 Billy's mother said, "You may play outdoors for 2 hours." Billy may play until half past _?_.

5. Rob has 3 dimes and 4 pennies. In all, he has _?_¢.

6. Sally has 5 rows of 10 stamps and 8 more stamps. In all, she has _?_ stamps.

7. Ted has 8 gumdrops. He wants to share them with Ann. If he keeps 5, Ann will get _?_.

8. Bob had a quarter changed into _?_ nickels.

9. Sue has 10¢. Jo has 6¢. Sue has _?_¢ more than Jo.

10. Joe Brown is keeping a record of his marks on Problem Tests. Joe had 9 problems right on the first test. He got 10 points for each problem. His mark was 9 tens, or _?_.

Joe's Problem Test Record	
Test	Marks
1	90
2	
3	
4	
5	
6	
7	
8	

How many problems did you have right on Problem Test 1? Give yourself 10 points for each right answer. What is your mark? Start a record, like Joe's, of your marks on the 8 Problem Tests in this book. Keep it in your folder.

To the Teacher: See Note 5, page 311.

Now is the time to test yourself

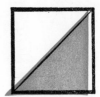

Work carefully. Check your answers.

1. How many months are there in a year?

2. What number means 7 tens and 5 ones?

3. What part of this square is each triangle?
Write your answer in figures.

4. 1 foot = __?__ inches.

5. How many pints are there in a quart?

6. What time is it by this clock? ⟶

7. Jane had 3¢. She earned a nickel. How much had she then?

8. Which one of these is an addition example? Copy it.

- 4 from 9 is 5
- 9 − 4 = 5
- 9 take away 4 is 5
- 9 minus 4 is 5
- 4 and 5 are 9

$$9$$
$$-\ 4$$
$$\overline{5}$$

9. Write in figures what this picture shows:

 and 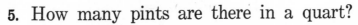 are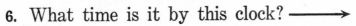

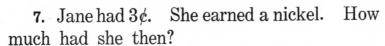

10. Jane has 4¢. She wants to buy an 8-cent pencil.
She needs __?__ ¢ more.

Just for fun

- I'm thinking of a number. If you put 3 with it, you will have 7. What is the number?

- I'm thinking of a number. If you divide it into 2 equal parts, you will have 4 in each part. What is the number?

- I'm thinking of a number. If you take away 5, you will have only 4. What is the number?

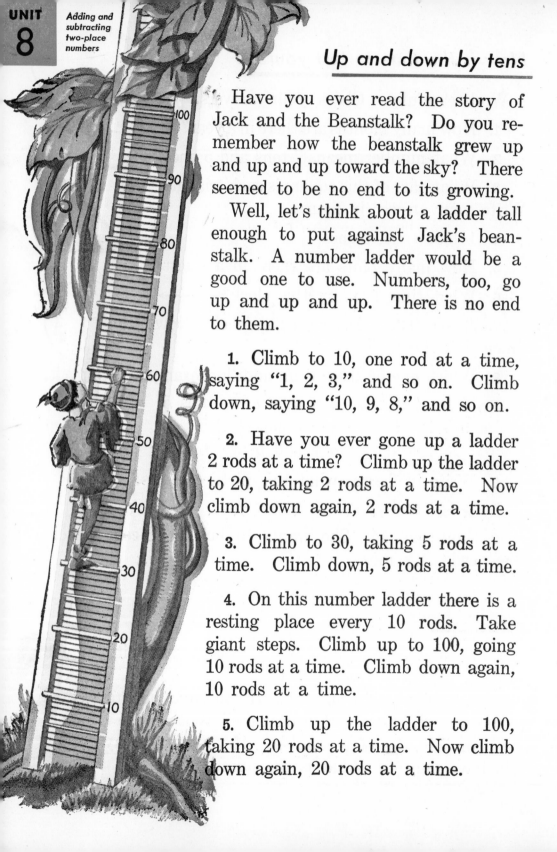

Up and down by tens

Have you ever read the story of Jack and the Beanstalk? Do you remember how the beanstalk grew up and up and up toward the sky? There seemed to be no end to its growing.

Well, let's think about a ladder tall enough to put against Jack's beanstalk. A number ladder would be a good one to use. Numbers, too, go up and up and up. There is no end to them.

1. Climb to 10, one rod at a time, saying "1, 2, 3," and so on. Climb down, saying "10, 9, 8," and so on.

2. Have you ever gone up a ladder 2 rods at a time? Climb up the ladder to 20, taking 2 rods at a time. Now climb down again, 2 rods at a time.

3. Climb to 30, taking 5 rods at a time. Climb down, 5 rods at a time.

4. On this number ladder there is a resting place every 10 rods. Take giant steps. Climb up to 100, going 10 rods at a time. Climb down again, 10 rods at a time.

5. Climb up the ladder to 100, taking 20 rods at a time. Now climb down again, 20 rods at a time.

Now you are ready to do some harder climbing.

1. Take 2 giant steps up the ladder, 10 rods at a time. That brings you to ___?___. Now take 3 more giant steps, 10 rods at a time. That brings you to ___?___.

2 tens and 3 tens are 5 tens.	2 tens 20
20 and 30 are 50.	+ 3 tens + 30
	5 tens 50

Go up the ladder to find:

2. 2 tens and 4 tens are ___?___ tens.
   20 and 40 are ___?___.

   2 tens 20
   + 4 tens + 40

3. 3 tens and 4 tens are ___?___ tens.
   30 and 40 are ___?___.

   3 tens 30
   + 4 tens + 40

4. 5 tens and 2 tens are ___?___ tens.
   50 and 20 are ___?___.

   5 tens 50
   + 2 tens + 20

5. Starting at 50, climb down the ladder. Take 3 giant steps, 10 rods at a time. That brings you to ___?___. How many more giant steps of 10 rods each do you have to take to get to the bottom?

Now go down the ladder to find:

6. 3 tens from 5 tens is ___?___ tens.
   30 from 50 is ___?___.

   5 tens 50
   − 3 tens − 30

7. 4 tens from 7 tens is ___?___ tens.
   40 from 70 is ___?___.

   7 tens 70
   − 4 tens − 40

8. 2 tens from 7 tens is ___?___ tens.
   20 from 70 is ___?___.

   7 tens 70
   − 2 tens − 20

9. Try climbing up and down the number ladder by yourself. Maybe you would like to climb above 100 to see what it is like up there.

1	2	3	4	5	6	7	8	9	10
11	12	13	14	15	16	17	18	19	20
21	22	23	24	25	26	27	28	29	30
31	32	33	34	35	36	37	38	39	40
41	42	43	44	45	46	47	48	49	50
51	52	53	54	55	56	57	58	59	60
61	62	63	64	65	66	67	68	69	70
71	72	73	74	75	76	77	78	79	80
81	82	83	84	85	86	87	88	89	90
91	92	93	94	95	96	97	98	99	100

1. On the chart find the number that is 10 more than 30. 3 tens and 1 ten are _?_ tens. 30 + 10 = _?_.

2. Find the number that is 2 tens more than 30; than 70; than 60; than 80; than 20.

3. Find 80. Take away 1 ten; 2 tens; 3 tens. 8 tens − 3 tens = _?_ tens. 80 − 30 = _?_.

Use the number chart to find these answers:

4. 70	70	30	50	60	90
+ 20	− 30	+ 30	− 30	+ 20	− 50

5. 4 + 3 = _?_   4 tens + 3 tens = _?_ tens   40 + 30 = _?_

6. 3 + 6 = _?_   3 tens + 6 tens = _?_ tens   30 + 60 = _?_

7. 8 − 5 = _?_   8 tens − 5 tens = _?_ tens   80 − 50 = _?_

8. 7 − 4 = _?_   7 tens − 4 tens = _?_ tens   70 − 40 = _?_

Dimes and tens

1. Yesterday Jack earned 3 dimes. Today he earned 2 dimes. All together he earned _?_ dimes.

2.

3 dimes	3 tens	30
+ 2 dimes	+ 2 tens	+ 20
? dimes	? tens	?

3. If you know that $5 + 2 = 7$, then you know that 5 tens + 2 tens = _?_ tens, and $50 + 20 =$ _?_.

4. Marie had 5 dimes. She spent 2 dimes. Then she had _?_ dimes left.

5.

5 dimes	5 tens	50
− 2 dimes	− 2 tens	− 20
? dimes	? tens	?

6. If you know that $9 − 5 = 4$, then you know that 9 tens − 5 tens = _?_ tens, and $90 − 50 =$ _?_.

7. Jane had 30¢. Her mother gave her 50¢ more. How much did Jane have then? Prove you are right.

8. Peter had 80¢. He lost 50¢. How much did he have left? Prove you are right.

Tell these answers. Then write them on folded paper.

9.

4 0	6 0	8 0	7 0	4 0	5 0
+ 2 0	+ 3 0	+ 1 0	+ 2 0	+ 3 0	+ 3 0

10.

6 0	9 0	9 0	7 0	8 0	9 0
− 2 0	− 3 0	− 1 0	− 3 0	− 3 0	− 2 0

Copy and find the answers:

11. $30 + 40$ $\qquad$ $50 + 20$ $\qquad$ $30 + 60$ $\qquad$ $40 + 20$

12. $60 − 40$ $\qquad$ $90 − 40$ $\qquad$ $80 − 60$ $\qquad$ $70 − 30$

1. Don had 13¢: → and

Don earned 32¢: → and

In all, Don had _?_ dimes and _?_ pennies, or 45¢. His coins show that 13¢ + 32¢ = _?_ ¢.

2. With the help of pictures, you have just seen that the sum of 13¢ and 32¢ is 45¢. Here is another way to find 13¢ + 32¢. Explain the addition.

13¢ = 1 dime and 3 cents
32¢ = 3 dimes and 2 cents
——————————————
4 dimes and 5 cents = 45¢

Use toy money (dimes and pennies) to do Exs. 3 to 10.

3. Jim needs 14¢ for bus fare and 25¢ for lunch. How much money does he need all together?

4. Mary had 43¢ in her bank. Her father gave her 25¢. How much money did she have then?

5. Judy earned 35¢ yesterday. She earned 24¢ today. How much did she earn on both days?

6. Show that 27¢ + 12¢ = 3 dimes and 9 cents, or 39¢.

7. Show that 35¢ + 23¢ = 5 dimes and 8 cents, or 58¢.

8. Show that 62¢ + 17¢ = 7 dimes and 9 cents, or 79¢.

9. Show that 51¢ + 25¢ = 7 dimes and 6 cents, or 76¢.

10. Show that 34¢ + 52¢ = 8 dimes and 6 cents, or 86¢.

11. Now tell how to do Exs. 6 to 10 without the help of toy money.

For Your Bird
Perch.....14¢
Swing...32¢

Adding two-place numbers

1. Joan wants to buy her bird a perch and a swing. She wonders how much money she needs. How many dimes does she need? How many pennies? How many cents in all?

▶ To add 14¢ and 32¢, write the example:——→

14¢
32¢

▶ Then think, "4 cents and 2 cents are 6 cents." Write the 6 in the cents column under the 4 and 2.
Does the 6 show how many pennies Joan needs?

▶ Next think, "1 dime and 3 dimes are 4 dimes." Write 4 in the dimes column under the 1 and 3.
Does the 4 show how many dimes Joan needs?
Joan needs __?__ ¢ to buy the perch and swing.

14¢
32¢
___
46¢

2. Peter had 32¢. Then he found a quarter. How much money did he have then?

3. Sue says the sum of 43¢ and 26¢ is 69¢. Is she right?

Copy and add:

4.	61¢	14¢	25¢	74¢	13¢	45¢	37¢
	32¢	55¢	31¢	13¢	16¢	52¢	32¢

5.	74¢	23¢	54¢	65¢	33¢	62¢	27¢
	24¢	54¢	42¢	23¢	52¢	16¢	21¢

Adding two-place numbers

1. There are 15 girls and 12 boys in Miss Hill's class. Miss Hill wants to give each child a card. Jack and Molly added to find how many cards are needed. Explain each one's work. Which way is the easiest to write?

MOLLY'S WAY	JACK'S WAY
15 cards = 1 ten and 5 ones 12 cards = 1 ten and 2 ones Cards for all = 2 tens and 7 ones = 27	15 cards + 12 cards 27 cards

2. Jane needs a yard of lace for a doll's dress and 12 inches more for a cap. How many inches does she need in all?

3. Joe has 2 boxes of cupcakes. There are 12 in each box. Write an addition to show how many cakes he has.

4. Explain these additions. Copy them without the answers and add.

43	52	68	45	34	56	73
25	22	11	31	14	31	21
68	74	79	76	48	87	94

Copy and add. Begin at the top each time.

5.

58	37	24	61	86	42	64
41	32	12	31	12	31	34

6.

52¢	61¢	43¢	18¢	42¢	34¢	42¢
33¢	22¢	24¢	71¢	47¢	25¢	16¢

7. David wants a cowboy hat which costs 45¢, and a 34-cent belt. How much will both cost?

8. Find out if each answer in Exs. 5 and 6 is right by *seeing in your mind* a number ladder.

Subtracting dimes and cents

1. Sally has 2 dimes and 8 pennies. She has __?__ ¢ in all.

Special Today
Sodas 13 ¢

Sally is buying an ice-cream soda. The soda will cost 13¢. 13¢ = __?__ dime and __?__ pennies.

The picture of her money is shown below. She has crossed off the 1 dime and 3 pennies she will spend.

The picture shows she will have left __?__ dime and __?__ pennies, or __?__ ¢. 13¢ from 28¢ is __?__ ¢.

2. To subtract 13¢ from 28¢:

You write	You think
28¢ = 2 dimes and 8 cents	3 cents from 8 cents is __?__ cents.
− 13¢ = − 1 dime and 3 cents	1 dime from 2 dimes is __?__ dime.
__?__ dime and __?__ cents	13¢ from 28¢ is __?__ ¢.

3. Use toy money (dimes and cents) to find these answers:

49¢	78¢	69¢	56¢	87¢	97¢	74¢
− 13¢	− 53¢	− 47¢	− 23¢	− 44¢	− 62¢	− 64¢

4. To subtract 13 from 28:

You write	You think
28 = 2 tens and 8 ones	3 ones from 8 ones is __?__ ones.
− 13 = − 1 ten and 3 ones	1 ten from 2 tens is __?__ ten.
__?__ ten and __?__ ones	13 from 28 is __?__.

Subtracting tens and ones

The 28 children in Miss Beck's class are making paper-plate false faces. They have 13 plates. How many more plates do they need?

▶ To find *how many more are needed,* you subtract. Write the smaller number under the larger number this way:————————→

$$\begin{array}{r} 28 \\ -13 \\ \hline \end{array}$$

▶ Subtract 3 ones from 8 ones. Write the 5 ones in the ones column under the 8 and 3.

▶ Subtract 1 ten from 2 tens. Write the 1 ten in the tens column under the 2 and 1.

▶ How many more plates are needed?

$$\begin{array}{r} 28 \\ -13 \\ \hline 15 \end{array}$$

Explain the subtractions in Ex. 1.

1.
46	79	95	56	95	38	67	48
25	64	21	24	53	26	25	13
21	15	74	32	42	12	42	35

Subtract. Write the answers on folded paper.

2.
89	48	27	69	98	87	97	98
28	35	14	37	57	52	61	72

3.
39	98	77	99	98	85	79	86
13	34	23	24	61	64	41	31

4. Do Exs. 2 and 3 by *seeing in your mind* a number ladder. Think, "20 taken from 89 brings you down to 69; and 8 more taken away brings you down to 61."

Put on your thinking cap

▶ **Oral review**

1. Count to 100 by 10's; by 5's; by 2's; by 1's.

2. Which is the larger, 79 or 97? 62 or 56?

3. Here is Johnny. Name the shapes of the parts of his body. ⟶

4. Name in order the months of the year.

5. Does $4 + 5 = 5 + 4$?

6. What time is it by this clock?

7. What number fact does this picture show?

8. What does 7 A.M. mean? 8 P.M.?

9. 1 yd. = _?_ in.
   1 ft. = _?_ in.
   1 yd. = _?_ ft.

10. 1 quarter = _?_ cents
    1 quarter = _?_ nickels
    1 qt. = _?_ pt.

▶ **Written review**

1. 53
   + 34

2. 27
   + 62

3. 89
   − 64

4. 75
   − 32

5. 94
   − 62

6. 86
   − 32

7. $6¢ + 4¢ =$ _?_ ¢; $10¢ − 7¢ =$ _?_ ¢; $9¢ − 4¢ =$ _?_ ¢

8. Write the number that means 3 tens and 9.

9. What part of this ball is red? Write your answer in figures.

49

Checking subtraction

1. Use toy coins (4 dimes and 8 pennies) to do the subtraction in Box A. When you take 35¢ from 48¢, you have __?__ ¢ left.

A THE SUBTRACTION		B THE CHECK	
Bill had at first	48¢	Bill had left	13¢
Bill spent	− 35¢	Bill spent	+ 35¢
Bill had left	13¢	Bill had at first	48¢

2. Now use the same toy coins to prove the answer to your subtraction in Ex. 1. Put the 13¢ Bill had left and the 35¢ he spent back together again. You should have the __?__ ¢ he had at first. Do you?

3. Look at Box B. There you see a short way to prove the subtraction in Box A without using coins.

Add the 13¢ Bill had left and the 35¢ he spent. Does the sum equal the 48¢ he had at first? If so, 13¢ is the right answer. Why?

In Box B you found that 13¢ is the right answer. You *checked* the subtraction. Can you make up a rule for checking a subtraction?

Peter did these subtractions and checked them. By *checking* he found that one subtraction is *wrong*. Find it. Copy it, subtract correctly, and check.

		CHECK				CHECK				CHECK
4.	56	32	**5.**	79	44	**6.**	87	43
	− 24	+ 24		− 35	+ 35		− 34	+ 34
	32	56		44	79		43	77

Phil did these subtractions. Two are wrong. Check to find the two that are *wrong*. Copy them, subtract correctly, and check.

1.	68	95	85	48	52	77	98
	− 44	− 32	− 73	− 16	− 21	− 45	− 45
	24	63	12	32	21	32	52

Subtract and check:

2.	24	56	84	73	36	49	68
	− 13	− 25	− 63	− 21	− 14	− 26	− 33

3.	98	76	54	39	58	74	69
	− 57	− 44	− 31	− 26	− 12	− 52	− 32

Subtract and check. Do not use a pencil.

4. 90 − 70   60 − 30   50 − 40   70 − 20

5. 80 − 50   90 − 10   90 − 60   80 − 40

Check your answer to each subtraction problem below:

6. Molly has 95¢. If she spends 32¢, she has _?_ left.

7. Bill has a quarter. He wants to buy a game that costs 49¢. How much more money does he need?

8. Tom weighs 69 pounds. Ann weighs 58 pounds. Tom is _?_ pounds heavier than Ann.

9. Jim earned 43¢ on Monday. He earned 35¢ on Tuesday. All together he earned _?_¢.

10. Mary has 2 red pencils, 5 green pencils, and 3 yellow pencils. How many pencils has she in all?

11. There are 28 children in Miss Green's class. Today only 23 children are present. How many are absent?

1. Look at the picture. How much does each toy cost?

2. Tom wants a whistle, a ball, and a boat. How much will the three toys cost?

To find the cost of the three toys, Tom wrote the addition like this:——————>

Whistle 2¢
Ball 3¢
Boat 4¢
———
9¢

He thought, "2¢ + 3¢ = 5¢; 5¢ + 4¢ = _?_ ¢."
A whistle, a ball, and a boat will cost _?_ ¢.

Add. Begin at the top.

	a	b	c	d	e	f	g	h	i	j
3.	2	6	4	5	4	1	2	1	2	3
	4	1	3	1	4	3	4	7	5	1
	3	2	1	3	1	5	2	2	2	4
4.	3	2	5	4	4	6	4	5	6	4
	3	3	2	2	1	1	1	4	2	1
	3	4	2	4	5	3	3	1	2	4

5. Use the picture above to find the cost of:

a plane, a marble, a whistle
a boat, a plane, a marble
a ball, a whistle, a plane

a whistle and 2 boats
a plane and 2 marbles
a boat and 2 whistles

6. Joe has 2 red pencils, 4 blue pencils, and 3 black pencils. How many pencils has he in all?

52

Checking addition

1. Mary made 1 airplane. Tom made 4. Dick made 5. How many airplanes did they make in all?
   Write the example like this:——→
   Add. Begin at the top.
   Think: $1 + 4 = 5$; $5 + 5 =$ _?_
   To see if 10 is the right answer,

$$\begin{array}{r} 1 \\ 4 \\ +5 \\ \hline \end{array}$$

add again. This time *begin at the bottom* and add up.
Think: $5 + 4 = 9$; $9 + 1 =$ _?_
   Did you get 10 for the answer again? If so, you have *checked* your addition. Why should you always check?

2. Jane made 24 chocolate cookies and 32 nut cookies. How many cookies did she make all together?
   Write the example like this:————————→
   Begin at the top.
   Add the ones. Think: $4 + 2 = 6$
   Add the tens. Think: $2 + 3 = 5$
   Jane made _?_ cookies.

$$\begin{array}{r} 24 \\ +32 \\ \hline \end{array}$$

Now check the answer to see if it is right.
Begin at the bottom.
Add the ones. Think: $2 + 4 = 6$
Add the tens. Think: $3 + 2 = 5$
Again you find that Jane made _?_ cookies.

Add and check:

3.	6	3	4	1	3	2	4
	2	4	1	5	4	3	1
	1	3	4	2	2	2	3

4.	32	38	21	45	36	74	42
	42	51	16	23	42	21	53

Adding zeros

1. The third-grade pupils were playing ring toss. Tom first threw 3 rings on the peg. So his first score was 3.

$$\begin{array}{r} 3 \\ +0 \\ \hline 3 \end{array}$$

His next turn he did not get any rings on the peg. So his second score was *zero*. *Zero* means *not any* or *none*. It is written *0*.

All together Tom threw 3 + 0, or ___?___, rings on the peg.

2. How many rings did each of these pupils get on the peg on the first turn? on the second turn? on both turns?

Ann	Bob	Don	Mary	Jack	Dick
3	2	0	1	2	0
+ 2	+ 0	+ 2	+ 3	+ 3	+ 0

3. $7 + 0 =$ ___?___
$0 + 7 =$ ___?___

4. $8 + 0 =$ ___?___
$0 + 8 =$ ___?___

5. $9 + 0 =$ ___?___
$0 + 9 =$ ___?___

6. At the right are Billy's three scores on a number game. To find his total score, Billy thought:

$$\begin{array}{r} 7 \\ 0 \\ +3 \\ \hline \end{array}$$

$$7 + 0 = 7; \quad 7 + 3 = \underline{}$$

7. Tell what you think when you check Billy's score.

8. Find the total score of each of the following. Check.

Jean	Susan	Jack	Jerry	Carl	Jim	Tom
3	4	2	0	3	5	0
0	0	0	4	5	4	1
4	2	5	3	0	0	0

9. When Jean found her score in Ex. 8, she thought, "3 and 4 are 7." She skipped the zero. Why?

10. Make a rule for finding the sum of zero and any number.

54

1. Susan spent 30¢ for a ball and 42¢ for a bat. To find how much she spent for both, Susan wrote:———→

30¢ = 3 dimes 0 cents
42¢ = 4 dimes 2 cents
———————————————
7 dimes 2 cents = 72¢

Explain Susan's addition. She spent __?__ cents for the ball and bat.

2. Susan could have used this short way to add 30 cents and 42 cents:————————————→

```
 30¢
+42¢
 72¢
```

0 cents + 2 cents = __?__ cents.
3 dimes + 4 dimes = __?__ dimes.
She spent __?__ ¢ in all.

3. Dan read 15 pages of a storybook yesterday and 10 pages today. To find how many pages he has read in two days, do this addition:————→

```
 15
+10
 25
```

5 ones + 0 ones = 5 ones; write the 5 in the ones column.
1 ten + 1 ten = 2 tens; write the 2 in the tens column.
In 2 days he has read __?__ pages. Check the addition.

Tell what addition facts you use to find these sums; to check the sums.

4.
23	40	36	28	70	53	30	46
20	25	50	60	12	20	68	50

5. Copy Ex. 4. Add and check.

Add. Do not use a pencil.

6.
20	30	10	50	70	40	30	60
40	15	45	40	21	18	42	29

7. Write an addition which shows the sum of a quarter and a dime.

1. Don helps his father in the store on Saturday. He sold Mrs. Smith bread for 15¢, eggs for 60¢, and tomato juice for 12¢. How much did Mrs. Smith pay?

Add the cents. $5 + 0 + 2 = 7$
Write 7 in the cents column.
Add the dimes. $1 + 6 + 1 = 8$
Write 8 in the dimes column. Mrs. Smith spent __?__ cents.

```
15¢
60¢
12¢
───
87¢
```

2. Mary helped Miss Bell check the school supplies. She counted 30 reading books, 20 spelling books, and 25 arithmetic books. How many books did she count?

Add the ones. $0 + 0 + 5 = 5$
Add the tens. $3 + 2 + 2 = 7$
Mary counted __?__ books.

```
30
20
25
──
75
```

Use toy money to prove these examples are right:

3.

25¢	40¢	16¢	30¢	20¢	20¢	12¢	43¢
20¢	10¢	30¢	15¢	50¢	30¢	27¢	20¢
+ 40¢	30¢	22¢	50¢	20¢	48¢	40¢	35¢
85¢	80¢	68¢	95¢	90¢	98¢	79¢	98¢

Copy, add, and check. Then do them without a pencil.

4.

23	10	73	30	45	40	30	50
24	49	10	50	13	20	35	24
30	30	12	10	20	30	22	12

Subtracting zeros

1. Tom had 5 cents; he spent 4 cents; he had _?_ ¢ left.

2. Jane had 5 cents; she spent 5 cents; she had _?_ ¢ left.

3. Carl had 5 cents; he spent 0 cents; he had _?_ ¢ left.

4. Think of some number. Now subtract 0 from it. What is your answer?

Make a rule about subtracting zero from any number.

5. Peter had 68 cents. He spent 40 cents. Here is one way to subtract to find how many cents he had left:

You write	*You think*
68¢ = 6 dimes 8 cents	8 cents − 0 cents = _?_ cents
40¢ = 4 dimes 0 cents	6 dimes − 4 dimes = _?_ dimes
2 dimes 8 cents = 28¢	Peter had _?_ ¢ left.

6. Explain this shorter way to find 68¢ − 40¢: ⟶

7. Check the subtraction in Ex. 6.

$$\begin{array}{r} 68¢ \\ -40¢ \\ \hline 28¢ \end{array}$$

8. John had 56 marbles. He lost some. Now he has only 20. Here is one way to subtract to find out how many he lost:

You write	*You think*
56 = 5 tens 6 ones	6 ones − 0 ones = _?_ ones
20 = 2 tens 0 ones	5 tens − 2 tens = _?_ tens
3 tens 6 ones = 36	Peter lost _?_ marbles.

9. Explain this shorter way to find 56 − 20: ⟶

$$\begin{array}{r} 56 \\ -20 \\ \hline 36 \end{array}$$

Copy, subtract, and check:

10.

38	57	89	67	98	87	40	58
− 10	− 20	− 40	− 50	− 70	− 70	− 30	− 50

11. Now do Ex. 10 without using a pencil.

1. Don had a pet show. There were 4 dogs, 3 cats, and 1 goat. How many pets were in the show?

2. The table in Miss Hill's room is 1 yard and 12 inches long. The class wants a tablecloth to cover it for a party. Molly can bring a cloth 50 inches long. Is that long enough?

3. Here is a picture of Jane's money. Can she buy a 25-cent comb?

4. There are 20 children in one class and 22 in another. How many are there in both classes?

5. Sue earned 9¢ last week. She put 5¢ in her bank. How much did she keep out to spend?

6. Jean wants a 28-cent doll. She has 15¢. She needs __?__¢ more.

7. There are 97 children in a camp. 63 are boys. How many are girls?

8. Dick wants to practice his music for 20 minutes. If he begins at 5 minutes after 8, when will he finish?

9.
$$\begin{array}{r} 12 \text{ months} \\ + 12 \text{ months} \\ \hline 24 \text{ months} \end{array}$$
This addition shows there are 24 months in __?__ years.

10. Ted wants 3 quarts of ice cream. The ice cream comes in pint bricks. How many pints should he buy?

___

What is your mark on Problem Test 2? Get out your Problem Test Record. Fill it in for Test 2.

Self-Help Test 1

If you make mistakes in a Self-Help Test, you can help yourself. If you make a mistake in Ex. 1 on this test, you can find help on page 46. Where can you find help for Ex. 2?

Copy, find the answers, and check:

1.   46
    + 32 (46)

2.   93¢
    − 62¢ (47–48)

3. 35 + 40 (55)

4. 79 − 52 (48)

5. Which number is larger, 57 or 75? (16–17)

6. Write the numbers from 88 to 92. (16–17)

7. What number means 8 tens and 4? (14–15)

8. What number is 10 larger than 35? than 29? (16–17)

9. Find the sum of 2, 0, and 3. (54)

10. Which of these is a square? a circle? a rectangle? a clock face   a page of this book   a paper napkin (10)

Self-Help Test 2

1. What part of this circle is white? Write your answer in figures. (11)

2. Which might show a baby's height? 22 pints; 22 pounds; 22 inches. (24–25)

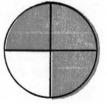

3. 1 ft. = _?_ in. (25)

4. 1 yd. = _?_ ft. (25)

5. 1 yd. = _?_ in. (25)

6. 1 qt. = _?_ pt. (28)

7. 1 pint = _?_ glasses (28)

8. 1 hour = _?_ minutes (3)

9. 1 dime = _?_ cents (4)

10. 1 quarter = _?_ cents (4)

UNIT
10

Thermometer
Money to one dollar
Roman numerals to XII

Using arithmetic

1. Miss Stone's class is going to visit the Public Library. It is 14 blocks to the library from their school. If the children walk to the library and back, how many blocks will they walk?

2. The bus fare is 5¢. If the class rides to the library and back, how much money will each child need?

3. The class decided to walk to the library and ride back. Each child will need __?__ cents. He will have to walk __?__ blocks.

4. The children brought notes from home saying that they might go on the trip. Andy counted the notes. At first there were only 15. There were 20 children in the class. How many notes were missing?

5. Sue counted the nickels the children brought. There were 19 nickels.

She placed the 19 nickels like this:⟶

Then she counted, "5, 10, 15, . . . 95."

Sue said, "We have 95 cents."

Do you agree that they had 95 cents?

6. When the last child brings his nickel, how much will they have?

7. Look at the picture. Then use your clock to find how many hours the library is open each day.

8. Look at the picture to see when the story hour starts. It takes half an hour to walk to the library. At what time should the class leave school to reach the library in time to hear the story?

9. Do you belong to a library? How long may you keep a book out of your library? Do you pay a fine if you do not return a book on time? Make up some arithmetic problems about using the library.

One morning when Betsy came into the class-room, she said, "It's cold in here, Miss Hart."

"Yes, it is cold," said Miss Hart. "Look at the thermometer. What is the temperature?"

Betsy looked at the thermometer. The top of the red liquid was at the line marked 60. The thermometer looked like the one shown here.

"Oh," said Betsy. "No wonder I'm cold! It's 60 degrees in here."

"Well, please go to the janitor's room and ask if we can have more heat," said Miss Hart.

Very soon the radiator began to sizzle. When Betsy looked at the thermometer again, the top of the red liquid was one line below 70.

"That means the temperature is 68 degrees. That's just what it should be," said Miss Hart.

About 11 o'clock, Paul asked, "May I open a window? I'm too hot. It's 74 degrees in here."

"We'll turn the radiator off. The room will cool down to 68 degrees again," said Miss Hart.

You use a thermometer to tell how hot or cold the air is. With it you measure the temperature of the air.

Temperature is measured in *degrees*. 68 degrees is written like this: 68°. The little circle means degrees. The numbers on a thermometer stand for degrees.

Is there a weather report in your newspaper? What was the lowest temperature yesterday? the highest? How much did the temperature change yesterday?

1. Read the thermometer in your classroom. What is the temperature? Are you warm enough?

2. Place the thermometer outside your window. What will happen to it? Check to see if you are right.

3. What is the temperature outdoors? Did you need to wear a coat to school this morning?

4. Show where the top of the red liquid is when the temperature is 0°; 10°; 20°; 30°; 40°; 50°; 60°.

5. What temperature is 10° higher than 20°? 50°? 70°?

6. What is the temperature if it falls 10° from 90°? from 80°? 70°? 60°? 50°? 40°? 30°? 20°? 10°?

7. Peter said, "A thermometer is just like a number ladder, except that it goes up by 2's instead of by 1's." Tell what Peter meant.

8. Show where the top of the liquid is when the temperature is 30°; 32°; 34°; 36°; 38°; 40°; 42°.

9. Tell what the temperature is when the liquid rises to each line on the thermometer between 50 and 60.

10. Water freezes at a temperature of 32°. Find 32° on the thermometer.

11. Mary saw ice on the sidewalk when she came to school one morning. The temperature was 27°. When she went home for lunch, the thermometer read 38°. The ice was gone. There was a puddle of water in its place. Why?

12. On the thermometer find 50°; 52°; 53°; 54°; 55°.

13. How much does the temperature rise or fall when it goes from 54° to 66°? 78° to 70°? 46° to 68°? 54° to 50°?

14. Tell some ways in which thermometers are used.

Every week Carl earns 20¢ from a neighbor for feeding her chickens. One day Carl said, "I don't earn enough to pay for all the things I need, Daddy. I wish you would give me an allowance."

"I will, Carl, if you can prove that you know a few things about money."

Carl's father asked him the questions below. Can you answer them? Carl could.

1. A dime is worth _?_ pennies; or _?_ nickels.

2. A quarter is worth _?_ pennies; or _?_ nickels; or _?_ dimes and 1 nickel.

> **LEARN THIS**
>
> A fifty-cent piece is called a *half dollar*. One hundred cents is a *dollar*.

3. A half dollar is worth _?_ pennies; or _?_ nickels; or _?_ dimes; or _?_ quarters.

4. A dollar is worth _?_ pennies; or _?_ nickels; or _?_ dimes; or _?_ quarters; or _?_ half dollars.

5. Name some things that cost a penny; a nickel; a dime.

6. Do you know some things that cost about a quarter? a half dollar? a dollar?

7. How much change will you get:
- from a nickel if you spend 3¢? 2¢? 1¢? 4¢? 5¢?
- from a dime if you spend 5¢? 3¢? 8¢? 6¢? 7¢? 9¢?
- from a quarter if you spend 20¢? 15¢? 10¢? 5¢? 1¢?
- from a half dollar if you spend 42¢? 37¢? 23¢? 16¢?
- from a dollar if you spend 85¢? 75¢? 40¢? 35¢? 15¢?

Carl's father said, "Good work, son. You know money well enough to have an allowance. Make a list of the things you need money for each week. Then we can find out what your allowance should be."

School supplies – 10¢
Sunday school – 5¢
To save in
  dime bank – 10¢
To spend for
  what I wish – 10¢
         Total – 35¢

8. Read Carl's list. How much does he need each week?

9. His father said, "Your list shows you need 35¢ a week. You earn only 20¢. I will give you the other __?__ ¢ each week."

10. Carl saves __?__ ¢ each week in his dime bank. How long will it take him to save 40¢?

11. Carl wants a 20-cent book called *Model Airplanes*. If he uses his spending money, can he buy the book at the end of 1 week? at the end of 2 weeks?

12. Do you have an allowance? Do you earn money? How do you earn it? How do you spend your money?

Do you save money each week? What do you plan to do with what you save?

What time is it by each of these clocks? Can you read the numbers on the cuckoo clock? Those numbers are called *Roman numbers*.

On clock faces the Roman number *four* is written IIII. But the more common way of writing *four* in Roman numbers is IV.

1	2	3	4	5	6	7	8	9	10	11	12
I	II	III	IV	V	VI	VII	VIII	IX	X	XI	XII

1. What does the Roman number I mean? the Roman number V? X? VI? VII? XI? XII? IX? IV?

2. Write the Roman numbers from I to XII. Where have you seen Roman numbers besides on a clock?

3. Billy kept a record of all the Roman numbers he saw. Here is a part of his record. Maybe you would like to keep one in your Arithmetic Folder.

Roman numbers that I have seen

1. V on an old nickel

2. I, II, III, IV, V, VI, VII, VIII, IX —
Chapter numbers in our
science book

Now is the time to test yourself

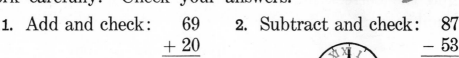

Copy the numbers correctly.
Work carefully.   Check your answers.

1. Add and check: 69
    + 20

2. Subtract and check: 87
    − 53

3. Find the sum of 3, 4, and 2.

4. What time is it by this clock?

5. This picture shows an addition.   Write the same addition in figures.

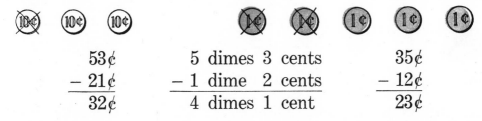

Cost of paper = (10¢)   and   (1¢) (1¢) (1¢)

Cost of paints = (10¢) (10¢)   and   (1¢) (1¢)

Cost of both = (10¢) (10¢) (10¢) and   (1¢) (1¢) (1¢) (1¢) (1¢)

6. Miss Bell's class gathered 24 maple leaves and 35 oak leaves.   In all, they gathered ? leaves.

7. Which one of the 3 subtractions below is shown by the picture?   Copy the subtraction.

53¢	5 dimes 3 cents	35¢
− 21¢	− 1 dime 2 cents	− 12¢
32¢	4 dimes 1 cent	23¢

8. Jerry has a quarter.   He wants to buy a flashlight for 49¢.   How much more money does he need?

9. Alice spent 30¢ in the toyshop.   She gave the clerk a half dollar.   How much change should she receive?

10. The temperature was 55° at 9 o'clock.   It was 65° at noon.   How much warmer was it at noon?

UNIT 11

*Reading and writing
three-place numbers
Reading money*

Number names

1. Write the numbers from 1 to 5 in a column. Then find the correct number word below to write beside each number.

three   two   five   one   four

2. Write the numbers from 6 to 10 in a column. Then find the correct number word below to write beside each number.

seven   six   nine   eight   ten

Write in figures the numbers in columns *a*, *b*, and *c*.

a	*b*	*c*
3. ten	zero	twenty-six
4. eleven	ten	sixty-two
5. twelve	twenty	forty-seven
6. thirteen	thirty	seventy-four
7. fourteen	forty	thirty-five
8. fifteen	fifty	fifty-three
9. sixteen	sixty	ninety-one
10. seventeen	seventy	nineteen
11. eighteen	eighty	eighty-four
12. nineteen	ninety	forty-eight
13. twenty	one hundred	sixty-seven

14. Write these words in a column in the right order:

first   sixth   ninth   fifth   seventh
eighth   second   tenth   fourth   third

Three-place numbers

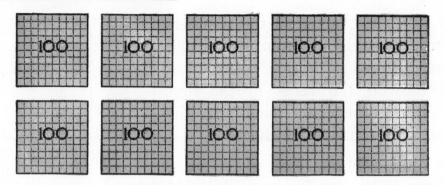

Some children are selling Christmas seals. There are 100 seals in each sheet. How many sheets are shown here?

In one sheet there are one hundred seals. In two sheets there are two hundred seals. Two hundred is a three-place number. It needs two zeros and is written like this: 200. The zeros mean there are no tens and no ones.

1. Point to the seals and count them by hundreds.

one hundred	100	six hundred	600
two hundred	200	seven hundred	700
three hundred	300	eight hundred	800
four hundred	400	nine hundred	900
five hundred	500	ten hundred	1000

In ten sheets there are _?_ hundred seals. Ten hundred is called *one thousand*. It is written: 1,000.

2. Dick had one sheet of seals to sell. He divided it into strips of ten. How many rows of ten could he make out of one sheet? 100 = _?_ tens.

3. Look at the picture at the top of the page. How many rows of ten are there in 1 sheet? 3 sheets? 6 sheets?

300 = _?_ tens   400 = _?_ tens   600 = _?_ tens

500 = _?_ tens   1000 = _?_ tens   900 = _?_ tens

69

1. In this chart read the numbers from 100 to 1000; from 10 to 100; from 1 to 10.

What do the zeros in the first column in the chart mean? in the second column in the chart?

100	10	1
200	20	2
300	30	3
400	40	4
500	50	5
600	60	6
700	70	7
800	80	8
900	90	9
1000	100	10

2. June sold one sheet of 100 seals, 2 rows of 10, and 5 more. She sold one hundred twenty-five seals.

This picture shows how many Christmas seals she sold.————>

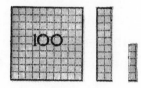

One hundred twenty-five is written: 125. It is a three-place number. 125 means 1 hundred, 2 tens, and 5 ones.

3. How many seals did each of these boys sell?

Dick sold   Tom sold   Jack sold

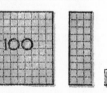 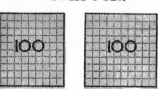 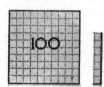

4. Dick sold 132 seals.

132 means _?_ hundred, _?_ tens, _?_ ones.

5. Tom sold 210 seals.

210 means _?_ hundred, _?_ ten, _?_ ones.

6. Jack sold 107 seals.

107 means _?_ hundred, _?_ tens, _?_ ones.

7. How many sheets of 100 seals, how many rows of 10 seals, how many separate seals are 375 seals? 205? 320?

A	B	C
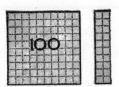	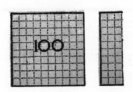	

1. How many seals are there in Picture A? in B? in C?

2. In which picture can you see 13 tens? 14 tens? 12 tens?

3. 120 = _?_ tens   130 = _?_ tens   140 = _?_ tens

4. 150 = _?_ tens   160 = _?_ tens   200 = _?_ tens

5. 1 hundred and 1 ten = _?_ tens.   110 = _?_ tens
   1 hundred and 8 tens = _?_ tens.   180 = _?_ tens
   1 hundred and 7 tens = _?_ tens.   170 = _?_ tens
   1 hundred and 10 tens = _?_ tens.   200 = _?_ tens

6. 10 tens = _?_ hundred.
   11 tens = _?_ hundred and _?_ ten.
   14 tens = _?_ hundred and _?_ tens.
   19 tens = _?_ hundred and _?_ tens.

7. Count by 25's to 400; by 30's to 150; by 40's to 200.

8. Count by 50's to 1000; by 20's to 500.

9. Count by 1's from 89 to 103; from 189 to 203.

10. Count by 2's from 146 to 156; from 294 to 304.

11. Count by 5's from 75 to 115; from 390 to 425.

12. Count by 10's from 150 to 230; from 640 to 710.

13. Count by 10's from 25 to 125; from 112 to 212.

14. What is the largest 2-place number? the smallest?

15. What is the largest 3-place number? the smallest?

16. What number comes next after: 909?   990?   999?

17. What number comes just before: 900?   910?   901?

Reading and writing three-place numbers

1. Miss Kane's class sold 785 seals. How many sheets of 100 seals, how many rows of 10 seals, and how many extra seals did they sell?

785 is ⎯?⎯ hundreds, ⎯?⎯ tens, and ⎯?⎯ ones

2. When you put together 400, 60, and 3, you have four hundred sixty-⎯?⎯.

3. When you put together 600, 50, and 4, you have ⎯?⎯ hundreds, ⎯?⎯ tens, and ⎯?⎯ ones.

4. When you put together 300 and 1, you have 3 hundreds, 0 tens, and 1 one, or 301. The zero in 301 shows there are ⎯?⎯ tens in the tens place.

5. What does the zero show in these numbers?

101　　105　　110　　107　　104　　120

6. Read each of these numbers. Then tell how many hundreds, tens, and ones there are in each.

169　　504　　401　　841　　119　　906
254　　669　　860　　732　　508　　700

7. Write the numbers above as your teacher reads them.

8. Write the number that means:

3 hundreds, 7 tens, 4 ones　　2 hundreds, 9 tens, 7 ones
6 hundreds, 3 tens, 0 ones　　7 hundreds, 0 tens, 6 ones
8 hundreds, 0 tens, 0 ones　　5 hundreds, 5 tens, 5 ones

9. Write these numbers in figures:

five hundred forty-five　　　two hundred fifty
nine hundred sixty-one　　　four hundred ninety-three

10. Write the numbers from 98 to 110; from 293 to 302.

11. Write the numbers by 100's from 100 to 1000.

72

Reading money numbers

Johnny likes these slacks. How much do they cost?

$9.50 means 9 dollars, 5 dimes, and no cents.

$9.50 is read "9 dollars and 50 cents."

The sign for dollars is $. The dot in $9.50 is the *cents point*. The figure to the left of the cents point tells the number of dollars. The two figures to the right of the cents point tell the number of cents.

SPORTS CLOTHES

SLACKS $9.50

1. $8.75 means __?__ dollars, __?__ dimes, __?__ cents. $8.75 is read __?__ dollars and __?__ cents.

2. $14.50 means __?__ dollars, __?__ dimes, __?__ cents. $14.50 is read __?__ dollars and __?__ cents.

3. $12.00 means __?__ dollars, __?__ dimes, __?__ cents. $12.00 is read __?__ dollars.

> 1 cent is written 1¢ or $.01
> 1 dollar is written $1 or $1.00

4. Tell how many dollars, dimes, and cents there are in:

| $2.25 | $6.43 | $3.05 | $6.00 | $11.50 |

5. Which is more: $87.00 or $.87? $7.06 or $7.60?

Read these prices. Which is largest? smallest?

6. 3¢ $.82 $.03 $.70 $4.00 $15.05

7. 8¢ $.28 $.08 $.35 $3.75 $12.02

Facts about 11

Miss Lee's class made 11 paper turkeys. They want to paste the turkeys on the 2 big doors of their classroom.

Jane said, "Let's put the same number on each door."

Jim said, "We can't do that." Prove that Jim is right.

How many turkeys can they put at the front door if they put 2 at the back door? if they put 3? 4? 5?

Dot Pictures about 11

1. Row A shows that 10 and 1 are ___?___. How many dots are there in each row of the chart? Show how Row B teaches you these four facts:

$$\begin{array}{cc} 9 \\ +2 \\ \hline 11 \end{array} \qquad \begin{array}{cc} 2 \\ +9 \\ \hline 11 \end{array} \qquad\qquad \begin{array}{cc} 11 \\ -9 \\ \hline 2 \end{array} \qquad \begin{array}{cc} 11 \\ -2 \\ \hline 9 \end{array}$$

2. What 2 addition facts does Row C teach? Row D? E? What 2 subtraction facts does each row teach?

3. Write the facts you taught yourself in Ex. 2.

4. Make up a problem about each fact you wrote in Ex. 3.

5. $9 + 1 = 10$, so $9 + 2 = $ ___?___.

6. $7 + 3 = 10$, so $7 + 4 = $ ___?___.

7. $8 + 2 = 10$, so $8 + 3 = $ ___?___.

8. $6+5=11$, so $11-6=$ ___?___.

9. $7+4=11$, so $11-7=$ ___?___.

10. $8+3=11$, so $11-3=$ ___?___.

Using coins to teach yourself about 11

1. Use 2 nickels and a penny to show these 4 facts:

$5 + 6 = 11$ $6 + 5 = 11$ $11 - 6 = 5$ $11 - 5 = 6$

2. Use 11 toy pennies to show that:

2 fives and 1 more are 11   3 threes and 2 more are 11
2 fours and 3 more are 11   5 twos and 1 more are 11

3. Jane says, "When I add 9¢ and 2¢, I change the 9 pennies and 2 pennies into 1 dime and 1 penny. That makes it easy to see that $9¢ + 2¢ = 10¢ + 1¢ = \underline{\ ?\ }¢$."

Use toy coins to prove your answers in Exs. 4 to 6.

4. $8¢ + 3¢ = \underline{\ 1\ }$ dime and $\underline{\ ?\ }$ cent. $8¢ + 3¢ = \underline{\ ?\ }¢.$

5. $7¢ + 4¢ = \underline{\ ?\ }$ dime and $\underline{\ ?\ }$ cent. $7¢ + 4¢ = \underline{\ ?\ }¢.$

6. $6¢ + 5¢ = \underline{\ ?\ }$ dime and $\underline{\ ?\ }$ cent. $6¢ + 5¢ = \underline{\ ?\ }¢.$

7. Bill had a dime and a cent. He gave the cent to Polly. What did he have to do to the dime to give a cent to Larry? Then Bill had $\underline{\ ?\ }¢$ left. Does $11¢ - 2¢ = 10¢ - 1¢$?

8. To take 3¢ from 1 dime and 1 cent, you take $\underline{\ ?\ }$ cents out of the dime. Does $11¢ - 3¢ = 10¢ - 2¢$?

9. To take 4¢ from 1 dime and 1 cent, you take $\underline{\ ?\ }$ cents out of the dime. Does $11¢ - 4¢ = 10¢ - 3¢$?

$\begin{array}{r} 9 \\ +2 \\ \hline 11 \end{array}$	$\begin{array}{r} 2 \\ +9 \\ \hline 11 \end{array}$	$\begin{array}{r} 8 \\ +3 \\ \hline 11 \end{array}$	$\begin{array}{r} 3 \\ +8 \\ \hline 11 \end{array}$	$\begin{array}{r} 7 \\ +4 \\ \hline 11 \end{array}$	$\begin{array}{r} 4 \\ +7 \\ \hline 11 \end{array}$	$\begin{array}{r} 6 \\ +5 \\ \hline 11 \end{array}$	$\begin{array}{r} 5 \\ +6 \\ \hline 11 \end{array}$
$\begin{array}{r} 11 \\ -9 \\ \hline 2 \end{array}$	$\begin{array}{r} 11 \\ -2 \\ \hline 9 \end{array}$	$\begin{array}{r} 11 \\ -3 \\ \hline 8 \end{array}$	$\begin{array}{r} 11 \\ -8 \\ \hline 3 \end{array}$	$\begin{array}{r} 11 \\ -7 \\ \hline 4 \end{array}$	$\begin{array}{r} 11 \\ -4 \\ \hline 7 \end{array}$	$\begin{array}{r} 11 \\ -6 \\ \hline 5 \end{array}$	$\begin{array}{r} 11 \\ -5 \\ \hline 6 \end{array}$

Write in 2 ways each number fact you use in Exs. 1 to 7.

1. Ann has 7 pictures of white horses and 4 pictures of black horses. In all, she has __?__ horse pictures.

2. Jack is 8 years old. Molly is 11 years old. So Jack is __?__ years younger than Molly.

3. Bill had 11 arithmetic problems to do. He has done 3. How many more does he have to do?

4. Eddie had 11¢. He spent a nickel. He has __?__ ¢ left.

5. Ted has 3 red marbles and 8 blue ones. He has __?__ marbles in all.

6. Ann had 6¢. Then she earned a nickel. Has she enough now to buy a 10-cent game? more than enough?

7. Joe wants to buy a 9-cent top and a 2-cent string for the top. To buy both, he needs __?__ ¢.

8. Tom and Bill found 11 marbles. If Tom keeps 2 marbles, Bill gets __?__. If Tom keeps 3, Bill gets __?__. Tell 6 other ways the boys could share the marbles. Don't give either boy more than 9. Can they share them equally?

Practice until you can say all the answers correctly:

$$
\textbf{9.} \quad
\begin{array}{r} 9 \\ +2 \end{array} \quad
\begin{array}{r} 5 \\ +6 \end{array} \quad
\begin{array}{r} 6 \\ +4 \end{array} \quad
\begin{array}{r} 11 \\ -4 \end{array} \quad
\begin{array}{r} 8 \\ +3 \end{array} \quad
\begin{array}{r} 11 \\ -9 \end{array} \quad
\begin{array}{r} 11 \\ -3 \end{array} \quad
\begin{array}{r} 7 \\ +4 \end{array} \quad
\begin{array}{r} 11 \\ -5 \end{array}
$$

$$
\textbf{10.} \quad
\begin{array}{r} 11 \\ -2 \end{array} \quad
\begin{array}{r} 3 \\ +8 \end{array} \quad
\begin{array}{r} 11 \\ -6 \end{array} \quad
\begin{array}{r} 4 \\ +7 \end{array} \quad
\begin{array}{r} 11 \\ -8 \end{array} \quad
\begin{array}{r} 2 \\ +9 \end{array} \quad
\begin{array}{r} 7 \\ +3 \end{array} \quad
\begin{array}{r} 11 \\ -7 \end{array} \quad
\begin{array}{r} 6 \\ +5 \end{array}
$$

11. Copy Exs. 9 and 10 and write the answers. Make Help-Yourself Cards for any facts you do not know. Study them; then write the answers again.

Be your own teacher

You can be your own teacher in arithmetic. You have never learned how to do the problems on this page, but you can do them. You may draw pictures to find the answers, if you want to.

See how many different ways the boys and girls in your class can find to do these problems.

1. How much money will Jack need to buy 3 games costing 15¢ each?

2. Billy wants a baseball suit costing $4.25 and a cap costing $.50. How much money will he need for both?

3. Four girls bought a box of lemon candies. There were 20 pieces in the box. If they share the candy equally, how many pieces should each girl take?

4. Tom's grandmother gave him $2.00 for his birthday. If he spends 35¢ to go to the movies, how much money will he have left?

5. Ann is making a costume. She measured with her foot ruler and found she needs 6 feet of cloth. But the cloth is sold by the yard. How many yards of cloth should she buy?

6. Jim's teacher asked him to find the sum of the numbers 1, 2, 3, 4, 5, 6, 7, 8, 9. Jim thought a minute and then said, "45."

His teacher asked how he found the sum so quickly. Jim showed her this picture and said, "This is what I thought." Can you understand Jim's picture?

$$1 \quad 2 \quad 3 \quad 4 \quad 5 \quad 6 \quad 7 \quad 8 \quad 9$$
$$4 + 6$$
$$3 + 7$$
$$2 + 8$$
$$1 + 9$$

To the Teacher: See Note 6 on page 311.

Dot Pictures about 12

A	• • • • • • • • • • • •
B	• • • • • • • • • • • •
C	• • • • • • • • • • • •
D	• • • • • • • • • • • •
E	• • • • • • • • • • • •

This chart will help you learn about the number 12.

1. Row A shows that 10 and 2 are __?__. How many dots are there in each row?

2. What 2 addition facts does Row B teach? Row C? Row D? What subtraction facts do these rows teach?

3. What 2 facts does Row E teach you?

4. Write the facts you taught yourself in Exs. 2 and 3. Make up a problem about each fact.

5. $9+1=10$, so $9+3=$ __?__.   7. $7+3=10$, so $7+5=$ __?__.

6. $8+2=10$, so $8+4=$ __?__.   8. $6+4=10$, so $6+6=$ __?__.

9. Use 2 nickels and 2 pennies to show these 4 facts:
$5+7=12$ $7+5=12$ $12-5=7$ $12-7=5$

10. $8+4=12$, so $4+8=$ __?__.   13. $9+3=12$, so $12-9=$ __?__.

11. $7+5=12$, so $5+7=$ __?__.   14. $12-4=8$, so $12-8=$ __?__.

12. $6+6=12$, so $12-6=$ __?__.   15. $12-5=7$, so $12-7=$ __?__.

16. Use toy pennies or draw dot pictures to show that:
3 fours are 12   4 threes are 12
2 sixes are 12   2 fives and 2 more are 12

1. Count these eggs by 4's. This shows that $4 + 4 =$? , and $8 + 4 =$? .

2. Cover a row of 4 eggs. $12 - 4 =$? .

3. Count backward by 4's from 12. This shows that $12 - 4 =$? , and $8 - 4 =$? .

4. Count the eggs by 3's. This shows that $3 + 3 =$? , $6 + 3 =$? , and $9 + 3 =$? .

5. Cover a row of 3 eggs. $12 - 3 =$? .

6. Count backward by 3's from 12. This shows that $12-3=$? ; $9-3=$? ; $6-3=$? .

7. Count these eggs by 6's. $6 + 6=$? . →

LEARN THIS

There are 12 things in a dozen.

8. Cover 6 eggs. Now how many eggs can you see? $12 - 6 =$? . How many eggs are there in half a dozen?

9. Your foot ruler is ? inches long. How many inches can you see if you cover 3 in.? 4 in.? 5 in.? 6 in.?

10. 9¢ + 3¢ = 1 dime and ? cents. 9¢ + 3¢ = ? ¢.

11. To take 3¢ from 12¢ (1 dime and 2 cents), you take 1¢ out of the dime. You have ? ¢ left. 12¢ − 3¢ = ? ¢.

9	3	8	4	7	5	6
+ 3	+ 9	+ 4	+ 8	+ 5	+ 7	+ 6
12	12	12	12	12	12	12
12	12	12	12	12	12	12
− 9	− 3	− 8	− 4	− 7	− 5	− 6
3	9	4	8	5	7	6

Write in 2 ways each number fact you use in Exs. 1 to 6.

1. Tom has 6 red pencils and 6 green pencils. All together he has __?__ pencils.

2. Diana has a dozen eggs. She is using 4 eggs in a cake. How many eggs will she have left?

3. Nick wants to buy a 12-cent ticket. He has only 7¢. He needs __?__ ¢ more.

4. Bill caught a fish a foot long. Sally caught one 8 inches long. Bill's fish was __?__ inches longer than Sally's.

5. Peter had 7¢. He was given a nickel. How much did he have then?

6. Jo has 12¢. Jane has 3¢. Jane has __?__ ¢ less than Jo.

7. Mary is buying a dozen cupcakes. How many yellow cakes can she have if she gets 9 white ones? 8? 7? 6? 5? 4? 3? Can she get an equal number of each?

8. Write 4 facts for each of these groups of numbers:

7, 4, 11   5, 6, 11   7, 5, 12   8, 3, 11

Practice until you can say every answer correctly:

9.	12	9	12	8	6	12	7	12
	− 8	+ 3	− 6	+ 4	+ 5	− 3	+ 5	− 9

10.	6	4	12	9	12	3	12	5
	+ 6	+ 8	− 7	+ 2	− 5	+ 9	− 4	+ 7

11. Write the answers to Exs. 9 and 10 on folded paper. Make and study Help-Yourself Cards for any facts you did not know. Then write the answers again.

No pencils, please

1. Tell the missing numbers:

   A dime = _?_ ¢   1 yard = _?_ feet
   A nickel = _?_ ¢   1 quart = _?_ pints
   A dollar = _?_ ¢   1 week = _?_ days
   A quarter = _?_ ¢   1 foot = _?_ inches
   A half dollar = _?_ ¢   1 year = _?_ months

2. IX = _?_   XII = _?_   IV = _?_   XI = _?_

3. Add and check:

a	b	c	d	e	f	g	h	i	j
3	4	7	4	2	5	2	5	5	4
2	0	2	3	4	4	4	0	2	4
1	5	1	5	4	3	6	7	4	4

4. Tell the answers to the examples on pages 22 and 37.

5. $9 + \_?\_ = 12$ $6 + \_?\_ = 10$ $4 + \_?\_ = 12$
   $8 + \_?\_ = 11$ $7 + \_?\_ = 11$ $8 + \_?\_ = 10$
   $5 + \_?\_ = 12$ $6 + \_?\_ = 12$ $9 + \_?\_ = 11$
   $6 + \_?\_ = 11$ $7 + \_?\_ = 10$ $7 + \_?\_ = 12$

6. Sue says she can't tell these missing numbers. Why not?

   $24 - 56 = \_?\_$ 1 qt. = _?_ yd. $8 + \_?\_ = \_?\_$

   Tell each answer. Then see if each answer is right by *seeing in your mind* a number ladder.

7.
98	87	69	86	75	87	79
− 42	− 34	− 37	− 42	− 30	− 57	− 53

8.
43	15	30	62	36	27	82
+ 35	+ 74	+ 57	+ 36	+ 40	+ 50	+ 13

Using a calendar

1. Why is the 25 red on the calendar in the picture?

2. A white circle is drawn around the day school closes for Christmas vacation. On what day of the month does school close? On what day of the week?

3. Friday, December 6, is Jean's birthday. Find the date on the calendar.

4. Paul's birthday is marked with a red circle, too. Can you find it? On what day of the month does his birthday come? On what day of the week?

5. Paul says his birthday is two weeks before Christmas. Do you agree with him?

6. Ted borrowed a book from the library on December 9. He may keep it two weeks. Look at the calendar in the picture and tell when he must take it back.

7. Don said their calendar showed three weeks of school in December. Do you agree with him?

8. Mary says there are five school days in a week. Name them. Is Mary right?

9. How many school days are there in three weeks? $5 + 5 + 5 = \underline{\ ?\ }$. How many days will the children in Miss Carter's class go to school in December?

You will need to look at your classroom calendar to answer the next questions.

10. What month is it now? What year? What day of the week?

11. On what day of the week is the first of December this year? On what day of the week is Christmas?

12. School closes for Christmas vacation this year on what day of the month? on what day of the week?

13. Which children in your class have birthdays in December? On what days of the month do they come? On what days of the week do they come this year?

14. Name the days of the week. Count them. What day of the month is a week before Christmas? What day of the week is that?

 *There are 7 days in a week.*

15. What day of the month is two weeks before Christmas? What day of the week is it?

16. What day of the month is the last day of December? What day of the week is it?

17. On what day of the week does December tenth come this year? December fifth? December twentieth?

18. Tell some ways you use a calendar at school; at home.

Making lollipops

Here are the things Miss Kane's class used to make lollipops:

3 cups of sugar	A few drops of flavoring
1 cup of Karo syrup	A few drops of coloring
2 cups of water	

First, the girls put the sugar, the syrup, and the water together and boiled them until a little dropped in cold water became brittle.

Then they divided the candy into three equal parts. Betsy poured $\frac{1}{3}$ of the candy into one pitcher, $\frac{1}{3}$ into a second pitcher, and $\frac{1}{3}$ into a third pitcher.

Jean added blue coloring to $\frac{1}{3}$ of the candy.

She added brown coloring to $\frac{1}{3}$ of the candy.

She added orange coloring to $\frac{1}{3}$ of the candy.

The children oiled the shiny white top of the kitchen table. They poured big drops of the candy on the table and stuck lollipop sticks into the drops.

1. Into how many equal parts did Betsy divide the candy? What part of the candy did Jean color blue? Write your answer in figures.

2. The girls made 11 blue lollipops and 13 brown lollipops. How many was that?

3. The boys made 15 orange lollipops. How many lollipops did the class make all together?

4. The lollipop sticks came in packages. The children had 2 packages. There were a dozen sticks in each package. How many sticks did they have?

5. They had enough candy for 39 lollipops. They had only 24 sticks. How many more sticks did they need?

6. Jane found 10 sticks in the closet. Then they had 24 sticks and 10 sticks. How many sticks was that?

7. They had candy enough for 39 lollipops. They had 34 sticks. How many lollipops had to go without sticks?

8. Have you ever made candy? If so, what measuring did you do? How long did you cook the candy?

Reading and writing dollars and cents

Look at the picture. Do you see anything you want for Christmas?

1. How much do the skates cost? Copy the price.

2. What is the price of the doll? the airplane?

3. Read the price tag on the sled. Copy the price.

4. Read the price of the football. Copy the price.

5. Make a list of toys that you think a boy would like. Where can you find the prices of these toys? Write the prices.

6. Make a list of toys that you think a girl would like. Write the prices of the toys.

Making a boat

Dave made a boat. This is the way he made it.

He took a piece of wood 4 inches wide and about 1 inch thick. He sawed off a piece 9 inches long. This was for the main part of the boat.

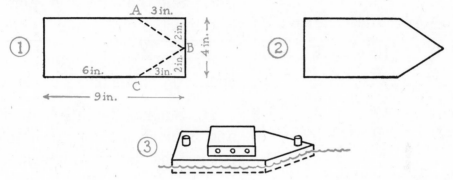

1. Look at the first picture. Tell how Dave measured to mark Point A; Point C; Point B.

He drew a line from A to B and from C to B.

Then he sawed off the corners along the lines. His piece of wood then looked like the second picture.

Next, Dave cut out a square piece of wood 3 inches long and 3 inches wide. This was for the cabin. He nailed the cabin to the boat.

2. His mother gave him two small spools for posts. Where did he put those? Look at the third picture.

He sandpapered the boat. Then he painted it. He used tacks for windows for the cabin.

3. Can you make a boat like Dave's? Make a paper pattern first. That will help you to measure correctly.

4. Have you ever needed to measure when you made something out of wood? out of paper? out of cloth? If possible, show the class what you made.

Put on your thinking cap

▶ Oral review

1. $8¢ + 3¢ = 10¢ + \underline{\ ?\ }¢ = \underline{\ ?\ }¢$

2. $9¢ + 2¢ = 10¢ + \underline{\ ?\ }¢ = \underline{\ ?\ }¢$

3. $7¢ + 4¢ = 10¢ + \underline{\ ?\ }¢ = \underline{\ ?\ }¢$

4.
```
  6     10      8     11
+ 4    - 6    + 3    - 8
```

5.
```
  3     12      4      9
+ 9    - 9    + 5    - 4
```

6. $12 - 6 = 6$, so $6 + 6 = \underline{\ ?\ }$.

7. $7 + 3 = 10$, so $3 + 7 = \underline{\ ?\ }$.

8. $9 + 1 = 10$, so $9 + 2 = \underline{\ ?\ }$.

9. Sue has 9 pansy plants. She wants to put each in a pot. She has only 5 pots. She must buy $\underline{\ ?\ }$ more pots.

10. Harry had a dime. He spent 6¢. He has $\underline{\ ?\ }$¢ left.

11. Sue has 3 white kittens and 3 black kittens. All together she has $\underline{\ ?\ }$ kittens.

12. Jean is 9 years old. Molly is 7. Molly is $\underline{\ ?\ }$ years younger than Jean.

▶ Written review

Add and check.

1.
```
2    5    5    6    1
3    2    0    1    2
4    1    4    3    6
```

2.
```
2    3    5    1    7
0    0    2    4    0
3    2    0    2    1
4    5    4    4    4
```

3.
```
3 5    4 6    5 5    6 7
2 0    3 3    2 4    2 2
```

Subtract and check.

4.
```
9 8    7 6    5 4    3 2
6 8    5 4    3 2    2 0
```

5.
```
5 8    6 7    8 5    9 6
5 4    6 3    4 4    7 1
```

6. What number means:
6 tens and 4? 5 tens and 5?
8 tens and 7? 4 tens and 9?

7. Do Exs. 9, 10, and 11 on pages 76 and 80.

Facts about 13

1. Ann and Polly together want to make 13 clothespin dolls. How many must Polly make if Ann makes 5? To find out, cover 5 of the 13 dolls.

2. How many must Polly make if Ann makes 7? 6? 9? 8?

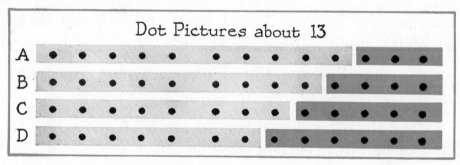

Dot Pictures about 13

A
B
C
D

3. Row A shows that 10 and 3 are __?__. How many dots are there in each row?

4. What 2 addition and subtraction facts does Row B teach? Row C? Row D?

5. $6+6 = 12$, so $6+7 = $ __?__. 7. $9+3 = 12$, so $9+4 = $ __?__.

6. $7+3 = 10$, so $7+6 = $ __?__. 8. $8+5 = 13$, so $13-8 = $ __?__.

9. Use 2 nickels and 3 pennies to show that:

$5+8 = $ __?__ $8+5 = $ __?__ $13-5 = $ __?__ $13-8 = $ __?__

10. Draw dot pictures to show that:

3 fours and 1 are 13   2 sixes and 1 are 13

4 threes and 1 are 13   2 fives and 3 are 13

Use toy coins (dimes and pennies) to show that:

1. $9¢ + 4¢ = 1$ dime and $\underline{\ ?\ }¢$ $9¢ + 4¢ = \underline{\ ?\ }¢$

2. $8¢ + 5¢ = 1$ dime and $\underline{\ ?\ }¢$ $8¢ + 5¢ = \underline{\ ?\ }¢$

3. $7¢ + 6¢ = 1$ dime and $\underline{\ ?\ }¢$ $7¢ + 6¢ = \underline{\ ?\ }¢$

4. To take 5¢ from 13¢ (1 dime and 3¢), you take $\underline{\ ?\ }¢$ out of the dime. $13¢ - 5¢ = \underline{\ ?\ }¢$.

5. To take 9¢ from 13¢ (1 dime and 3¢), you take $\underline{\ ?\ }¢$ out of the dime. $13¢ - 9¢ = \underline{\ ?\ }¢$.

6. To take 7¢ from 13¢ (1 dime and 3¢), you take $\underline{\ ?\ }¢$ out of the dime. $13¢ - 7¢ = \underline{\ ?\ }¢$.

7. To take 8¢ from 13¢ (1 dime and 3¢), you take $\underline{\ ?\ }¢$ out of the dime. $13¢ - 8¢ = \underline{\ ?\ }¢$.

8. Tell the other 3 members in the Number Family of each of these facts:

$$\begin{array}{ccc} 6 & 13 & 13 \\ +7 & -8 & -4 \\ \hline \end{array}$$

9. $8 + \underline{\ ?\ } = 13$ $7 + \underline{\ ?\ } = 13$ $4 + \underline{\ ?\ } = 13$

10. $9 + \underline{\ ?\ } = 13$ $5 + \underline{\ ?\ } = 13$ $6 + \underline{\ ?\ } = 13$

11. Write 4 facts about each of these groups of numbers:

     6, 7, 13   9, 4, 13   8, 5, 13

12. Do the examples on pages 22 and 37 today.

$$\begin{array}{cccccc} 9 & 4 & 8 & 5 & 7 & 6 \\ +4 & +9 & +5 & +8 & +6 & +7 \\ \hline 13 & 13 & 13 & 13 & 13 & 13 \end{array}$$

$$\begin{array}{cccccc} 13 & 13 & 13 & 13 & 13 & 13 \\ -9 & -4 & -8 & -5 & -7 & -6 \\ \hline 4 & 9 & 5 & 8 & 6 & 7 \end{array}$$

Using facts about 13

Write in 2 ways the number facts you use in Exs. 1 to 6.

1. Harry has a dime and 3 pennies. How much will he have left if he spends 4¢?

2. There are 6 white stripes and 7 red stripes in the flag of the U.S.A. How many stripes are there in all?

3. John went to see Miss Bell. She said, "I'm busy now. Come back in 5 minutes." John looked at the clock. It was 13 minutes of two. At what time should he go back? Use a clock to prove your answer.

4. Don had a nickel and 3 pennies. He earned another nickel. Then he had _?_ ¢.

5. On December 6 Harry said, "A week from today is my birthday." His birthday must be on December _?_. Use a calendar to prove your answer.

6. The temperature was 13°. An hour later it was 9°. The temperature had fallen _?_ degrees. Use a thermometer to prove your answer.

Practice until you can say every answer correctly:

7.

9	13	8	7	13	7	9	13
+4	−7	+5	+4	−8	+6	+3	−9

8.

13	5	13	8	4	13	6	9
−6	+8	−5	+3	+9	−4	+7	+2

9. Write the answers to Exs. 7 and 8. Make Help-Yourself Cards for facts you do not know. Study the cards. Then write the answers again.

Practice until you can say every answer in 3 minutes:

1.	5 + 6	13 − 6	7 + 4	12 − 5	9 + 2	8 + 4	4 + 7	4 + 9
2.	11 − 7	9 + 4	12 − 4	13 − 7	11 − 2	6 + 6	12 − 8	13 − 9
3.	7 + 6	12 − 7	11 − 9	5 + 8	12 − 6	11 − 3	3 + 8	11 − 4
4.	11 − 8	8 + 5	13 − 4	6 + 7	12 − 9	2 + 9	4 + 8	13 − 8
5.	3 + 9	12 − 3	7 + 5	9 + 3	5 + 7	13 − 5	8 + 3	6 + 5

Mary writes down the addition and subtraction facts she doesn't know. Her paper looks like this. What facts does she need to learn? How does she help herself learn them?

Facts I don't know	Facts I do know that help me
5 + 6 = ?	5 + 5 = 10, so 5 + 6 = 11 6 + 6 = 12, so 5 + 6 = 11 6 + 5 = 11, so 5 + 6 = 11
12 − 7 = ?	7 + 5 = 12, so 12 − 7 = 5 12 − 5 = 7, so 12 − 7 = 5 12 − 6 = 6, so 12 − 7 = 5

6. Make a study paper like Mary's to help you learn the facts you couldn't remember in Exs. 1 to 5.

7. Write the answers to Exs. 1 to 5 on folded paper. Make Help-Yourself Cards for any facts you do not know. Study your cards. Then write the answers again.

Facts about 14

1. Joan and David found a box with 2 nickels and 4 pennies in it. How much money was in the box all together?

2. They want to share the 14¢. How much will David get if Joan gets 5¢? 6¢? 7¢? 8¢? 9¢? Cover coins in the picture to prove your answers.

3. What would be the fairest way to share 14¢?

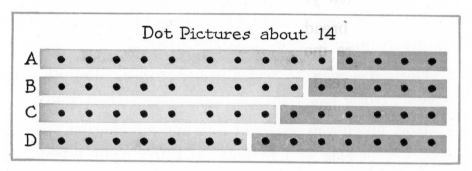

Dot Pictures about 14

4. Row A shows that 10 and 4 are __?__. How many dots are there in each row?

5. What addition and subtraction facts do Rows B, C, and D teach? Write the facts. Make a problem for each.

6. $6+7=13$, so $7+7=$ __?__.   **8.** $8+6=14$, so $14-8=$ __?__.

7. $10+4=14$, so $9+$ __?__ $=14$.   **9.** $6+6=12$, so $6+8=$ __?__.

9	5	8	6	7
+ 5	+ 9	+ 6	+ 8	+ 7
14	14	14	14	14
14	14	14	14	14
− 9	− 5	− 8	− 6	− 7
5	9	6	8	7

Write in 2 ways the fact you use to find each answer:

1. Peter has a dime and 4 pennies. If he spends 5¢, how much will he have left?

2. When the temperature rises from 8° to 14°, how many degrees does it rise? Use a thermometer to prove your answer.

3. How many days are there in 2 weeks? Use a calendar to prove your answer.

4. A loaf of bread costs 14¢. Jane has a nickel and 4¢. How much more money does she need?

5. Doris has read 14 pages in her reader. Polly has read 6 pages. Doris has read ‿?‿ more pages than Polly.

6. How much will a 9-cent kite and a 5-cent ball of string cost? Use nickels and pennies to prove your answer.

7. Mary has a nickel and 3 pennies. Bill has a nickel and 1 penny. Together they have ‿?‿ nickels and ‿?‿ pennies. This proves that 8¢ + 6¢ = ‿?‿ ¢.

Practice until you can say every answer correctly:

8.	9	6	14	8	6	14	12	7
	+ 5	+ 7	− 8	+ 5	+ 8	− 5	− 5	+ 7

9.	13	8	7	5	12	14	14	14
	− 9	− 6	+ 4	+ 9	− 6	− 7	− 6	− 9

10. Write the answers to Exs. 8 and 9. Make Help-Yourself Cards for facts you do not know. Study the cards. Then write the answers again.

Put on your thinking cap

▶ Oral review

1. Name the other three members in the Number Family of each of these facts:

$4 + 8 = 12$ $11 - 4 = 7$
$7 + 6 = 13$ $12 - 3 = 9$

2. Count to 1,000 by 100's; by 50's; by 25's.

3. What time is it? What is the temperature in your room? What is the date today?

4. Jim has 3 fifty-cent pieces and a dime. How much money has he in all?

5. What number is 10 more than 57? than 157? than 257?

6. What number is 10 less than 69? than 109?

7. 1 year = __?__ months.
1 quarter = __?__ nickels.
1 quart = __?__ pints.

8. What numbers do these Roman numerals equal?

X VI III V IX IV VIII

9. How do you check an addition example? a subtraction example?

▶ Written review

1. $\begin{array}{r} 46 \\ + 33 \\ \hline \end{array}$ **2.** $\begin{array}{r} 35 \\ + 54 \\ \hline \end{array}$ **3.** $\begin{array}{r} 87 \\ - 62 \\ \hline \end{array}$

4. $\begin{array}{r} 95 \\ - 73 \\ \hline \end{array}$

5. $9¢ + 4¢ = $ __?__ $¢$

6. $12¢ - 7¢ = $ __?__ $¢$

7. Write the number that is 10 more than 152.

8. What number is 20 less than 89?

9. Write the number that means 3 hundreds, 7 tens, and 5 ones.

10. Write the largest number you can with the figures 2, 4, 6; the smallest number.

11. Write the number that means 7 tens and 3 ones.

12. $200 + 70 + 6$ is __?__.

Using key facts in addition

1. Use dimes and pennies to find:

$4\cent + 3\cent$ $14\cent + 3\cent$ $24\cent + 3\cent$ $34\cent + 3\cent$ $44\cent + 3\cent$

2. Use the number chart to find $4 + 3$. Put your finger on 4; count 3 more. You stop at __?__. In the same way show how to find $14 + 3$; $24 + 3$; $34 + 3$; $44 + 3$.

If 3 is added to a number ending in 4, the sum ends in __?__.

1	2	3	4	5	6	7	8	9	10
11	12	13	14	15	16	17	18	19	20
21	22	23	24	25	26	27	28	29	30
31	32	33	34	35	36	37	38	39	40
41	42	43	44	45	46	47	48	49	50

3. Use the chart to find:

$$\begin{array}{ccccc} 3 & 13 & 23 & 33 & 43 \\ +2 & +2 & +2 & +2 & +2 \end{array}$$

If 2 is added to a number ending in 3, the sum ends in __?__.

4. Use the chart to find:

$3 + 3$ $5 + 2$ $4 + 5$
$13 + 3$ $15 + 2$ $14 + 5$
$23 + 3$ $25 + 2$ $24 + 5$
$33 + 3$ $35 + 2$ $34 + 5$
$43 + 3$ $45 + 2$ $44 + 5$

5. Mary says the first fact in each column in Ex. 4 is the *key fact* for the other additions in the column. What does she mean?

6. Tell the key fact in finding each of these sums:

$$\begin{array}{ccccc} 24 & 16 & 27 & 54 & 84 \\ +5 & +3 & +2 & +4 & +3 \end{array}$$

7. Sue wants a 25-cent game and a 3-cent puzzle. She needs __?__ $\cent$ in all.

Add 1 to each of the numbers below:

	a	b	c	d	e	f	g	h	i
1.	1	11	21	31	41	91	51	81	71
2.	2	12	22	32	42	52	62	72	82
3.	3	23	43	63	86	13	55	96	30
4.	4	14	54	75	26	84	45	36	60

5. Add 2 to each of the numbers in Exs. 1 to 4; **add** 3.

Add 5 to each of the numbers below; add 4.

6.	1	13	34	22	11	73	92	84	53
7.	3	61	12	51	74	82	33	42	14

Add down. Check by adding up. Write your answers on folded paper.

8.	5	7	6	7	6	7	4	6	5
	6	7	8	6	5	4	6	7	8
	8	4	3	2	7	8	8	5	4
9.	4	7	5	8	6	3	2	5	9
	9	4	9	5	6	7	8	9	5
	3	6	4	6	7	7	5	4	5

Write in columns. Add and check.

10. $3 + 8 + 5$ $7 + 4 + 8$ **$7 + 7 + 5$**

11. $8 + 6 + 5$ $8 + 3 + 7$ $6 + 6 + 5$

12. In a game of ring toss Peter won 5, 6, and 7 points. In all, he won __?__ points.

13. Find the cost of a 5-cent balloon, an 8-cent ice-cream cone, and a 6-cent candy bar.

14. Find the cost of two 3-cent stamps and a 1-cent stamp.

Adding

tens

1. Patsy and Jim are playing a game of ring toss. If Patsy gets a ring on hooks 30 and 50, what is her score?

2. Jim got a ring on hooks 70 and 30. Do these additions both show how to find his score? Which way do you like better?

70 =	7 tens		70
30 =	3 tens		+ 30
	10 tens = 100		100

3. Count by 10's from 100 to 200.

4. 10 tens = 100, so 11 tens = __?__, and 12 tens = __?__.

5. 13 tens = __?__   15 tens = __?__   17 tens = __?__

6. 14 tens = __?__   16 tens = __?__   18 tens = __?__

7. Patsy threw a ring on hooks 50 and 70. Do these additions both show how to find her score? Which way do you like better?

50 =	5 tens		50
70 =	7 tens		+ 70
	12 tens = 120		120

8. Who made the highest score below?

Jane	Bob	Tom	Polly	Sue	John
70	90	60	60	80	70
40	30	80	60	50	60

Find the sums and check:

1. | 60 | 90 | 60 | 50 | 50 | 90 | 30 |
    |----|----|----|----|----|----|----|
    | 50 | 40 | 80 | 50 | 70 | 50 | 90 |

2. | 40 | 70 | 80 | 70 | 50 | 70 | 60 |
    |----|----|----|----|----|----|----|
    | 80 | 60 | 30 | 70 | 80 | 40 | 60 |

3. Their teacher asked Mary Lu and Dan to find the sum of 62 and 74. Here is their work. Explain Mary Lu's work; Dan's work. Whose way do you like better?

Mary Lu
62 → 6 tens and 2 ones
74 → 7 tens and 4 ones
_____
13 tens and 6 ones = 136

Dan
62
+74
____
136

Find the sums and check. Use Dan's way of adding.

4. | 82 | 45 | 73 | 36 | 94 | 64 | 65 |
    |----|----|----|----|----|----|----|
    | 44 | 90 | 56 | 82 | 51 | 64 | 74 |

5. | 80 | 45 | 52 | 55 | 24 | 75 | 96 |
    |----|----|----|----|----|----|----|
    | 68 | 71 | 87 | 62 | 93 | 73 | 31 |

6. Tom gathered 62 shells. Polly gave him 53 more. How many shells did he have then?

7. David collects stamps. He had 74. His uncle gave him 50 more. Then he had __?__ stamps.

8. There are 85 third-grade children and 63 fourth-grade children. In both grades there are __?__ children.

The Broadway Movie Theater sent 70 free tickets to the Park Street School. There are 120 children in the school. How many children will not get a ticket this time?

To find out, Doris and Bill did these subtractions. Explain each. Whose work do you like better?

Doris	Bill
$120 \rightarrow 12$ tens	120
$70 \rightarrow -7$ tens	-70
5 tens $= 50$	50

1. 13 tens − 6 tens = __?__ tens.   130 − 60 = __?__.
2. 12 tens − 5 tens = __?__ tens.   120 − 50 = __?__.

Subtract and check:

3.	130	110	120	130	140	110	120
	90	20	60	60	80	30	80

4.	140	130	110	120	140	120	110
	50	50	70	50	70	30	60

5. Here are 2 ways to subtract 73 from 129.   Explain each.

129 =	12 tens and 9 ones		129
73 =	7 tens and 3 ones		− 73
	5 tens and 6 ones = 56		56

Subtract and check:

6.	145	124	135	116	139	148	127
	93	62	61	70	46	73	34

7.	136	117	132	123	104	147	129
	75	57	81	52	64	82	83

Facts about 15

1. Don has 2 nickels and 5 pennies. In all, he has __?__ ¢.

2. Don wants to buy a horn and a ball. How much can he spend for the ball if the horn costs 6¢? 7¢? 8¢? 9¢? Cover coins in the picture to prove each answer.

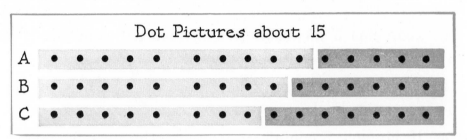

Dot Pictures about 15

A

B

C

3. Row A shows that 10 and 5 are __?__. How many dots are there in each row?

4. What addition and subtraction facts does Row B teach? Row C? Write the facts. Make a problem for each.

5. $7 + 7 = 14$, so $7 + 8 = ?$ **8.** $15 - 10 = 5$, so $15 - 9 = ?$

6. $14 - 9 = 5$, so $15 - 9 = ?$ **9.** $15 - 5 = 10$, so $15 - 6 = ?$

7. $15 - 8 = 7$, so $15 - 7 = ?$ **10.** $6 + 9 = 15$, so $15 - 9 = ?$

	a	*b*	*c*	*d*
11.	$8 + 7 = ?$	$7 + 8 = ?$	$15 - 7 = ?$	$15 - 8 = ?$
12.	$9 + 6 = ?$	$6 + 9 = ?$	$15 - 9 = ?$	$15 - 6 = ?$
13.	$8 + ? = 15$	$9 + ? = 15$	$6 + ? = 15$	$7 + ? = 15$

8	7	15	15	9	6	15	15
+7	+8	−8	−7	+6	+9	−9	−6
15	15	7	8	15	15	6	9

Using facts

about 15

1. Can 2 boys share 15 marbles equally? What is the best they can do?

2. Joan has 3 nickels. If she buys a 6-cent candy bar, how much money will she have left?

3. Tom has 9¢. How much more does he need to buy a 15-cent comic book?

4. If January 8 comes on Monday, the next Monday will be January ___?___.

5. John has a nickel and 4 pennies. Peter has a nickel and 1 penny. Together they have ___?___ nickels and ___?___ pennies, or ___?___ cents. This shows that 9¢ + 6¢ = ___?___ ¢.

Practice until you can say every answer correctly:

	a	*b*	*c*	*d*	*e*	*f*	*g*	*h*
6.	13 − 9	14 − 8	7 + 8	15 − 8	7 + 6	8 + 7	15 − 9	13 − 5
7.	6 + 8	15 − 7	9 + 6	7 + 7	15 − 6	9 + 5	6 + 9	9 + 4

8. Write the answers to Exs. 6 and 7 on folded paper. Make Help-Yourself Cards for any facts you do not know. Study your cards. Then write the answers again.

Everyday problems

1. Sam and Mike found a box with 14 pennies in it. If Sam keeps 7¢, Mike will get _?_¢.

2. Tell 4 other ways the boys (Ex. 1) could share the 14¢. Don't give either boy less than 5¢.

3. Bill had 12¢. He spent a nickel. He had _?_¢ left.

4. Marie's doll is 13 inches tall. Lucy's doll is 4 inches taller. Lucy's doll is _?_ inches tall.

5. Ken had 14 arithmetic examples to do. He has done 6 of them. He has _?_ more to do.

6. Jane has a nickel and 3 pennies, or _?_¢. Tom has a nickel and 2 pennies, or _?_¢. Together they have _?_ nickels and _?_ pennies, or _?_¢.

7. Andy is 8 years old. Betty is 11 years old. How much older is Betty than Andy?

8. Bill wants to buy a 12-cent puzzle. He has only 7¢. He needs _?_¢ more.

9. Ted has 13¢. Ed has 4¢. Ed has _?_¢ less than Ted.

10. Tom had 13¢. He found a nickel. Then he had _?_¢.

11. Dick and Don together bought a box of 15 peppermint candies. If Dick takes 7 pieces, Don can have _?_ pieces.

12. Lucy's birthday is Dec. 15. On Dec. 8 she said, "One week from today will be my birthday." Was she right?

13. Mike asked for a dozen cookies. The baker gave him 6 nut cookies and 7 sugar cookies. Did the baker give him an extra cooky?

Edith made paper baskets for the Christmas tree. This is the way she made them:

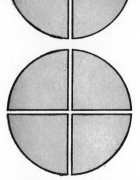

She cut 4 large circles from red paper. She drew around a plate to make her circles.

She folded each circle and cut it into 2 equal parts.

She folded and cut each half circle into 2 equal parts.

How many pieces did she have from each circle?

Each piece of paper had two straight edges. Edith pasted these edges together. Then each piece of paper looked like this:——————→ *paste*

She used a paper clip to hang each basket.

1. How many baskets can Edith make from 1 circle? How many can she make from 2 circles? from 3 circles? from 4 circles?

2. If Edith puts 9 of her 16 baskets on the classroom tree, how many can she take home for her own tree?

$$16 - 9 = 7 \qquad 9 + 7 = 16$$
$$16 - 7 = 9 \qquad 7 + 9 = 16$$

3. If Edith puts 8 of her baskets on the classroom tree, how many can she take home for her own tree?

$$16 - 8 = 8 \qquad 8 + 8 = 16$$

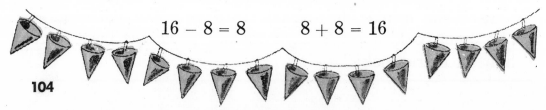

How quickly can you tell the answers in Exs. 4–8?

4. $\begin{cases} 16 - 7 \\ 16 - 8 \\ 16 - 9 \end{cases}$ **5.** $\begin{cases} 16 - 9 \\ 16 - 7 \\ 16 - 8 \end{cases}$ **6.** $\begin{cases} 7 + 9 \\ 8 + 8 \\ 9 + 7 \end{cases}$ **7.** $\begin{cases} 9 + 7 \\ 15 - 7 \\ 8 + 8 \end{cases}$ **8.** $\begin{cases} 8 + 8 \\ 7 + 9 \\ 16 - 7 \end{cases}$

9. Edith had 3 paper clips. Dick gave her 4 more. Then she had __?__ clips.

10. When Edith had 7 clips, how many more did she need for her 16 baskets?

11. Ann gave Edith 1 clip. Then she had 7 and 1, or __?__ clips.

12. When Edith had 8 clips, how many more did she need for her 16 baskets?

13. Edith had 8 clips. Dan gave her 1 more. Then she had __?__ clips.

14. When Edith had 9 clips, Sally gave her 7 more. Did she have enough then for her 16 baskets?

15. Billy brought to school 5 Christmas-tree balls, Ann brought 4 balls, and Jack brought 7 balls. Together they brought __?__ balls.

16. Ted brought 2 strings of Christmas-tree lights. There were 8 lights on each string. That was __?__ lights.

Practice until you can say every answer correctly:

17.

16	8	16	9	7	16	6	9
− 7	+ 8	− 9	+ 5	+ 9	− 8	+ 7	+ 7

18. Write the answers to Ex. 17 on folded paper. Make Help-Yourself Cards for any facts you do not know. Study your cards. Then write the answers again.

UNIT
17

Addition and
subtraction facts
about 17 and 18
Tests of basic facts

Facts about 17

1. Alice and Tom found 10 paper stars in one box and 7 stars in another. All together they had _?_ stars.

2. Alice said, "If we had 16 stars, we could divide the stars equally. We could put 8 stars on one poster and 8 on the other." Do you agree with Alice?

3. Tom said, "Well, we have 17 stars, so we can't divide them equally. We shall do the best we can. We'll put 9 stars on one poster and 8 on the other." Do you agree with Tom? $17 - 9 =$ _?_.

4. Four of the 17 stars are red. Four are blue. The other _?_ stars are green. $17 - 8 =$ _?_.

5. $8 + 8 = 16$, so $8 + 9 =$ _?_. Why?

6. $17 - 10 = 7$, so $17 - 9 =$ _?_. Why?

7. $16 - 8 = 8$, so $17 - 8 =$ _?_. Why?

8. Jane has a nickel and 3 pennies, or _?_ ¢. Tom has a nickel and 4 pennies, or _?_ ¢. Together they have _?_ nickels and _?_ pennies, or _?_ ¢. $8¢ + 9¢ =$ _?_ ¢.

$$8 + 9 = 17 \qquad 17 - 8 = 9$$
$$9 + 8 = 17 \qquad 17 - 9 = 8$$

Practice until you can say every answer correctly:

9.

9	17	14	8	15	13	8	17
$+8$	-9	-6	$+8$	-9	-4	$+9$	-8

10. Write the answers to Ex. 9 on folded paper. Make Help-Yourself Cards for any facts you do not know. Study your cards. Then write the answers again.

This is Mary Lu. She says, "I have $9 + 6$ jelly beans in my right hand. I have $6 + 8$ jelly beans in my left hand. Which hand do you take?"

Which hand do you take in each of these?

NUMBER OF JELLY BEANS IN		NUMBER OF JELLY BEANS IN	
RIGHT HAND	LEFT HAND	RIGHT HAND	LEFT HAND
1. $12 - 5$	$14 - 6$	6. $13 - 9$	$11 - 5$
2. $8 + 9$	$9 + 7$	7. $18 - 9$	$16 - 8$
3. $15 - 7$	$12 - 3$	8. $13 - 5$	$17 - 8$
4. $8 + 8$	$6 + 9$	9. $7 + 4$	$3 + 9$
5. $6 + 7$	$4 + 8$	10. $12 - 4$	$14 - 5$

1. Lucy and Ben bought a box of chocolate drops. They wanted to share the candies equally. Ben placed the candies as shown here. How many candies are in the top row? in the bottom row? in both rows together?

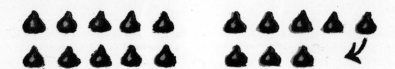

2. Ben said, "If I move the last candy from the top row into the bottom row, there will be __?__ candies in each row. That shows if we share 18 candies equally we each get 9 candies."

3. Ben's candies show that $9 + 9 = $ __?__ ; $18 - 9 = $ __?__ ; two 9's = __?__ .

4. $8 + 9 = 17$, so $9 + 9 = $ __?__   **5.** $17 - 9 = 8$, so $18 - 9 = $ __?__

$$9 + 9 = 18 \qquad 18 - 9 = 9$$

Practice until you can say every answer correctly:

6.

15	9	16	9	17	7	18	15
− 9	+ 8	− 8	+ 9	− 9	+ 8	− 9	− 6

7. Write the answers to Ex. 6 on folded paper. Make Help-Yourself Cards for any facts you do not know. Study your cards. Then write the answers again.

8.

54	98	73	56	84	75	44
+ 63	+ 31	+ 62	+ 73	+ 64	+ 42	+ 95

9.

119	148	127	137	118	148	129
− 25	− 74	− 46	− 50	− 82	− 93	− 67

Playing Push-Over

The boys and girls in Miss Bell's class like to play this game of Push-Over. A player pushes 3 wooden blocks each time he has a turn.

Bill has just had a turn. His blocks landed on 8, 9, and "outside." His score is $8 + 9 + 0$, or __?__.

What scores did each of these children make?

Jack	8, 7, outside	Alice	10, outside, 10 off
Tom	7, outside, 10	Molly	7, 9, 10
Jean	outside, 9, 7	Sam	8, 8, 10 off
Nancy	8, 10, outside	Peter	10, 10, 7
Billy	7, 8, 10	Sue	7, 7, 10 off
Ted	9, 8, 10 off	Betty	9, 9, 10

Tell the answers to these addition examples. Then write the answers on folded paper in 5 minutes. Make Help-Yourself Cards for any facts you do not know. You can find the correct answers on page 309. Study your cards. Then write the answers again.

1.
7	2	2	2	4	4	3	7	6	5
1	9	5	8	4	1	1	7	1	4

2.
3	1	9	1	2	2	5	7	6	3
3	1	2	7	1	2	5	2	2	6

3.
2	4	8	6	9	6	3	2	9	6
4	5	2	4	1	6	2	6	3	5

4.
3	3	3	7	2	8	4	5	5	8
8	4	9	3	7	4	8	2	1	5

5.
7	5	5	7	8	9	5	8	8	9
9	8	7	8	7	6	9	9	6	5

6.
9	6	5	4	7	1	9	1	5	1
4	7	6	6	6	8	9	2	3	5

7.
8	1	2	6	6	3	6	1	8	9
8	3	3	8	9	5	3	9	1	8

8.
3	4	4	8	7	4	7	9	4	1
7	7	2	3	5	9	4	7	3	6

Test on subtraction facts

Tell the answers.   Then write the answers on folded paper in 5 minutes.   Make Help-Yourself Cards for any facts you do not know.   You can find the correct answers on page 310. Study your cards.   Then write the answers again.

1.
$$\begin{array}{cccccccccc} 3 & 3 & 7 & 5 & 8 & 9 & 7 & 7 & 12 & 4 \\ -3 & -2 & -7 & -1 & -8 & -3 & -3 & -2 & -6 & -1 \end{array}$$

2.
$$\begin{array}{cccccccccc} 12 & 15 & 14 & 12 & 12 & 11 & 11 & 13 & 7 & 6 \\ -3 & -6 & -8 & -5 & -7 & -4 & -6 & -7 & -5 & -4 \end{array}$$

3.
$$\begin{array}{cccccccccc} 12 & 10 & 8 & 8 & 6 & 16 & 14 & 17 & 4 & 6 \\ -9 & -5 & -1 & -4 & -5 & -9 & -5 & -9 & -2 & -6 \end{array}$$

4.
$$\begin{array}{cccccccccc} 13 & 11 & 14 & 8 & 10 & 9 & 5 & 10 & 14 & 10 \\ -8 & -3 & -6 & -2 & -4 & -6 & -5 & -6 & -7 & -3 \end{array}$$

5.
$$\begin{array}{cccccccccc} 16 & 18 & 11 & 8 & 11 & 10 & 6 & 2 & 5 & 6 \\ -8 & -9 & -9 & -6 & -2 & -7 & -1 & -1 & -2 & -3 \end{array}$$

6.
$$\begin{array}{cccccccccc} 9 & 4 & 9 & 9 & 5 & 5 & 1 & 3 & 7 & 4 \\ -8 & -4 & -1 & -9 & -3 & -4 & -1 & -1 & -1 & -3 \end{array}$$

7.
$$\begin{array}{cccccccccc} 9 & 9 & 14 & 13 & 15 & 17 & 15 & 13 & 13 & 16 \\ -7 & -4 & -9 & -4 & -9 & -8 & -7 & -9 & -5 & -7 \end{array}$$

8.
$$\begin{array}{cccccccccc} 10 & 6 & 10 & 7 & 9 & 8 & 8 & 11 & 11 & 9 \\ -1 & -2 & -2 & -6 & -5 & -7 & -5 & -5 & -8 & -2 \end{array}$$

9.
$$\begin{array}{cccccccccc} 11 & 13 & 15 & 12 & 10 & 7 & 12 & 8 & 10 & 2 \\ -7 & -6 & -8 & -4 & -8 & -4 & -8 & -3 & -9 & -2 \end{array}$$

1. Miss Hand's pupils had a party. They served an ice-cream cone to each child. Try to find out how much money the class needed for the ice-cream cones. These facts will help you.

- There were 20 children at the party.
- Empty cones cost 1¢.
- A quart of ice cream fills 10 cones.
- The ice cream costs $.60 a quart.

2. At the party the boys and girls divided into 4 teams. Look at the picture. How many children were on each team? Did all 20 children play?

Each child took a turn pushing down on scales as hard as he could. Bob pushed so hard the hand on the scale moved to show 51 pounds. Which child on each team pushed the hardest?

Green Team	Blue Team	Red Team	Yellow Team
Bob – 51	Frank-52	Roy – 41	Phil-49
Dick-46	Tom – 45	Ted – 54	Sue – 33
Judy-30	Betty-40	Ann – 35	Jane-29
Bill – 43	Alice-33	Molly-28	Pete – 43
Joan – 32	Fred-41	Sally-34	Jim-45

Make Sensible Sentences

1. tens three is four Forty-three and.
2. quarter nickels a Five equal.
3. pints equals quart two One.
4. feet three yard in are There a.
5. foot twelve One inches equals.
6. There thirty-six are yard in a inches.

3. The children played a Sensible Sentences game at the party. Billy won. He made 6 sensible sentences out of the words on the board. It took him 3 minutes. Can you do it as fast as Billy did?

4. Miss Hand asked the class these number riddles at the party. Can you answer them?

- What has 3 feet but can't walk?
- Tom thought of the number 7. He added a number to it. His answer was 7. What number did Tom add to the 7?
- Jack thought of the number 8. He subtracted a number from it. His answer was 8. What number did he subtract from the 8?
- Ted thought of a number. He took 8 away and had 9 left. What number did he think of?
- Mary thought of a number. She took 9 away from it and had 6 left. What was the number?

1. Ned is reading *The Brave Cowboy*. He is ready to start Chapter VIII. How many chapters has he read?

2. Jane ironed 9 white handkerchiefs and 6 colored ones. How many did she iron?

3. Ellen is sending 16 invitations. She has written 9. She has _?_ more to write.

4. Bob sold 4 tickets on Monday, 3 on Tuesday, and 6 on Thursday. How many did he sell in all?

5. At 6 A.M. the temperature was 32°. At 8 A.M. it was 48°. How much did it rise in 2 hours?

6. John's father went to take a nap. He asked John to call him in 20 minutes. John looked at the clock. It was 10 minutes after 3. At what time should John wake his father?

7. Sally sold a box of cookies for 40¢. Mrs. Smith gave Sally $1.00. Sally gave Mrs. Smith _?_ dimes in change.

8. Jane had a quarter. She earned 4¢ more. How much money did she have then?

9. Bob is saving his money to buy a football. He has a dollar bill, 8 dimes, and 5 pennies. How much money has he all together? Write the answer. Use a dollar sign and cents point.

10. John had 64 savings stamps. His uncle gave him 55 more. How many did he have then?

_____

Get your Problem Test Record out of your Arithmetic Folder. Write on it your score on this test.

Self-Help Test 3

Copy, find the answers, and check:

1. 75
   + 24 (46)
2. 67
   + 72 (99)
3. 94
   − 63 (48)
4. 128
   − 63 (100)
5. 140
   − 80 (100)

6. 4¢ + 2¢ + 3¢ (52)   7. 8 + 7 + 4 (97)

8. 572 = _?_ hundreds, _?_ tens, _?_ ones. (70)

9. Six boys need 6 pennies to be weighed. They have a dime and 5 pennies. How much will they have to use out of the dime? How many cents will they have left? (101)

Self-Help Test 4

1. What part of this square is white? (11)

2. Write with dollar sign and cents point: four dollars and forty-nine cents. (73)

3. Write these Roman numbers in figures: V X III XII IV VIII IX (66)

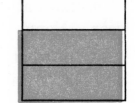

4. Jean is buying a 10-cent ice-cream cone. How much change should she receive from a half dollar? (57)

5. Tom has a piece of wood a foot long. He wishes to make a boat 9 in. long. His wood is _?_ inches too long. (79)

6. At 9 o'clock the thermometer read 16°. At 10 o'clock it read 9°. In one hour the temperature fell _?_ degrees. (63)

7. 1 yd. = _?_ in. (25)   10. 1 wk. = _?_ da. (83)

8. 1 yd. = _?_ ft. (25)   11. 1 qt. = _?_ pt. (28)

9. 1 yr. = _?_ mo. (26)   12. 1 hr. = _?_ min. (3)

Look at your calendar for the new year.

1. What year is this? What does New Year's Day mean?

2. What is the first month of the year? the last?

3. How many months are there in a year? Name them.

4. How many days are there in a week? Name them.

5. How many days are there in January? June? May?

6. How many Sundays are there in January this year? On what days of the month do these Sundays come?

7. On what day of the week does the 10th of January come? the 16th? the 21st? the 31st?

8. In what months do you have summer vacation?

9. Look at the pictures below. Name the 4 seasons of the year. Name the months in each season.

10. In what season does New Year's Day come? Fourth of July? April Fools' Day? Halloween?

11. Make a drawing for your folder about the 4 seasons of the year. Your drawing should show: (1) the names of the seasons; (2) something you like to do in each season.

116

September • October • November

FALL

December • January • February

WINTER

Kate's little sister, Carol, was born on January 15, 1950. January 15, 1950 is the date of Carol's birth.

Notice that a date has three parts: *the month, the day of the month,* and *the year.*

1. Tell what date it is today. Name the month, the day of the month, and the year. Write the date. Be sure to place a comma after the day of the month.

2. What date is a week from today? Write it.

3. What date is next Saturday? a week from next Saturday? Write the dates.

4. On January 8, Judy said, "I can tell what date is a week from today without looking at the calendar." How can she do that?

5. On what day of the week do these days come this year? In what season does each come?

New Year's Day   (Jan. 1)   Fourth of July   (July 4)
Valentine's Day   (Feb. 14)   Columbus Day   (Oct. 12)
Flag Day   (June 14)   Christmas Day   (Dec. 25)

6. Thanksgiving Day is the fourth Thursday in November. In what season does it come? On what day of the month does it come this year?

March   •   April   •   May   June   •   July   •   Augus

SPRING

SUMMER

Tell whether the missing word in each example is *add* or *subtract*.

1. Bob wants to buy a ball and a bat. You know the cost of each. To find the cost of both, you _?_.

2. You know how much money Tom had, and how much he spent. To find how much he has left, you _?_.

3. You know how much money Ann has. You know how much Sue has. To find how much more Ann has than Sue, you _?_.

4. You know the cost of the pencil, the notebook, and the crayons Jean bought. To find how much they cost all together, you _?_.

5. You know how much money Jim has. You know how much skates cost. To find how much more money Jim needs to buy the skates, you _?_.

6. You know how many children are in class. You know how many pencils your teacher has. To find how many more are needed for each child to have one, you _?_.

7. You know how old Polly is. You know how old Bob is. To find how much younger Polly is than Bob, you _?_.

8. You know how many boys are in your class, and how many girls. To find the number of children, you _?_.

9. You know how many pretzels you had. You know how many are left. To find how many you ate, you _?_.

10. You know how much a comic book costs. You know how much money you have. To find how much more you must get before you can buy the book, you _?_.

Put on your thinking cap

▶ Oral review

1. What kinds of things do you buy by the yard? by the quart?

2. Jane knows that $8 + 7 = 15$. Then she should also know that $15 - 7 = \underline{?}$; $15 - 8 = \underline{?}$.

3. Read these temperatures: 32° 68° 0° 72°

4. Jack has a yardstick. How can he use it to measure off a stick 1 ft. long? 2 ft. long? 3 ft. long?

5. How many nickels are there in a dime? a quarter? a half dollar? a dollar?

6. Read these: 5¢ $.05 $3.10 $1.01 $12.25

7. Beginning with 5, count by 10's to 95.

8. $8 + 6$ is as much as $10 + \underline{?}$.

9. Tell the sum of 4, 5, 3, and 6.

10. Read these: 745 608 IV VII XI

▶ Written review

Check your answers to these examples:

1.	2.	3.	4.	5.
64 + 32	75 + 63	59 - 23	106 - 42	85 - 30

6. Sue is going to the museum. She needs 20¢ for bus fare and 60¢ for lunch. In all, she needs $\underline{?}$ ¢.

7. In one whole there are $\underline{?}$ fourths.

8. How much change will Bob get from a quarter if he spends 14¢?

UNIT 19

*Adding by endings
with bridging
Readiness for multiplying*

More key facts in addition

1	2	3	4	5	6	7	8	9	10
11	12	13	14	15	16	17	18	19	20
21	22	23	24	25	26	27	28	29	30
31	32	33	34	35	36	37	38	39	40
41	42	43	44	45	46	47	48	49	50

1. Sue spent 17¢ for envelopes and 3¢ for a stamp. To find the cost of both, put your finger on 17 on the chart. Count 3 more. That brings you to 20. 17¢ + 3¢ = _?_.

Use the number chart to find these sums:

2. $7 + 3$ $17 + 3$ $27 + 3$ $37 + 3$ $47 + 3$

3. $8 + 2$ $18 + 2$ $28 + 2$ $38 + 2$ $48 + 2$

4. $6 + 4$ $16 + 4$ $26 + 4$ $36 + 4$ $46 + 4$

5. $9 + 1$ $19 + 1$ $29 + 1$ $39 + 1$ $49 + 1$

6. Peter added 18 and 5 this way: "18 and 2 are 20, and 3 more are 23. So $18 + 5 = 23$." Explain his work.

7. Ted added 36 and 6 this way: "36 and 4 are 40, and 2 more are 42. So $36 + 6 = 42$." Explain his work.

8. To add 27 and 5, think, "27 and _?_ are 30, and 2 more are 32. So $27 + 5 = 32$."

9. To add 46 and 5, think, "46 and _?_ are 50, and 1 more is 51. So $46 + 5 = $ _?_."

10. $7+3=10$, so $7+4=$_?_.   **12.** $27+3=30$, so $27+4=$_?_.

11. $17+3=20$, so $17+4=$_?_.   **13.** $37+3=40$, so $37+4=$_?_.

1. Put your finger on 18 on the number chart. Find:

$$18 + 2 \qquad 18 + 4$$
$$18 + 3 \qquad 18 + 5$$

2. Put your finger on 26 on the number chart. Find:

$$26 + 4 \qquad 26 + 6$$
$$26 + 5 \qquad 26 + 7$$

3. Put your finger on 35 on the number chart. Find:

$$35 + 5 \qquad 35 + 7$$
$$35 + 6 \qquad 35 + 8$$

4. Use the number chart to prove these additions:

8	18	28	38
+ 4	+ 4	+ 4	+ 4
12	22	32	42

5. Look at the answers in Ex. 4. How does knowing that $8 + 4 = 12$ help you to know the other 3 answers?

6. Knowing that $8+5=13$ helps you do this addition: $38 + 5 = \underline{}$.

7. $9+3=12$, so $19+3=\underline{}$.

8. $8+3=11$, so $18+3=\underline{}$.

9. $7+6=13$, so $27+6=\underline{}$.

10. $6+8=14$, so $36+8=\underline{}$.

11. Tom said, "$5 + 5$ is the *key fact* in these additions." What did he mean?

5	15	25	35
+ 5	+ 5	+ 5	+ 5

Tell the key fact in these:

12.
6	16	26	36
+ 5	+ 5	+ 5	+ 5

13.
8	18	28	38
+ 6	+ 6	+ 6	+ 6

14.
8	18	28	38
+ 3	+ 3	+ 3	+ 3

Find these sums. Say, "5 and 6 are 11, so 15 and 6 are 21"; and so on.

15.
15	12	26	37
+ 6	+ 8	+ 6	+ 6

16.
16	24	36	24
+ 8	+ 7	+ 7	+ 8

17. Carl did 16 addition examples and 6 subtraction examples. All together he did __?__ examples.

18. Nancy has a ribbon 1 yard and 8 inches long. The ribbon is __?__ inches long.

1. Jim made 9 snowballs, Bobby made 4, Don 5, and Jack 2. How many snowballs was that?

2. Tom made 8 snowballs, Jerry made 5, Carl 8, and Dick 6. How many snowballs was that?

Add 5 to each of the numbers below:

3. 15	25	35	45	55	65	75
4. 16	26	46	66	76	86	96
5. 17	27	37	47	57	77	97
6. 18	28	48	58	68	78	88
7. 29	39	49	59	69	89	99
8. 36	67	38	98	95	56	87

9. Add 6 to each number in Exs. 3 to 8. Add 7; 8; 9.

10. $15 + 7$ $12 + 8$ $28 + 4$ $36 + 7$ $16 + 8$

11. $16 + 6$ $17 + 6$ $26 + 6$ $21 + 9$ $28 + 8$

12. $24 + 8$ $18 + 7$ $38 + 5$ $32 + 8$ $18 + 9$

Add and check: (Begin at the top.)

	a	b	c	d	e	f	g	h	i
13.	5	8	9	7	8	9	7	8	8
	2	7	2	7	5	9	8	4	9
	3	7	6	7	8	6	8	3	4
14.	5	8	4	9	4	6	6	5	9
	6	6	6	6	5	7	8	7	4
	2	5	8	5	5	7	8	7	4
	6	4	2	3	8	2	3	6	7

At a lunch counter

Here is what the 3 boys ordered at the lunch counter. Figure out each boy's bill. Did the boys choose wisely?

GEORGE	PETER	ROBERT
Lamb stew	Roast beef	1 Ham sandwich
Apple pie	Ice cream	1 Cheese sandwich
Milk	Cocoa	2 pieces of pie
		Milk

The waitress punched these three tickets. They show how much the boys should pay at the desk on the way out. Which ticket is George's? Peter's? Robert's?

BLAKE'S LUNCH COUNTER

$	DIMES	CENTS
1	1	1
2	2	2
3	3	3
4	4	4
5	5	○
6	6	6
7	7	7
8	○	8
9	9	9

BLAKE'S LUNCH COUNTER

$	DIMES	CENTS
○	1	1
2	2	2
3	3	3
4	4	4
5	5	5
6	6	6
7	7	7
8	8	8
9	9	9

BLAKE'S LUNCH COUNTER

$	DIMES	CENTS
○	1	1
2	2	2
3	3	3
4	4	4
5	5	○
6	6	6
7	7	7
8	8	8
9	9	9

123

Making pot holders

Judy is making her mother a pair of pot holders. Jack is making her a rack to hang the holders on.

1. A pair of pot holders is ⟶?⟵ pot holders.

2. The pot holders are square. They are 6 inches on each side. Draw a pattern for the pot holders.

3. Judy has the red material for the holders. She needs to buy the tape to bind the edges. How many inches of tape does she need for 1 side? for 2 sides? for 3? for 4?

4. If she needs 24 inches of tape for 1 holder, how many inches does she need for 2 holders?

5. A roll of tape costs 10¢. It contains 54 inches. Will 1 roll of tape be enough?

6. Judy needs to sew a ring on each holder. The rings cost a cent apiece. How much will the tape and rings cost all together?

7. Jack needed 2 screws for the rack for the pot holders. The sign on the screws at the store said "5 for 5¢." How much did the 2 screws cost?

8. 2 and 2 are 4, so two 2's are ⟶?⟵.

9. 5 and 5 are 10, so two 5's are ⟶?⟵.

10. 3 and 3 are 6, so two 3's are ⟶?⟵.

11. 4 and 4 are 8, so two 4's are ⟶?⟵.

Now is the time to test yourself

1. Which of these 3 additions is *not* shown by the picture?

- $17 + 3 + 3 = 23$
- $18 + 6 = 24$
- $17 + 6 = 23$

2. Sally said, "My new coat cost seven dollars and eighty-nine cents." Write in figures the cost of Sally's coat.

3. Larry has 3 one-dollar bills, 5 dimes, and 4 cents. Write a number to show how much money he has. Use a dollar sign and cents point.

Add and check:

4. $4 + 3 + 6 + 2 = \underline{\ ?\ }$.   **5.** $6 + 8 + 0 + 7 = \underline{\ ?\ }$.

6. Nancy is 8 years old. Her sister is 15 years old. Nancy is $\underline{\ ?\ }$ years younger than her sister.

7. What is the date today? Look at your calendar.

8. Betty went to visit her aunt for a week, but she stayed 12 days. She stayed $\underline{\ ?\ }$ days longer than she had planned.

9. Jim has three red airplanes, eight blue ones, and four silver ones. How many airplanes has he all together?

10. Eight boys and eight girls are going on a picnic. If they take 4 quarts of tomato juice, can each child have a glass of tomato juice? This picture will help you.

125

Adding with carrying

Jim is saving to buy a fishing rod.

In his bank he has 27¢: ➤ 10¢ 10¢ 1¢ 1¢ 1¢ 1¢ 1¢ 1¢ 1¢

He just earned 35¢: ⟶ 10¢ 10¢ 10¢ 1¢ 1¢ 1¢ 1¢ 1¢

1. How many dimes has he now? How many pennies?

2. Jim said, "12 pennies = 1 dime and 2 pennies. So my 5 dimes and 12 pennies = 6 dimes and 2 pennies, or 62¢." Use toy coins (dimes and pennies) to prove that Jim is right.

3. Here is another way to show Jim's addition of 27¢ and 35¢:

> In his bank, 27¢:⟶ 2 dimes and 7 pennies
> Just earned, 35¢:⟶ 3 dimes and 5 pennies

- Money he has in all:➤ 5 dimes and 12 pennies
- Change the 12 pennies to 1 dime and 2 pennies.
- Put the dime over with the 5 dimes.
- Keep the 2 pennies in the cents column.
- Then Jim has in all 6 dimes and _?_ pennies, or _?_ ¢.

Use toy coins (dimes and pennies) to prove that:

4. 4 dimes and 13 pennies = 5 dimes and 3 pennies = 53¢.

5. 2 dimes and 14 pennies = 3 dimes and 4 pennies = 34¢.

6. 3 dimes and 12 pennies = 4 dimes and 2 pennies = 42¢.

7. John has 24¢:⟶ 2 dimes and 4 pennies
Bill has 39¢: ⟶ 3 dimes and 9 pennies
Together they have:➤ 5 dimes and 13 pennies = _?_ ¢

Do John and Bill together have 53¢, 63¢, or 81¢?

Here is a short way to find the sum of 27¢ and 35¢:

▶ Write the addition this way: ⟶

$$\begin{array}{r} 27¢ \\ +35¢ \\ \hline \end{array}$$

▶ Think, "27¢ = 2 dimes and 7 cents.
　　　　35¢ = 3 dimes and 5 cents."

▶ Think, "7¢ + 5¢ = 12¢." *Change the 12¢ to 1 dime and 2 cents.*

▶ Write the 2 in the cents column.
▶ *Carry* the dime to the dimes column: ⟶

$$\begin{array}{r} {}^{1}\\ 27¢ \\ +35¢ \\ \hline 2¢ \end{array}$$

▶ Think, "1 dime + 2 dimes + 3 dimes = _?_ dimes." Write the 6 in the dimes column: ⟶

▶ The sum of 27¢ and 35¢ is 6 dimes and 2 cents, or _?_ ¢. Check by adding up.

$$\begin{array}{r} {}^{1}\\ 27¢ \\ +35¢ \\ \hline 62¢ \end{array}$$

1. Do these additions orally. Then copy the examples without the answers. Add and check.

59¢	67¢	26¢	45¢	78¢	65¢	39¢
18¢	29¢	37¢	29¢	15¢	27¢	36¢
77¢	96¢	63¢	74¢	93¢	92¢	75¢

2. Copy, add, and check. Use toy coins to prove each answer.

56¢	47¢	19¢	34¢	73¢	48¢	44¢
37¢	45¢	16¢	27¢	18¢	26¢	37¢

3. Carl is going to earn 25¢ for scraping the skating pond, and 35¢ for shoveling snow. How much will he earn in all?

4. Billy earns 35¢ a week for keeping the wood basket filled. He earns 17¢ a week selling papers. How much does he earn each week?

5. Don needs 75¢ to buy a Cub Scout flashlight. If he earns 46¢ and 27¢, will he have enough to buy the light?

127

Miss Bell's pupils ordered 28 bottles of milk on Monday and 34 on Tuesday. Can you find out how many bottles they ordered in the 2 days?

Here is a short way to add 28 and 34 to find the answer:

▶ Write the addition this way: ───────────→

$$\begin{array}{r} 28 \\ +34 \\ \hline \end{array}$$

▶ Think, "28 = 2 tens and 8 ones.
      34 = 3 tens and 4 ones."

▶ Think, "8 ones + 4 ones = 12 ones." *Change 12 ones to 1 ten and 2 ones.*

▶ Write the 2 in the ones column.
▶ *Carry* the 1 ten to the tens column.

$$\begin{array}{r} 1 \\ 28 \\ +34 \\ \hline 62 \end{array}$$

▶ Think, "1 ten + 2 tens + 3 tens = 6 tens." Write the 6 in the tens column. Miss Bell ordered _?_ bottles of milk.

1. There are 15 boys and 19 girls in Dan's class. How many children are there all together?

2. Mary counted 16 books on one shelf and 28 on another. How many books were on the two shelves?

3. Yesterday 37 third-grade children and 34 fourth-grade children visited the airport. How many visited the airport?

4. Last week Harry sold 14 magazines. This week he sold 18. How many did he sell in the two weeks?

Tell how you should think in finding these sums. Then copy, add, and check.

5.	45	53	78	12	37	43	65	39
	29	36	18	18	58	29	28	24

6.	38	65	47	26	30	28	52	27
	26	29	48	59	45	49	47	47

Carrying in longer columns

Tell how Ex. 1 will help you with Exs. 2 and 3.

1.	9 + 6	12 + 4	15 + 5	14 + 7	16 + 7	10 + 6	15 + 8

1. 9 +6   12 +4   15 +5   14 +7   16 +7   10 +6   15 +8

2. 4 5 +6   7 5 +4   8 7 +5   7 7 +7   8 8 +7   3 7 +6   6 9 +8

3. 24 35 16   17 25 44   18 17 35   17 27 37   38 28 27   23 7 16   16 59 8

4. Find the example with the wrong answer. Copy that example and add correctly.

34	51	83	26	8	26	35
40	36	9	48	29	47	8
19	84	25	9	35	18	29
93	171	117	83	72	81	72

Add and check. Use folded paper.

5. 25 36 24   38 26 15   56 8 37   27 35 6   63 8 19   60 28 17   75 24 7

6. 34 17 18   26 39 18   27 9 36   9 45 38   37 8 46   27 26 13   68 30 56

7. Find the sum of 29, 34, and 16.

8. Jane needs 14 inches of ribbon for each of 2 hair bows, and 8 inches of ribbon for a bow on her dress. If she buys a yard of ribbon, will she have enough for the 3 bows?

Beads 60¢

Jane has 27¢. Sara has 35¢. Below is the way the girls added to find out if together they have enough to buy a string of beads. How are their additions alike? different? Have they enough to buy a string of beads?

JANE'S ADDITION	
Jane has	27¢
Sara has	+ 35¢
Both have	62¢

SARA'S ADDITION	
Jane has	$.27
Sara has	+ .35
Both have	$.62

1. Copy without the answers. Add. See if your answers are right. Don't forget dollar signs and cents points.

$.35	$.74	$.60	$.28	$.18	$.24
.28	.18	.28	.35	.09	.38
$.63	$.92	$.88	.16	.25	.18
			$.79	$.52	$.80

2. Copy, add, and check:

$.14	$.42	$.26	$.38	$.47	$.25
.25	.20	.07	.26	.28	.35
.36	.34	.15	.36	.13	.15

3. $.75 + $.16   4. $.26 + $.35 + $.24   5. $.17 + $.06

6. Tom wants to buy a key chain which costs $.39, and a whistle for $.25. How much will both cost?

7. A flashlight battery costs $.15. Add to find the cost of 2 batteries; 3 batteries; 4 batteries.

8. Ted earned 12 dimes for the March of Dimes. Write the amount Ted earned. Use a dollar sign and cents point.

Subtraction of two-place
numbers with borrowing
(regrouping tens and
ones)

UNIT
21

Borrowing in subtraction

1. Tom swept out Mrs. Kane's garage. She wants to pay Tom 25¢. She has 6 dimes and 2 pennies, or 62¢.

▶ Pick up 6 dimes and 2 pennies in toy coins. Using only these coins, try to hand someone 25¢. Can you do it? Why not?

▶ Change one of the 6 dimes to 10 pennies. Then you have 5 dimes and __?__ pennies. Now hand someone 25¢ (2 dimes and 5 pennies).

▶ How many dimes do you have left? How many pennies? How much money in all? Then 62¢ − 25¢ = __?__ ¢.

2. In Ex. 1 you subtracted 25¢ from 62¢. Here is a way to write that subtraction:

Mrs. Kane had 62¢ ⟶	$\overset{5}{\cancel{6}}$ dimes and $\overset{12}{\cancel{2}}$ pennies
She gave Tom 25¢ ⟶	2 dimes and 5 pennies
She has left ⟶	3 dimes and 7 pennies = 37¢

Answer these questions about this subtraction:

▶ How many dimes and pennies did Mrs. Kane have at first?

▶ How many dimes and pennies must she give Tom for the work he did?

▶ Could she give Tom 2 dimes and 5 pennies at first? Why not? What did she do about it?

▶ Why is the 6 crossed off and the 5 written above it?

▶ Why is the 2 crossed off and the 12 written above it?

▶ 12 pennies minus 5 pennies = __?__ pennies;
   5 dimes minus 2 dimes = __?__ dimes.

▶ How many dimes and pennies did Mrs. Kane have left? How much money in all? 62¢ − 25¢ = __?__ ¢.

Borrowing in subtraction

1. On page 131 you learned how to find 62¢ – 25¢. Here is a shorter way to write that subtraction.

▶ Write the subtraction with the smaller number under the larger number: ⟶

$$\begin{array}{r} 6\,2¢ \\ -\,2\,5¢ \end{array}$$

▶ Think, "62¢ = 6 dimes and 2 cents.
     25¢ = 2 dimes and 5 cents."

▶ Think, "I can't take 5¢ from 2¢, so I'll *borrow* one dime from the 6 dimes and change it into 10¢. Then 62¢ becomes 5 dimes and 12 cents."

$$\begin{array}{r} {}^{5\;12} \\ \not{6}\,\not{2}¢ \\ -\,2\,5¢ \\ \hline 3\,7¢ \end{array}$$

▶ Think, "5¢ from 12¢ = 7¢."

▶ Write the 7 in the cents column.

▶ Think, "I borrowed 1 dime from the 6 dimes, so the 6 dimes became 5 dimes. 2 dimes from 5 dimes = 3 dimes."

▶ Write the 3 in the dimes column.

▶ 62¢ – 25¢ = _?_ ¢. Check by adding 25¢ and 37¢.

Tell what you think when you do these subtractions. Use coins to check.

2.
33¢	45¢	64¢	53¢	87¢	56¢	66¢	84¢
19¢	29¢	28¢	17¢	39¢	27¢	37¢	59¢
14¢	16¢	36¢	36¢	48¢	29¢	29¢	25¢

3. Dick has 63¢. How much will he have left if he buys a 25-cent book? a 39-cent knife?

4. Betty has a quarter. How much more does she need to buy a 40-cent ticket? a 72-cent scarf?

Copy and subtract. Use coins to check.

5.
52¢	75¢	63¢	76¢	83¢	71¢	64¢	55¢
38¢	48¢	29¢	37¢	57¢	27¢	26¢	26¢

More about borrowing

Jack and Jim measured to see how far each could throw a ball. Jack threw it 27 feet. Jim threw it 43 feet.

Jane subtracted this long way to find how much farther Jim threw the ball than Jack. First she wrote this:

$$43 = 4 \text{ tens and } 3 \text{ ones}$$
$$27 = 2 \text{ tens and } 7 \text{ ones}$$

Could she take 7 ones from 3 ones? Why not?

She borrowed 1 ten from the 4 tens and changed it into 10 ones. She said, "4 tens and 3 ones = 3 tens and 13 ones."

She finished the subtraction this way:

$$43 = \overset{3}{4} \text{ tens and } \overset{13}{3} \text{ ones}$$
$$27 = 2 \text{ tens and } 7 \text{ ones}$$
$$1 \text{ ten and } 6 \text{ ones } = 16$$

Answer these questions about Jane's subtraction:

1. Why is the 4 crossed off and the 3 written above it?

2. Why is the 3 crossed off and the 13 written above it?

3. Where do the 6 ones come from in the answer?

4. Where does the 1 ten come from in the answer?

5. 1 ten and 6 ones = __?__.

6. Jim threw the ball how many feet farther than Jack?

On the next page you will find a short way to write this subtraction. Most third-grade children like it better than the long way that Jane used. See if you do, too.

You have already learned one way to find how much farther Jim threw the ball than Jack. Here is a shorter way.

▶ To find how much more 43 is than 27, write the subtraction this way: ⟶

$$\begin{array}{r} 4\,3 \\ -2\,7 \\ \hline \end{array}$$

▶ Think, "43 is 4 tens and 3 ones.
     27 is 2 tens and 7 ones."

▶ Think, "I can't take 7 ones from 3 ones. I'll *borrow* 1 ten from the 4 tens and change it into 10 ones. Then 43 becomes 3 tens and 13 ones."

▶ Think, "13 ones − 7 ones = 6 ones."

▶ Write the 6 in the ones column.

▶ Think, "3 tens − 2 tens = 1 ten."

$$\begin{array}{r} {}^{3}\!\!\!\!\!\diagup^{13} \\ 4\,3 \\ -2\,7 \\ \hline 1\,6 \end{array}$$

▶ Write the 1 in the tens column.

▶ Jim threw the ball 16 feet farther than Jack. Check.

1. Miss Bell's class set out 42 tomato plants. The frost killed 18 of them. There are ＿?＿ plants left.

2. Mary jumped rope 41 times without missing. Susan jumped 29 times. Mary jumped ＿?＿ times more than Susan.

3. Betty weighs 52 pounds. Susan weighs 44 pounds. Betty is ＿?＿ pounds heavier than Susan.

4. The first picture below shows the cookies Bob's mother baked. The second picture shows the cookies that were left after Bob and Don were in the kitchen. Write a subtraction to show how to find how many cookies the boys ate.

Subtraction practice

▶ How can you tell in a subtraction whether you need to borrow?

▶ In which of the subtractions in Ex. 1 do you need to borrow?

▶ Copy, subtract, and check these examples:

	a	*b*	*c*	*d*	*e*	*f*	*g*	*h*
1.	51	84	63	77	65	92	47	81
	29	37	19	25	32	48	19	27
2.	95	82	91	74	75	56	84	38
	28	49	68	38	59	37	49	15
3.	66	47	75	76	50	52	80	62
	48	28	39	39	39	28	26	37
4.	67	57	76	64	78	85	45	58
	28	24	49	28	39	27	19	19
5.	98	54	67	75	63	82	78	43
	39	39	49	28	39	69	28	28
6.	83	86	86	67	83	96	96	36
	59	49	38	48	57	77	39	18
7.	46	67	86	74	66	91	87	53
	27	39	47	50	49	58	69	37

8. Some pupils made a list of 6 things they knew about subtraction. How many things do you know about subtraction?

1. Joan and Molly together have 38¢. They want to buy a book that costs 65¢. To find out how much more money they need, they subtracted 38¢ from 65¢. How are their subtractions alike? different?

JOAN'S SUBTRACTION	MOLLY'S SUBTRACTION
65¢	$.65
− 38¢	− .38
27¢	$.27

2. Find the subtraction with the wrong answer. Copy it and subtract correctly.

$.76	$.38	$.55	$.63	$.47	$.77
− .27	− .19	− .38	− .47	− .39	− .53
$.49	$.19	$.17	$.16	$.09	$.24

3. $.75 is equal to 6 dimes and ? cents.

4. $.60 is equal to 5 dimes and ? cents.

Copy, subtract, and check:

5.	$.67	$.75	$.70	$.46	$.94	$.68
	.28	.28	.65	.29	.48	.20

6.	$.65	$.97	$.74	$.80	$.85	$.56
	.27	.34	.27	.32	.39	.38

7.	$.84	$.78	$.47	$.63	$.90	$.58
	.45	.25	.29	.35	.54	.19

8. $.75 − $.29   **9.** $.63 − $.48   **10.** $.80 − $.45

11. Bill has $.60. How much will he have left if he spends $.25 for a magnet? $.39 for fishhooks?

136

Written review

1. Write the numbers by 2's from 2 to 24.

2. Write the numbers by 3's from 3 to 30.

3. 1 qt. = _?_ pt.   1 yr. = _?_ mo.   1 ft. = _?_ in.
   1 yd. = _?_ ft.   1 yd. = _?_ in.   1 dime = _?_ ¢

4. What time is it when the long hand of the clock points to 12 and the short hand points to 5?

Copy, add, and check:

	a	b	c	d	e	f	g
5.	3	9	8	6	8	9	4
	7	8	5	7	9	7	9
	8	6	9	6	8	5	7
6.	39	29	43	54	25	49	38
	76	78	25	60	86	52	83

Copy, subtract, and check:

7.	178	169	45	49	85	157	87
	95	76	28	47	38	69	78

8. How much will it cost to buy a doll for $.25 and a doll-coat pattern for $.15?

9. Ann has read 49 pages in her new reader. Alice has read only 33 pages. How many pages must Alice read to catch up with Ann?

10. Jean has 89¢. She wonders how much she will have left if she spends 15¢ to go to the movies. Do you know?

11. Yesterday Bob said 79 addition facts correctly. Today he said 87 correctly. He knows _?_ more addition facts today than he did yesterday.

137

Sensible answers in addition

Bill bought a 49-cent kite and some string for 29¢. The clerk said, "88 cents, please."

Bill thought, "49¢ is about 50¢; 29¢ is about 30¢; so my bill should be about 50¢ + 30¢, or 80¢."

Bill said to the clerk, "Did you add right? I don't think I owe you as much as 88¢."

The clerk wrote down this example: ⟶

$$\begin{array}{r} 49¢ \\ +29¢ \\ \hline \end{array}$$

She added. How much did she find Bill owed? She said, "I'm sorry. You owe only 78¢."

"That's better," said Bill. "I knew I owed about 80¢."

Bill *estimated* the sum of 49¢ and 29¢. That means he found out *about how much* he owed; so he knew that 88¢ was not a *sensible answer*.

There are 3 answers given for Exs. 1 to 4. Tell how you find the one that is most sensible. In Ex. 1 say: "39 is almost 40; 22 is about 20. The sum should be about 40 + 20, or 60. I see that 61 is the most sensible answer."

1. Does 39 + 22 = 52, or 61, or 73?

2. Does 28 + 63 = 71, or 81, or 91?

3. Does 32 + 50 + 48 = 110, or 120, or 130?

4. Does 43 + 39 + 60 = 132, or 142, or 152?

Do these additions. Check each answer by estimating.

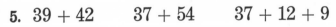

5. 39 + 42	37 + 54	37 + 12 + 9
6. 28 + 73	49 + 13	48 + 15 + 12
7. 18 + 69	88 + 23	67 + 14 + 39

Sensible answers in subtraction

I have about 70¢
I spend about 50¢
I'll have left about 20¢

Bill had 72 cents. He wondered how much he would have left if he bought a knife for 49 cents. He thought:————————————→

Then he subtracted 49 cents from 72 cents to find exactly how much he would have left. He knew that his answer, 23 cents, was sensible.

$$\begin{array}{r} 72 \\ -49 \\ \hline 23 \end{array}$$

Estimate the answers to these subtractions. In Ex. 1 say: "71 is about 70; 48 is about 50; so the answer is about _?_."

1.	71 − 48	71 − 22	80 − 48	100 − 47
2.	83 − 39	89 − 51	79 − 38	100 − 26
3.	92 − 61	90 − 21	91 − 32	100 − 78
4.	58 − 31	98 − 69	69 − 21	100 − 89
5.	61 − 39	100 − 22	120 − 19	120 − 89
6.	72 − 43	100 − 39	140 − 39	130 − 21
7.	83 − 54	100 − 52	150 − 98	171 − 29
8.	94 − 58	100 − 69	160 − 79	189 − 48

9. John now has $19.80. He wants to buy a radio that costs $30.00. Estimate how much more he must save.

10. Mary wants to buy a used bicycle for $21.00. She has saved $10.85. Estimate how much more she must save.

11. Carl has $9.95. Estimate how much he will have left if he buys skates for $3.98.

12. Timmy's aunt sent him $5.00 for his birthday. Estimate how much he will have left if he spends $2.95 for a cowboy shirt.

▶ **Oral review**

1. 5 hundreds + 7 tens + 4 ones = __?__.

2. Count by 2's to 20; by 5's to 50.

3. Add 3 to each of the numbers below; add 8.

   22   14   31   33   75   96   80   54

4. Does the tenth of this month come on Monday?

5. 87 is __?__ tens and __?__ ones.

6. 5 dimes and 14 pennies = __?__ dimes and 4 pennies.

7. 7 dimes and 3 pennies = 6 dimes and __?__ pennies.

8. 9 tens and 5 ones = 8 tens and __?__ ones.

9. 75 = 6 tens and __?__ ones.

10. 1 yd. = __?__ ft.; 1 yd. = __?__ in.; 1 ft. = __?__ in.

11. Which is more, IX or 10?

12. Does 59 + 31 equal about 80, or 90, or 100?

13. 9 tens = __?__; 10 tens = __?__; 11 tens = __?__.

▶ **Written review**

Check your answers to these examples:

1. 3 + 4 + 7   2. 6 + 5 + 3   3. 9 + 5 + 2 + 8

4.   75   5.   93   6.   159   7.   94   8.   96
   + 44   + 58   − 63   − 76   − 28

9. Write in figures: sixty dollars and six cents.

10. The temperature is 52°. If it gets 10° cooler, what will the temperature be?

Using common sense

1. Bob and Ann are eating breakfast. One of the clocks in the picture has stopped. The other tells the right time. What is the right time?

2. Does a quart of milk cost about 5¢, 23¢, or 50¢?

3. Will 5 books at $.98 each cost about $2.00, $5.00, or $50.00?

4. Is the height of an eight-year-old girl nearer 4 inches, 4 feet, or 4 yards?

5. Would a boy's shoes cost about $.05, $.50, $5, or $50?

6. Should it take you about ½ hour, about 1 hour, or about 2 hours to eat your lunch?

7. Is the age of a boy's grandfather about 10 years, 20 years, 55 years, or 150 years?

8. On an all-day hike would some Boy Scouts be likely to walk ½ mile, 12 miles, 75 miles, or 100 miles?

1. $9 + \underline{\ ?\ } = 17$ $\qquad \underline{\ ?\ } + 4 = 13$ $\qquad 8 + \underline{\ ?\ } = 14$

2. $5 + \underline{\ ?\ } = 13$ $\qquad 8 + \underline{\ ?\ } = 17$ $\qquad 7 + \underline{\ ?\ } = 16$

3. Tell 2 other facts that belong with each of these pairs:

$\begin{cases} 14 - 5 = 9 \\ 14 - 9 = 5 \end{cases}$ $\begin{cases} 13 - 9 = 4 \\ 13 - 4 = 9 \end{cases}$ $\begin{cases} 9 + 6 = 15 \\ 6 + 9 = 15 \end{cases}$ $\begin{cases} 8 + 9 = 17 \\ 9 + 8 = 17 \end{cases}$

4. Tell the *key facts* that help you find these sums:

34 + 5	18 + 7	43 + 9	17 + 6
32 + 8	27 + 3	38 + 6	34 + 4

5. What "doubles" facts help you know these sums?

7	6	9	4	6	8	8
+8	+5	+8	+5	+7	+9	+7

6. Add 9 to each of these numbers:

27 16 35 24 29 33 21 32

7. Add 8 to each number in Ex. 6. Add 7; 6; 5.

Find the sums and check:

	a	b	c	d	e	f	g	h
8.	98	86	75	66	64	77	89	64
	69	67	69	98	83	57	55	55
9.	65	50	65	23	58	98	94	72
	89	77	46	96	48	43	98	45
10.	3	9	7	4	6	3	2	6
	9	2	3	6	9	6	4	8
	4	7	4	3	5	7	9	4
	5	6	8	9	4	8	5	7

Can you tell?

Tell whether to add or subtract to find the answers to these problems. Then work the problems.

1. Tony has a half dollar. He wants to buy a book that costs 89¢. To find how much more he needs, he should __?__.

2. Teddy earned 65¢ shoveling snow and 20¢ running errands. To find how much he earned in all, he should __?__.

3. Four children are planning a boat trip. There is room for 12 children in the boat. To find how many children they can invite, they should __?__.

4. Susan is 8 years old. Ann is 13 years old. To find how much younger Susan is than Ann, you should __?__.

5. Judy saved 25¢. Her brother saved 10¢ more than Judy. To find how much her brother has, you should __?__.

6. Some boys had 26 snowballs ready for the snowball fight. When they won the fight, they had 11 snowballs left. To find how many snowballs they threw, the boys should __?__.

7. Nine of the girls and 7 of the boys in a class have skates. To find how many children have skates, you should __?__.

8. Art had 15 comic books. He gave 8 books to Jack. To find how many books Art has left, you should __?__.

9. To find the total score of each of these teams, you should __?__. Which team made the best total score?

| SCORE BOARD | | |
Spitfires	Indians	Rangers
42	75	28
35	24	32
72	83	46

1. Count by 10's from 14 to 94; by 20's from 17 to 97; by 100's from 67 to 867.

2. What is the sum of 20 and 50?

3. If you put 600 pins, 80 pins, and 5 pins together, you will have _?_ pins.

4. Jane wishes to buy a doll for 25¢. She has 14¢. How much more does she need?

5. Bobby is 58 inches tall. Dick is 53 inches tall. Bobby is _?_ inches taller than Dick.

6. How much more is 87¢ than 60¢?

7. What is today's date?

8. What time is it now?

9. What is the temperature in your classroom?

10. 9+6 is as much as 10+_?_.
8+4 is as much as 10+_?_.

11. 6+6=12, so 6+7=_?_.
8+8=16, so 9+8=_?_.

12. 10+7=17, so 9+7=_?_.
10+4=14, so 9+4=_?_.

13. Is 76 larger than 67?

14. Which of these numbers is larger than 36?

| 20 | 6 | 13 | 42 |

15. Which number is nearest 10?

| 5 | 4 | 11 | 7 |

16. Which number is nearest 100?

| 30 | 70 | 20 | 50 |

17. Which number is nearest 60?

| 50 | 53 | 58 | 52 |

18. Find the sum of:

| 3 | 5 | 8 | 7 |

19. Tom went to the store with 70¢. When he got there, he had half a dollar. He had lost _?_ cents.

20.

$$159 - 76 \qquad 158 - 95 \qquad 165 - 95$$

21.

$$83 + 92 \qquad 74 + 53 \qquad 68 + 80$$

22.

$$175 - 90 \qquad 90 - 23 \qquad 138 - 72$$

144

About Eskimos

1. One day, when the thermometer looked like the one in the picture, Mary Jane said, "The temperature is _?_ degrees today. The Eskimos have much colder weather than this."

2. The temperature in Greenland often goes down as low as 50° below zero. How low does the temperature go where you live? How high?

3. It is dark all day and all night in the far north during the winter. An Eskimo often sees the stars shining brightly at 11 A.M. Where you live can the stars be seen at 11 A.M.? at 11 P.M.?

4. Eskimo children do not have a regular bedtime. An Eskimo boy might go out for a swift ride over the snow behind his dog team at 2 A.M.
Do you ever go out to play at 2 A.M.? at 2 P.M.?

5. In the winter the Eskimos live in houses made of blocks of frozen snow. These houses are called igloos. An Eskimo can build an igloo in about 3 hours.
To build a house in your town, does it take a group of men about 3 hours? 3 days? 3 weeks? 3 months? 3 years?

6. Eskimos are strong, short people. An Eskimo father is usually little more than 5 feet tall. Show how tall an Eskimo man is. About how tall is your father?

1. Jerry's teacher sent him to the supply room for colored paper. He brought 100 sheets of red paper, 80 sheets of green, and 9 sheets of blue. How many was that in all?

2. Ann has 38¢ in her bank. She earned 17¢ more. How much has she all together?

3. Buddy wants to buy a 50-cent siren for his bicycle. He has saved a quarter, a nickel, and a dime. Does he have enough money?

4. The Girl Scouts are selling cookies. Ann sold 8 boxes, Judy sold 5, Alice 7, and Rita 3. Together these girls sold ? boxes.

5. Jerry caught a fish 1 foot and 7 inches long. Ned caught one 20 inches long. Whose fish was longer? How much longer?

6. Nancy had a yard of ribbon. She cut off some for a bow. She had 17 inches left. She must have used ? inches for the bow.

7. Jack bought a dozen doughnuts. He ate some. There are only 9 left in the box. How many did he eat?

8. Betty wants to listen to a radio program at half past three. It is now 5 minutes to 3. Betty said, "I must wait ? minutes for the program."

9. Mary needs 24 in. of tape for one apron string. How much does she need for two apron strings?

10. Dan would like to buy a book for 49¢. He has only 23¢. How much more does he need?

Write your score on your Problem Test Record.

Self-Help Test 5

Copy, find the answers, and check:

1. $3 + 2 + 4$ (52)

2. $8 + 6 + 3$ (97)

3. $2 + 7 + 5 + 3$ (97)

4. $8 + 6 + 7 + 2$ (120–122)

5. $\begin{array}{r} 43 \\ + 25 \end{array}$ (46)

6. $\begin{array}{r} 27 \\ + 35 \end{array}$ (126–128)

7. $\begin{array}{r} 42 \\ + 97 \end{array}$ (99)

8. $\begin{array}{r} \$.65 \\ + .25 \end{array}$ (130)

9. $\begin{array}{r} 96 \\ - 23 \end{array}$ (47–48)

10. $\begin{array}{r} 82 \\ - 47 \end{array}$ (131–135)

11. $\begin{array}{r} 146 \\ - 74 \end{array}$ (100)

12. $\begin{array}{r} \$.82 \\ - .46 \end{array}$ (136)

Self-Help Test 6

1. Write the number that means 2 hundreds, 3 tens, and 4 ones. (70)

2. Write the numbers by 100's from 100 to 1000. (70)

3. Write the next five numbers after 79. (16–17)

4. What time is it by this clock? (2–3)

5. Bob has 28¢. He wants to buy a flashlight that costs a half dollar. How much more does he need? (132)

6. Jim will have a birthday party on Saturday of this week. On what date will he have the party? (117)

7. Tom says he is 1 yard and 16 inches tall. How many inches tall is he? (128)

8. Jack went to the store to get two quart bottles of grape juice. He can get only one quart bottle and the rest in pint bottles. How many pint bottles should he get? (28)

UNIT
23

Adding and subtracting money
and three-place numbers — no
carrying or borrowing

Adding money

Billy wants to buy a bicycle light for $1.25 and a bicycle horn for $1.34. Can you figure out without help how much both will cost?

Long way to find the sum of $1.25 and $1.34:

Cost of light = 1 dollar 2 dimes 5 cents
Cost of horn = 1 dollar 3 dimes 4 cents
Cost of both = 2 dollars 5 dimes 9 cents = $2.59

Short way to find the sum of $1.25 and $1.34:

▶ Think, "5 cents and 4 cents are 9 cents." Write the 9 in the cents column.

▶ Think, "2 dimes and 3 dimes are 5 dimes." Write the 5 in the dimes column.

▶ Think, "1 dollar and 1 dollar are 2 dollars." Write the 2 in the dollars column.

$\begin{array}{r} \$1.25 \\ 1.34 \\ \hline \$2.59 \end{array}$

▶ Put the cents point in the sum right under the cents points in the example. The sum is $2.59.

▶ Notice that the dollar sign is written in two places, before the first amount of money to be added and before the sum.

▶ Check the addition by adding up.

Use the *long way* and the *short way* to find these sums:

1.
$1.37	$2.35	$6.72	$5.42	$4.31	$2.40	$1.23
8.10	7.21	3.16	2.05	1.58	.26	.36

2.
$7.15	$6.31	$1.53	$2.13	$2.48	$1.48	$7.51
2.70	2.46	5.30	4.44	2.51	.30	.40

3. $2.43 + $3.45   4. $1.83 + $7.14   5. $5.60 + $.38

Adding three-place numbers

Can you figure out from the picture how many carnival tickets the boys and girls sold all together?

Long way to find the sum of 234 and 253:

Tickets girls sold   = 2 hundreds 3 tens 4 ones
Tickets boys sold   = 2 hundreds 5 tens 3 ones
Tickets sold in all = 4 hundreds 8 tens 7 ones = 487

Short way to find the sum of 234 and 253:

▶Think, "4 ones and 3 ones are 7 ones." Write the 7 in the ones column.

▶Think, "3 tens and 5 tens are 8 tens." Write the 8 in the tens column.

▶Think, "2 hundreds and 2 hundreds are 4 hundreds." Write the 4 in the hundreds column.

```
234
253
487
```

▶Check by adding up.

▶The addition shows the third-grade children sold __?__ tickets all together.

Use the *long way* and the *short way* to find these sums:

1.	371	32	874	561	256	321	764	331
	410	41	124	314	603	523	20	17

2. $124 + 553$ 4. $320 + 341$ 6. $231 + 26$

3. $542 + 450$ 5. $425 + 261$ 7. $245 + 13$

Show that you understand these problems by working Exs. 1 and 2 in two ways. Use the long way first.

1. Peter wants a baseball mitt marked $1.45 and a bat marked $1.50. How much will both cost?

2. Dick has 275 stamps and his brother has 310 stamps. How many do they have together?

3. There are 423 boys and 374 girls in the Adams School. How many children are there in the school?

4. Eddie bought a basketball for $2.65 and a building set for $1.34. How much money did he spend?

5. Jane's mother bought her a pair of boots for $2.40 and a jacket for $6.50. How much did both cost?

6. Carl's grandmother lives on a farm. She sold 120 eggs one week and 144 eggs the next week. How many eggs did she sell?

7. Today 252 boys and 246 girls ate lunch in the lunch-room. How many children ate lunch at school today?

8. Billy and his father went to his grandmother's. They drove 375 miles the first day and 224 miles the second day. How far did they drive in two days?

9. A punching bag costs $2.40. Find the cost of 2 punching bags by adding.

10. Janet wants to buy these twin dolls. How much will the twins cost?

Molly and Polly
are twins
Price $3.24 each

How much money?

Dave and Kay were making plans to buy their little sister a birthday present. They shook the coins out of their banks to see how much money they had saved to buy her present.

1. Dave has 1 quarter, 4 dimes, and 3 nickels. How much money has he?

2. Kay has a half dollar, a quarter, a dime, and 6 pennies. How much money has she?

3. Who has saved more money, Dave or Kay?

How much money has each of the children in Exs. 4 to 9?

4. Ann has a quarter, a dime, and a nickel.

5. Patty has a half dollar, a quarter, and a dime.

6. Alice has 2 quarters, 2 nickels, and 3 pennies.

7. Dick has 1 half dollar, 5 nickels, and 4 cents.

8. Carl has 1 half dollar, 1 quarter, and 2 dimes.

9. Jim has a dollar, a quarter, and 3 dimes.

Write in figures, using the dollar sign and cents point:

10. Thirty-three dollars and three cents.

11. Twelve dollars and fifty-two cents.

12. Forty dollars and ten cents.

13. In Joan's coin purse she has __?__ quarters, __?__ dimes, __?__ nickels, __?__ pennies. In all she has __?__ ¢.

STOCKING CAPS
$2.45 each

Subtracting money

Molly has $5.69. She wants to buy this stocking cap. How much does the cap cost?

Can you figure out without help how much she will have left if she buys the cap? This is the way she subtracted to find out:

Molly has ⟶ 5 dollars 6 dimes 9 cents
Cap costs ⟶ 2 dollars 4 dimes 5 cents
She will have left ⟶ 3 dollars 2 dimes 4 cents = $3.24

Here is a shorter way to subtract $2.45 from $5.69:

▶ Think, "5 cents from 9 cents is 4 cents." Write the 4 in the cents column.

▶ Think, "4 dimes from 6 dimes is _?_ dimes." Write the 2 in the dimes column.

▶ Think, "2 dollars from 5 dollars is _?_ dollars." Write the 3 in the dollars column.

$$\begin{array}{r} \$5.69 \\ -2.45 \\ \hline \$3.24 \end{array}$$

▶ Where is the cents point written in the answer? the dollar sign? Molly will have _?_ left. Check the subtraction.

1. How much will these girls have left if each buys a stocking cap for $2.45? Jane has $3.95. Ann has $4.48.

Copy, subtract, and check:

2.

$5.98	$6.73	$9.76	$8.74	$6.65	$6.75
− 2.40	− 2.42	− .05	− 3.00	− 4.25	− .45

3.

$8.09	$8.54	$3.00	$7.50	$8.73	$5.47
− 4.09	− .24	− 2.00	− .20	− .63	− .43

4. $9.45 − $7.32   **5.** $7.98 − $.43   **6.** $8.96 − $.64

Subtracting three-place numbers

John and Jim collect pins and badges. You can see some of John's pins on his cap. He has 267 pins. Jim has 135.

Can you figure out how many more pins John has than Jim? This is the way John subtracted to find out:

Pins John has ⟶ 2 hundreds 6 tens 7 ones
Pins Jim has ⟶ 1 hundred 3 tens 5 ones

How many more John has than Jim } ⟶ 1 hundred 3 tens 2 ones = 132

Here is a shorter way to subtract for finding how much more 267 is than 135. Explain it. →

$$\begin{array}{r} 267 \\ -135 \\ \hline 132 \end{array}$$

The subtraction shows John has _?_ more pins than Jim. Check the subtraction.

Copy, subtract, and check:

	a	b	c	d	e	f	g	h
1.	751	865	963	862	456	872	943	874
	221	431	361	621	151	162	21	73
2.	653	653	985	863	647	876	847	948
	442	530	430	503	41	845	23	905

3. Dan can get a plastic harmonica for 275 box tops. He has 152 box tops. How many more does he need?

4. Tom can get a horseshoe-nail ring for 235 box tops. He has 110 box tops. How many more does he need?

5. Bobby has saved $2.20. How much more does he need in order to buy gloves for $2.75?

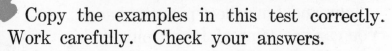

Copy the examples in this test correctly. Work carefully. Check your answers.

1. Billy got his dog, Molly, on January 17, 1951. Two weeks later Molly's puppies were born. On what date were the puppies born?

2.   827
     + 162

3. $4.22
     + 8.37

4. $9.79
     − 3.35

5. 75
     − 48

6. Don would like to buy skates that cost $3.25. He has saved $2.10. How much more does he need in order to buy the skates?

7. Susan has 70¢. If she spends 39¢ to have her skates sharpened, she estimates that she will have _?_ left.

8. Write this addition in a short way, using figures only:

$$\begin{array}{l} 2 \text{ hundreds } 3 \text{ tens } 4 \text{ ones} \\ + 4 \text{ hundreds } 0 \text{ tens } 5 \text{ ones} \\ \hline 6 \text{ hundreds } 3 \text{ tens } 9 \text{ ones} \end{array}$$

9. There are 425 children in the Hillside School and 354 in the Wilson School. How many are there in both schools?

10. A skating cap is marked $.95 and mittens are marked $.79. How much more does the cap cost than the mittens?

Just for fun

Tell the missing numbers in these examples. Prove that you are right.

[?] 2	7 [?]	6 4	[?] [?]	2 3 [?]
− 5 6	− 3 5	− [?] [?]	+ 7 2	+ 1 [?] 5
3 6	4 0	1 7	1 3 1	[?] 9 9

Carrying from cents to dimes

Tom wants cowboy boots that cost $6.49 and a belt that costs $1.35. Can you find out how much both will cost? Tom added this way to find out:

Cost of boots = 6 dollars   4 dimes   9 cents
Cost of belt = 1 dollar   3 dimes   5 cents
───
Cost of both = 7 dollars   7 dimes 14 cents

Tom had trouble writing 7 dollars 7 dimes 14 cents with a dollar sign and cents point. Can you do it?

The 14¢ = 1 dime and 4 cents. Put the dime over with the 7 dimes and keep the 4 cents in the cents column. So the cost of both = 7 dollars 8 dimes 4 cents = $7.84.

Here is a short way to do this addition:⟶

▶ Think, "9 cents and 5 cents are 14 cents. Change the 14 cents into 1 dime and 4 cents." Write the 4 in the cents column.

$$\begin{array}{r} {\scriptstyle 1} \\ \$6.49 \\ 1.35 \\ \hline \$7.84 \end{array}$$

▶ Carry the dime from the 14¢ to the dimes column.

▶ Think, "1 dime and 4 dimes are 5 dimes, and 3 dimes are 8 dimes." Write the 8 in the dimes column.

▶ Tell how to finish the addition.

▶ Check by adding up. What is the total cost?

1. Tom earned $2.25 and $1.65. In all, he earned __?__.

2. Copy these examples without the answers. Add and check. Then see if your answers are right.

$1.49	$2.37	$7.25	$.59	$1.09	$1.77	$1.32
1.36	1.57	6.05	.18	.83	.16	.39
$2.85	$3.94	$13.30	$.77	$1.92	$1.93	$1.71

Copy, add, and check:

1. $1.35	$2.49	$1.69	$3.75	$5.56	$6.28	$5.27
1.59	2.25	3.15	1.19	.37	.45	1.67

2. $4.07	$3.67	$5.29	$6.86	$ .47	$3.75	$4.39
3.86	4.19	9.59	7.08	6.45	2.06	.26

3. Ann's mother bought her mittens for $1.29 and a skating cap for $2.35. How much did she spend?

4. Paul wants a sled which costs $4.75 and skates which cost $3.05. How much will both cost?

5. Tom saved $2.48. His aunt gave him $1.25. Did he have enough then to buy a four-dollar camera?

Examples 6, 7, and 8 will help you do Ex. 9.

6. 16	13	15	16	15	12	11
+3	+3	+8	+5	+9	+3	+9

7. 9	5	6	8	9	4	7
7	8	9	8	6	8	4
+3	+3	+8	+5	+9	+3	+9

8. How many tens and ones are there in each of these?

19	16	23	21	24	15	20

9. Copy, add, and check:

$1.29	$5.25	$4.16	$2.28	$3.59	$3.24	$5.07
5.17	1.48	2.39	.18	2.16	.38	1.34
1.43	2.23	1.18	2.45	.09	2.13	2.29

10. Do you think the sum of $4.06 + $3.12 + $5.00 would be about $12 or about $20? Why?

Carrying from ones to tens

Tom had 237 stamps in one book and 356 stamps in another. He wondered how many stamps he had all together. He knew he should add to find out.

▶ Tom thought,"7 ones and 6 ones are 13 ones, but 13 = 1 ten and 3 ones." He wrote the 3 in the ones column.

```
  1
237
356
593
```

▶ Then he carried the one ten to the tens column.

▶ He thought, "1 ten and 3 tens are 4 tens, and 5 tens are 9 tens." He wrote the 9 in the tens column.

▶ Then he thought, "2 hundreds and 3 hundreds are 5 hundreds." He wrote the 5 in the hundreds column.

▶ He checked his addition by adding up. How many stamps did he have all together?

1. Cover the answers to these additions. Do each example on folded paper. Then look to see if your answers are correct.

256	107	406	275	657	557
+ 314	+ 483	+ 284	+ 718	+ 26	+ 33
570	590	690	993	683	590

Add and check:

2.

275	847	367	285	354	467
+ 116	+ 125	+ 428	+ 707	+ 18	+ 28

3.

467	238	406	125	789	375
+ 519	+ 657	+ 389	+ 46	+ 201	+ 608

4. 206 + 375 + 214   **5.** 406 + 338 + 25

6. Harry has a game called Up to a Thousand. He made 208 points his first turn and 462 points his next turn. How many points did he make in all?

Nancy wants a shoulder-strap bag which costs $3.75 and a scarf which costs $1.60. Can you find out without help how much both will cost? Nancy added this way to find out:

Cost of bag = 3 dollars 7 dimes 5 cents
Cost of scarf = 1 dollar 6 dimes 0 cents
Cost of both = 4 dollars 13 dimes 5 cents

Try to write 4 dollars 13 dimes 5 cents with a dollar sign and cents point. Can you do it?

Nancy thought, "10 dimes make a dollar. So 13 dimes would be 1 dollar and 3 dimes. That makes the cost of the bag and scarf 5 dollars 3 dimes 5 cents, or $5.35."

Here is a shorter way to do the addition: ⟶

```
  1
$3.75
+1.60
$5.35
```

▶Think, "5 cents and 0 cents are 5 cents." Write the 5 in the cents column.

▶Think, "7 dimes and 6 dimes are 13 dimes; 13 dimes = 1 dollar and 3 dimes."

▶Write the 3 in the dimes column.

▶Carry the 1 dollar to the dollars column.

▶Think, "1 dollar and 3 dollars are 4 dollars, and 1 dollar are 5 dollars." Write the 5 in the dollars column.

Write the dollar sign and cents point in the sum.

▶Check by adding up. What is the cost of both?

Copy, add, and check:

1.
| $5.64 | $7.95 | $6.76 | $3.83 | $1.86 | $.84 | $4.75 |
| 2.83 | 4.34 | 1.43 | 2.34 | 6.70 | .54 | 1.63 |

2.
| $2.72 | $3.86 | $3.70 | $6.81 | $3.76 | $.80 | $6.72 |
| 2.95 | 5.43 | 3.58 | 2.95 | .80 | .85 | .75 |

Carrying from tens to hundreds

There are 382 children in the Webster School and 583 children in the Lincoln School. Can you find out without help how many children there are in both schools?

Here is a short way to add 382 and 583: →

```
  1
  382
+ 583
  965
```

▶ Think, "2 ones and 3 ones are 5 ones." Write the 5 in the ones column.

▶ Think, "8 tens and 8 tens are 16 tens; 16 tens = 10 tens and 6 tens, or 1 hundred and 6 tens."

▶ Write the 6 in the tens column.

▶ Carry the 1 hundred to the hundreds column.

▶ Think, "1 hundred and 3 hundreds are 4 hundreds, and 5 hundreds are 9 hundreds."

▶ Write the 9 in the hundreds column.

▶ Check the addition by adding up.

▶ How many children are there in both schools?

1. Dan's hobby is collecting shells. He has 152 large shells and 166 small shells. How many shells has he all together?

2. Pete's hobby is collecting rocks. He has 230 rocks in one collection and 182 in another. How many rocks has he in both collections?

3. Janet collects butterflies. She has 124 butterflies in one collection and 84 in another. How many butterflies has she in all?

Copy, add, and check:

4. $243 + 185$	7. $473 + 283$	10. $534 + 83$
5. $370 + 294$	8. $594 + 160$	11. $653 + 96$
6. $563 + 375$	9. $472 + 277$	12. $765 + 84$

Sporting Goods Sale ~ ~

	OLD PRICE	SALE PRICE
Roller Skates	$4.75	$4.50
Ice Skates	$5.98	$4.75
Football	$3.69	$3.00
Baseball Glove	$2.35	$2.10
Baseball Bat	$1.98	$1.90
Baseball	$.85	$.69

1. How much can Jim save by buying roller skates at the sale? How much can he save on each of the other things that are on sale?

2. At the sale, find the cost of:

a pair of roller skates and a baseball bat

a pair of ice skates and a baseball glove

a baseball and a baseball bat

a baseball and a pair of roller skates

3. Jim has $3.40. How much more does he need to buy roller skates? ice skates?

4. Peter has $3.75. How much will he have left if he buys a football? a baseball glove?

5. How much more do ice skates cost than roller skates?

Keeping in practice

Examples 1, 2, and 3 will help you with Ex. 4.

1. Tell these sums. Add down.

4	10	11	12	16	17
+6	+4	+2	+5	+4	+5

2. Add down. Check by adding up.

2	5	5	5	8	9
2	5	6	7	8	8
6	4	2	5	4	5

3. Tell how many dollars and dimes there are in:

10 dimes	13 dimes	20 dimes
14 dimes	17 dimes	22 dimes

4. Copy, add, and check:

$2.23	$3.51	$2.50	$ .50	$4.83	$1.92
1.22	2.53	.65	4.72	.80	2.86
3.60	1.42	1.24	3.57	3.45	3.50

5. Take the tests on pages 110 and 111.

Subtract and check. Use folded paper.

6.

69	98	87	98	69	78	59
35	24	32	15	46	56	23

7.

167	157	136	143	185	174	126
80	95	74	92	90	84	56

8.

83	76	85	62	74	88	57
26	27	38	49	67	79	49

Addition with two-place carrying

Two stamp clubs are planning a Stamp Trade Day. One club has 168 stamps to trade. Another has 174 stamps.

This is the way Jim added to find out how many stamps the two clubs had to trade:

▶ He thought, "8 ones and 4 ones are 12 ones, but 12 = 1 ten and 2 ones."

```
 1 1
 168
 174
 342
```

▶ He wrote the 2 in the ones column.

▶ He carried the 1 ten to the tens column and thought, "1 ten and 6 tens are 7 tens, and 7 tens are 14 tens, but 14 tens are 1 hundred and 4 tens."

▶ He wrote the 4 in the tens column.

▶ Then he carried the 1 hundred to the hundreds column.

▶ He thought, "1 hundred and 1 hundred are 2 hundreds, and 1 hundred are 3 hundreds."

▶ He wrote the 3 in the hundreds column.

▶ He checked his addition by adding up. How many stamps did the two clubs have?

Copy these examples without the answers. Add and check. Then look to see if your answers are correct.

1.
386	249	835	57	$1.48	$ .64
245	163	92	78	4.75	.87
631	412	927	135	$6.23	$1.51

2. Jim has 235 stamps in one book and 356 stamps in another book. How many stamps has he all together?

3. Jerry has 196 stamps in one book and 219 stamps in another book. How many stamps has he all together?

4. Ed had 256 stamps. His uncle sent him 175 more. How many stamps did he have then?

Adding with carrying

Copy, add, and check:

	a	b	c	d	e	f	g
1.	152	789	456	467	157	357	735
	463	201	284	446	386	463	183
2.	754	647	367	288	275	467	386
	165	285	482	563	163	283	378
3.	275	283	436	256	170	375	560
	718	675	387	354	483	548	295

Copy Exs. 4 to 7, add, and check. Keep the cents points in straight lines. Don't forget to write a dollar sign and a cents point in each answer.

4. $4.00	$4.39	$ .67	$1.04	$1.25	$ .98	$ .05
3.00	2.73	.52	.76	1.25	.43	.07
5. $ .76	$1.76	$1.73	$4.50	$5.60	$ .04	$1.00
.54	.24	1.24	5.04	3.80	.74	2.00
.32	2.46	.59	6.30	4.30	.69	2.00

6. $2.46 + $3.75 $4.36 + $3.75 $2.84 + $3.65

7. $2.86 + $5.54 $2.87 + $4.65 $9.04 + $4.03

8. Here are some additions that have not been checked. Find the additions that are *wrong*. Then do them correctly.

$1.25	$.20	$.48	$ .75	$1.68	$ .63	$ .84
1.30	.70	.50	.50	.50	1.74	.99
$2.55	$.90	$.98	$1.25	$3.18	$1.37	$1.83

$3.00
1.39
.40
——
$4.79

Sally went shopping. She saw shoes for $3, a sweater for $1.39, and socks for $.40. She wondered how much they would all cost.

Sally wrote the prices as shown. She kept the cents points in a straight line. Notice that she wrote the three dollars this way: $3.00. Is her addition correct?

Find the sum for each shopping list below:

1. Shoes, $4.00; hat, $2.19; rubbers, $1.19.

2. Coat, $8.98; cap, $1.29; tie, $.39.

3. Raincoat, $4.98; dress, $1.94; gloves, $1.

4. Jane wished to find the sum of $4.25, $.03, and $5. Here is the way she copied the numbers. Did she copy them correctly? If not, what mistake did she make?

$4.25
.30
5.00

Write in columns, add, and check. Be sure to keep the cents points in a straight line. Put a dollar sign and a cents point in each answer.

5. $1.98+$2.54

6. $.45+$1.98

7. $.54+$.69+$2

8. $1.58+$.09+$4

9. $3+$.25

10. $4+$.28

11. $2.00+$4

12. $6+$8+$.50

13. $5+$.25+$.08

14. $7.57+$2+$4

15. $6.50+$3+$.05

16. $4+$.40+$.04

Put on your thinking cap

▶Oral review

1. Is a foot more than 10 inches?
2. Is the length of this book more or less than a foot?
3. Is your teacher's desk longer than a yard?
4. Name the third month of the year.
5. Are 3 cups of milk more or less than a pint?
6. 90 minutes is how much more than an hour?
7. 20 dimes = __?__ dollars.
8. Which number is larger, 895 or 598? 208 or 280?
9. Count from 97 to 103 by 1's.
10. Count from 65 to 105 by 5's.

▶ Written review

1. Look at your classroom thermometer. Write the temperature of the room.

2. Al wants a sled.   He can get one for $5.78 or another for $4.19.   How much more does one cost than the other?

3. Mary went to the store for her mother.   She bought a loaf of bread for 12¢, a pineapple for 29¢, and cherries for 38¢. Estimate how much she spent.

4. Alice has a dime, four pennies, and a quarter in her bank.   How much money has she in her bank?

5. The wingspread of Billy's airplane is one foot.   The wingspread of Dick's airplane is sixteen inches.   How much wider is Dick's plane than Billy's?

Problems to solve

1. Emily is making a birthday present for her cousin. His birthday is on February 10. She wants to mail the present a week before. On what date should she mail it?

2. There are 12 boys and 10 girls in a class. Each one is to have a notebook. How many notebooks will be needed?

3. Leo earned $.75. He is going to spend $.59 for a knife. How much will he have left?

4. Paul would like to buy skates that cost $2.59. He has $1.13. How much more does he need?

5. Janet has 9 eggs. She needs _?_ more to make a dozen.

6. Susan had 63¢ in her bank. She put in 2 dimes. How much did she have in her bank then?

7. Bob made a boat 7 inches long. Billy's was 2 inches longer. How long was Billy's?

8. Alice weighed 51 pounds in September when school opened. She says she has gained 4 pounds. How much does she weigh now?

9. Judy's mother bought her a snow suit for $7.50 and a pair of boots for $1.49. How much did they both cost?

10. The temperature was 54° at 7 A.M. and 58° at noon. How much did the temperature rise during the morning?

11. Jean is baking cookies. She put them in the oven at 7 minutes after 4. They should bake for 15 minutes. At what time should she take them out?

What you should know

Add down. Check by adding up.

1.

4	84	27	8	$.75	$4.25
8	37	36	69	.69	5.49
7	12	35	54	.25	.36

Subtract and check:

2.

78	869	74	71¢	$8.75	$5.00
43	242	49	29¢	3.35	3.00

3. _?_ feet in a yard

4. _?_ inches in a foot

5. _?_ inches in a yard

6. _?_ pints in a quart

7. _?_ glasses in a pint

8. _?_ months in a year

9. _?_ days in a week

10. _?_ minutes in an hour

11. Write the date for today; a week from today.

12. What time is it by each of these clocks?

13. How much change will you get from a quarter if you spend 22¢? 20¢? 15¢? 10¢?

14. What part of an apple will each boy get if 2 boys share it equally? 3 boys? 4 boys?

15. 642 = _?_ hundreds, _?_ tens, _?_ ones.

16. If 7 + 7 = 14 shows there are 14 days in 2 weeks, how can you show how many days there are in 3 weeks?

17. 86¢ = 8 dimes 6 cents = 7 dimes _?_ cents.

18. 19 dimes = _?_ dollar and _?_ dimes.

Does your class feed the birds while the ground is covered with snow? One class had fun doing it.

1. They bought 4 bags of peanuts at 5¢ a bag. Do you know how much the peanuts cost?

2. They paid 34¢ for grain and 15¢ for grit. What did the grain and grit cost?

3. They bought 3 pounds of suet at 10¢ a pound. How much did the suet cost?

4. They made baskets for the suet from grapefruit skins. Find the cost of 3 grapefruit at 8¢ each.

5. They cut each grapefruit in half. They made a basket from each half. How many baskets could they make from 3 grapefruit?

6. They tied each basket on a tree with 4 pieces of red tape. Each piece of tape was ½ yard long. Use the yardstick to show how long each piece of tape was.

Using money

1. Tom saw a flashlight marked $1.29. He has 2 half dollars, a dime, and 3 nickels in his wallet. Has he enough to buy the flashlight?

2. A quart of milk costs 24¢. The Outdoor Club needs 2 quarts to make cocoa. How much will the milk cost?

3. Ann needs a quarter for her share in a party and a dime for bus fare. How much money does Ann need?

4. Tickets for the movies cost 25¢ each. How much will Jack need if he invites a friend to go with him?

Copy, solve, and check:

	a	b	c
5.	$2.46 + $7.28	$3.45 + $1.00	$8.64 − $8.52
6.	$.45 + $.38	$.67 + $.75	$.76 − $.40
7.	$1.35 + $.35	$5.98 − $2.78	$8.00 − $5.00
8.	$.25 + $3.27	$.78 − $.75	$6.87 − $.42

9. Which of these costs about $1? about $2? about $3?

bat $2.98   ball $.95   mitt $2.09

Write in figures, using dollar sign and cents point:

10. Sixty-seven dollars and forty cents.

11. Fifty dollars and five cents.

12. Seventy-seven cents.

13. In the picture at the right, how much money does Bill have in his hands?

▶ Oral review

1. What will the date be a week from today?
2. Count by 3's to 30; by 4's to 40; by 5's to 50.
3. Name the months of the year in order.
4. Add 7 to each of the numbers below. Then add 8.

    15   36   24   41   77   89   65   58

5. $9 + 8$ equals the same number as $10 +$ _?_.
6. Read these: III   VI   X   IV   IX   VII
7. Is $81 + 49 + 30$ about 150, or 160, or 170?
8. Is $98 - 31$ about 50, or 60, or 70?
9. 9 dimes and 8 cents = 8 dimes and _?_ cents.
10. 6 dimes and 15 cents = _?_ dimes and 5 cents.
11. 8 tens and 3 ones = 7 tens and _?_ ones.
12. 5 tens and 19 ones = 6 tens and _?_ ones.

▶ Written review

1. How much of a peppermint stick will each boy get if 2 boys share it equally? 3 boys? 4 boys?

Add and check:

2. $6¢ + 5¢ + 4¢ + 8¢$ 4. $219 + 194$ 6. $\$.78 + \$.65$
3. $\$.16 + \$.32 + \$.08$ 5. $346 + 235$ 7. $\$1.42 + \$2.85$

Subtract and check:

8. $83 - 26$ 9. $\$8.93 - \$5.33$ 10. $\$7.49 - \$.45$

11. Nancy has saved $3.20. How much more does she need for skates marked $5.50?

Sensible answers

No pencils, please. Just estimate each answer.

1. Jerry wants a ball that costs 49¢ and a bat that costs 98¢. He thought, "The ball costs about 50 cents and the bat costs about ___?___, so both will cost about ___?___."

2. It takes 3 yards of gingham to make a dress for Alice. The gingham Alice wants costs 49¢ a yard. Alice thought, "49¢ is about ___?___, so 3 yards will cost about ___?___."

3. Alice would like to have a silk dress. The silk she wants costs 98¢ a yard. She needs 3 yards. About how much would the silk for her dress cost?

4. Tom earned $3.03 last week. If he buys the fishing rod that he wants for $1.99, about how much money will he have left?

5. Jean earned 53¢ last week. She would like to earn a half dollar this week. If she does, she will have about ___?___ all together.

6. John has a dollar. If he buys a knife for 69¢, about how much will he have left?

In the following examples, estimate the answer. Then check the estimate by measuring.

7. About how tall is your desk?

8. About how tall is your teacher?

9. About how long is your teacher's desk?

10. About how long is a new pencil?

11. Is there anything in your schoolroom that would hold about 2 quarts?

171

Using dimes

Miss Bell's pupils decided to have a puppet show and charge 10¢ a ticket.

1. John said, "For 1 ticket I shall charge 10¢; for 2 tickets I shall charge 20¢." Was he right?

2. Make a table like this to show how much the children should charge for 1 ticket; 2 tickets; 3; 4; 5; 6; 7; 8; 9; 10. Use dimes to prove that your table is right.

Tickets	1	2	3	4	5	6	7	8	9	10
Cents	10	20	30	40	50	60	70	80	90	100

3. Practice until you can tell without looking at your table how much to charge for these numbers of tickets at 10¢ each:

4   6   3   2   8   1   5   9   10

Price List
Balloons   10¢ each
Balls   10¢ each
Popcorn   10¢ a bag
Whistles   5¢ each
Bubble Pipes   5¢ each
Puzzles   4¢ and 10¢
Candy Bars   10¢ each
Gumdrops   1¢

PUPPET SHOW
3 o'clock • Tickets 10¢

The children had a table at the Puppet Show, where they sold toys and candy.

4. How much should Ann pay for 3 balls?

5. How much will 5 balloons cost?

6. Dick sold 8 bags of popcorn. How much did he take in?

7. Mary has 10¢. Has she enough to buy a 5-cent whistle and 3 cents' worth of candy?

8. How much will a 5-cent soap-bubble pipe and a 4-cent puzzle cost?

9. Tom sold 6 bags of candy at 10¢ a bag. How much did he take in?

10. How much should Peggy pay for a 10-cent candy bar and 6 cents' worth of peanuts?

11. Sue asked Don for two 10-cent puzzles. She gave him a dime and 2 nickels. Should he have given her any change?

12. Mrs. White gave Jack 3 dimes and 2 pennies to spend at the Puppet Show. She gave Betsy a quarter, a nickel, and 2 pennies. Did she give them each the same amount?

1. When John was selling tickets for the Puppet Show, Jim put 30¢ on the table for tickets. John gave Jim 3 tickets. Was that right?

2. This table shows how many tickets John should give for 10¢, 20¢, and so on. Use dimes to prove the table is right.

Cents	10	20	30	40	50	60	70	80	90	100
Tickets	1	2	3	4	5	6	7	8	9	10

Read the table. Begin this way:

For 10¢ give 1 ticket
For 20¢ give 2 tickets; and so on.

3. Look at the table. Tell how many 10's there are in 10; in 20; in 30; 40; 50; 60; 70; 80; 90; 100.

4. Practice until you can tell how many 10-cent tickets to give for these amounts:

20¢   40¢   10¢   30¢   50¢   80¢   60¢   70¢

5. How many 10-cent toys can Susan buy for 40¢?

6. Mary has 20¢. How many 10-cent balls can she buy?

7. Marshmallows are 10¢ a package. Betsy gave Tom 30¢. How many packages of marshmallows should he be able to buy for her?

8. How many 10-cent games can Alice buy with a half dollar? with a dollar?

9. How many piles of pennies, each pile 10 pennies high, can you make with 70 pennies? 90 pennies? 100 pennies?

Getting change at the Puppet Show

1. Jack gave John a quarter for one 10-cent ticket. How much change should Jack get?

2. Ann gave John a quarter for two 10-cent tickets. How much did the tickets cost? How much change should Ann get from the quarter?

3. Betsy bought four 10-cent tickets. She gave John a half dollar. How much did her tickets cost? How much change should she get?

4. Don bought two 10-cent tickets. How much did the tickets cost? How much change should he get from a half dollar?

5. What change will you get from a quarter after buying one 10-cent ticket? 2 tickets?

6. What change will you get from a half dollar after buying one 10-cent ticket? 3 tickets? 5 tickets? 2 tickets? 4 tickets?

7. What change will you get from a dollar after buying five 10-cent tickets? 8 tickets? 9 tickets? 4 tickets? 6 tickets? 7 tickets?

8. Alice has a quarter and a dime. That is _?_ cents. She wants three 10-cent tickets. How much will the tickets cost? What change should she get?

9. Tell the class about the last time you went shopping. What did you buy? How much money did you give the clerk? How much change did you get?

10. When you get change, do you count it to make sure you are getting the right amount? You should always count your change.

Giving change at the Puppet Show

● When Jack bought his 10-cent ticket from John, he gave John a quarter. This is what John did in giving Jack his change.

John said, "10¢ for the ticket." Then, dropping a nickel into Jack's hand, he said, "15." Dropping a dime into Jack's hand, he said, "25. Thank you!"

● Ann gave John a quarter for two 10-cent tickets. John gave her two tickets and said, "20." Then, dropping a nickel into her hand, he said, "25."

● At the counter Betsy gave Don a nickel to pay for 2 cents worth of candy. Don said, "2." Then, dropping 3 pennies into her hand, he said, "5."

1. Tell what Don would say and what coins he would give in change for a nickel after selling 1 cent's worth of candy; 3 cents' worth; 4 cents' worth.

2. Tell what Don would say and what coins he would give in change for a dime after selling 6 cents' worth of candy; 7 cents' worth; 8 cents' worth; 9 cents' worth.

3. Tell what Don would say and what coins he would give in change for a dime after selling 1 cent's worth of candy; 2 cents' worth; 3 cents' worth; 4 cents' worth.

Tell what Don would say and what coins he would give in change for a quarter after he had made a sale of each of the following amounts:

4. 21¢	7. 17¢	10. 12¢	13. 8¢	16. 2¢
5. 22¢	8. 16¢	11. 14¢	14. 7¢	17. 4¢
6. 24¢	9. 19¢	12. 11¢	15. 6¢	18. 3¢

Self-Help Test 7

Add and check:

1. 6
   9
   <u>4</u> (97)

2. 7
   8
   <u>9</u> (120–122)

3. 58
   5
   <u>27</u> (129)

4. 469
   <u>327</u> (157)

5. 46¢
   <u>32¢</u> (44–45)

6. 456
   <u>487</u> (162–163)

7. $1.85 + $4.63 (158)

8. $7 + $.36 + $2.75 (164)

Subtract and check:

9. 105
   <u>62</u> (100)

10. 86
    <u>37</u> (131–135)

11. $3.75 − $1.60 (152)

12. 685 − 253 (153)

Self-Help Test 8

1. Tom has 2 dollar bills, a half dollar, and a nickel. Write the amount of money he has. (73)

2. Jake has 8 lemon sourballs, 5 cherry ones, and 8 orange ones. How many sourballs has he in all? (120–122)

3. Nancy is making muffins that need to bake 20 minutes. If she puts them in the oven at 10 minutes after 8, when should she take them out? (55)

4. Al earned $2.45. Jerry earned $3.95. Who earned more? How much more? (152)

5. There are 348 children in the West Side School and 483 children in the Park Street School. To give each child in both schools a pencil, __?__ pencils are needed. (162–163)

6. Draw a triangle. Make one side 2 inches long and the other sides as long as you wish. (10)

Pints — quarts — gallons

1. Miss Bell's class is going to have a Valentine party. Valentine's Day is on February 14. The children have from February 9 to February 14 to get ready for the party. That is _?_ days.

2. The party is to begin at quarter after two. How much time will the children have for their party before school closes at three o'clock?

Use a toy clock to prove your answer.

3. In planning for the party, the children wondered how much fruit juice they would need so that each of the 20 children could have a glass of juice.

They knew they could fill 4 glasses from 1 quart of juice. How many quarts of juice would they need to fill 20 glasses? Explain how the picture helps you answer this problem.

4. Sally said, "Mother's gallon thermos jug and my quart thermos bottle together hold 4 quarts and 1 quart, or 5 quarts." Do you agree with Sally?

| 1 qt. | 1 qt. | 1 qt. | 1 qt. | | 1 gal. |

5. Prove the facts Ann has written in the picture at the bottom of the page. Learn them.

6. A gallon of water equals _?_ quarts of water.

7. A quart of milk equals _?_ pints of milk.

8. A gallon of milk will fill _?_ quart bottles.

9. A quart of milk will fill _?_ pint bottles.

10. Write in a short way: pint; quart; gallon.

11. Name some things sold by the gallon; quart; pint.

12. Mary bought a pint of vanilla ice cream, 2 pints of chocolate, and a pint of strawberry. Did she buy 2 quarts?

2 glasses = 1 pint
2 pints = 1 quart
4 quarts = 1 gallon

pt. means pint
qt. means quart
gal. means gallon

Understanding numbers in reading

Pedro lives high on a mountain outside Mexico City. Tall trees grow near his home.

From the trees Pedro gets firewood. He cuts the wood into pieces about sixteen inches long. Then he ties the pieces into bundles.

Every Monday, Wednesday, and Friday Pedro loads the bundles on his donkey's back and goes down to Mexico City. Carlos and Tonio, two little Indian boys, go along to help sell the wood.

They start down the mountain at eight o'clock in the morning. It is noon when they get to the little inn where they sell the wood.

Carlos and Tonio walk all the way to the inn. After the wood has been sold, there is room on the donkey for them. They may ride back home.

Mexico City is warm during the day. The temperature then is about 80°. When the sun goes down, the temperature falls to 60°. Some of the wood is burned in a fireplace then. Some is burned in a cookstove during the day.

Pedro gets a high price for his wood. In the United States you would have to pay about a dollar for the wood Pedro's donkey carries. Pedro gets twice as much as that. This is because there is very little coal and wood in Mexico.

Now answer these questions on the story:

1. How long are the pieces of firewood that Pedro sells? On the blackboard draw a line that you think is as long as a piece of his wood. Use a ruler to see if your line is about the right length.

2. How many times a week does Pedro go to the city?

3. At what time does Pedro leave home? At what time does he get to the inn? How long does the trip take?

4. Do you think Carlos and Tonio are tired when they get to the inn? Why?

5. What is the temperature in Mexico City during the day? How much does the temperature fall after the sun goes down?

6. Why does Pedro get such a high price for his firewood?

The problems on page 183 are like the ones on this page, but are much easier. If you have trouble with Problem 1 below, do Problem 1 on page 183. Then come back and try Problem 1 below again, and so on.

1. Jane wants a box of crayons for 25¢ and a crayon book for 12¢. How much will both cost?

2. Tom's grandmother gave him $.75 for his birthday. If he spends $.29 for a ball, how much will he have left?

3. Susan is going to Chicago on February 16 to spend a week. On what date will she come home?

4. Ann wants to buy a 49-cent box of crayons. She has only 23¢. How much more money does she need?

5. Carl has 297 stamps. Jerry has 267 stamps. How many more stamps has Carl than Jerry?

6. Alice has a quarter, a dime, and eight pennies in her bank. How much money has she?

7. Mary said, "I need only 28 inches of this yard of ribbon." How many inches of ribbon will be left?

8. Dick wants to buy a snow shovel for 89¢ and a hockey stick for 35¢. How much does he need for both?

9. Don can get a pair of skates for $2.89 or for $2.65. How much will he save if he buys the cheaper pair?

10. Bob has 132 stamps in his book of United States stamps and 245 stamps in his book of stamps from other countries. How many stamps has he in both books?

11. Pete has two 25-cent stamps. Do an addition to show how much his stamps are worth.

Easier problems to solve

If you had every problem on page 182 correct, you may skip this page.

Write the addition or subtraction fact you use to find the answer to each problem below.

1. Jane buys an ice-cream cone for 5¢ and a lollipop for 1¢. How much does she pay for both?

2. Tom has 5¢. If he spends 2¢ for a pencil, how much money will he have left?

3. How many days are there in a week? What date is it a week from February 2? a week from February 3? a week from February 4?

4. Ann wants to take 6 cents to school. She has 4 cents. How many more cents does she need?

5. Carl has 5 tops. Jerry has 2 tops. How many more tops has Carl than Jerry?

6. Alice has 3 red crayons, 2 blue ones, and 4 green ones. How many crayons has she all together?

7. Mary said, "I need only 7 inches of this 10-inch piece of ribbon." How many inches of ribbon will be left?

8. Dick wants to buy a ball for 5¢ and a pencil for 2¢. How much money does he need for both?

9. Don can get a pencil for 10¢ or one for 5¢. How much does he save if he buys the cheaper pencil?

10. Bob has 3 marbles in one pocket and 6 marbles in the other pocket. How many marbles has he?

11. Do an addition to find out how much two 8-cent candy bars will cost.

1. Billy said, "I'll give 10 peanuts to the one who makes the best guess as to the number of peanuts in this bag."

Tom guessed 290   Jack guessed 289
Jean guessed 215   Sally guessed 268

There are 275 peanuts in the bag.   Who won?

2. Count by 100's from 100 to 1000; from 18 to 518.

3. Tell the number which is 100 more than 198; 100 more than 52; 100 more than 610; 100 more than 3; 100 less than 888; 100 less than 550.

4. $5.75 = 5 dollars, 7 dimes, and __?__ cents.

5. $1.00 = 1 half dollar and __?__ quarters.

6. $3.00 = 2 dollars and __?__ quarters.

7. $4.00 = 3 dollars and __?__ dimes.

8. Read these numbers.   Then write the numbers as your teacher says them.

629	407	770	666	193	420	576
504	960	831	909	139	382	805
432	509	680	890	208	476	970

9. What does the 6 mean in each of these numbers?

624   264   246

10. Write the largest number you can using a 2, a 7, and a 5; write the smallest number.

11. Write these numbers in order, from the smallest to the largest: 460   604   700   532

12. How do you write your house number? your telephone number? How do you read these numbers?

Problem Test 5

1. Ted saw a magnet marked 39¢. He has a quarter. To buy the magnet, he needs __?__ ¢ more.

2. This morning Jerry's cow gave enough milk to fill a gallon pail and 5 quart bottles. In all, the cow gave __?__ quarts of milk this morning.

3. When the thermometer falls from 13° to 6°, the air becomes __?__ degrees colder.

4. On December 8 Alice said, "A week from today will be my birthday." Alice's birthday comes on December __?__.

5. Bob had $4.65 in the school bank. He has just put in $1.75 more. He now has __?__ in the bank.

6. Bobby is making a treasure chest. He spent 37¢ for leather for the hinges and 59¢ for a lock and key. How much did he spend in all?

7. Tom has 3 dollars, 6 dimes, and 7 pennies in his wallet. He saw a football marked $2.45. If he buys it, how much will he have left?

8. Jane bought a coat for $9.98 and a hat for $2.50. How much did Jane's new clothes cost?

9. Molly wants new curtains for her room. She measured and found the curtains should be 1 yard 18 inches long. She can buy curtains 54 inches long or 63 inches long. Which ones should she take?

10. In the "Lost and Found" box there are 15 black pencils and 7 colored ones. How many pencils are in the box?

Write your score on your Problem Test Record.

Changing nickels to pennies

Miss Bell said, "Let's go to the drugstore to be weighed."

"We'll each need a cent to put in the slot," said Joe. "There are 20 of us. We'll need 20 pennies."

Miss Bell said, "I have four nickels. If you have them changed into pennies, will you have enough pennies?"

Joe laid the four nickels in a row, like this:

He pointed to them in order, saying, "5, 10, 15, 20."

1. For 4 nickels the children got ＿?＿ pennies. Can each of the 20 pupils be weighed?

2. Use this picture to find how many pennies you can get for 3 nickels; for 5 nickels; for 6 nickels.

3. If 1 toy costs a nickel, how much will 4 toys cost?

Think, "If 1 toy costs a nickel, 4 toys will cost 4 nickels. Four nickels equal _?_ cents."

4. If 1 ball costs a nickel, how much will 5 balls cost?

Think, "If 1 ball costs a nickel, 5 balls will cost 5 nickels. Five nickels equal _?_ cents."

5. If 1 ice-cream cone costs a nickel, how much will 8 cost?

Think, "If 1 cone costs a nickel, 8 cones will cost 8 nickels. Eight nickels equal _?_ cents."

6. Each of these toys costs a nickel. Tell what you think when you find the cost of:

3 balls   7 tops   6 cars   5 planes   7 dolls   8 boats

7. Practice until you can tell how many pennies you can get for 3 nickels; 6 nickels; 9; 2; 5; 8; 1; 4; 7; 10.

8. Make a table to show how many pennies you can get for 1 nickel; 2 nickels; 3; 4; 5; 6; 7; 8; 9; 10. Use toy coins (nickels and pennies) to prove that your table is correct.

Nickels	1	2	3	4	5	6	7	8	9	10
Pennies	5	10	15	20	25	30	35	40	45	50

9. Tom made up a rule to use in these examples. Figure out his rule; then tell the missing number in the last example.

- 2 nickels = 10 cents, so   4 nickels = _20¢_.
- 3 nickels = 15 cents, so   6 nickels = _30¢_.
- 4 nickels = 20 cents, so   8 nickels = _40¢_.
- 5 nickels = 25 cents, so   10 nickels = _50¢_.
- 10 nickels = 50 cents, so   20 nickels = _?_.

187

PARK HERE
1 hour - 5¢
Deposit Nickel in Meter

Changing pennies to nickels

Bob and his father wanted to park their car on Market Street for 3 hours. For each hour of parking they had to put a nickel in the parking meter. They needed ＿?＿ nickels.

Bob had 15 pennies. He laid out the pennies by fives, like this:

He thought, "For the first five cents I'll get 1 nickel. For the next five cents I'll get another nickel," and so on.

1. How many nickels did Bob get for the 15 pennies? Did he have enough money to park for 3 hours?

2. Make a table to show how many nickels you can get for 5 pennies; for 10 pennies; 15; 20; 25; 30; 35; 40; 45; 50. Use toy coins to prove your table is right.

Pennies	5	10	15	20	25	30	35	40	45	50
Nickels	1	2	3	4	5	6	7	8	9	10

3. How many nickels can you get for 15 pennies? for 30 pennies? for 45? 10? 25? 40? 5? 20? 35? 50?

4. If 1 ball costs a nickel, how many can you get for 20¢?

Think, "One ball costs a nickel; 20¢ is worth 4 nickels. So for 20¢ you can get _?_ balls."

5. If 1 balloon costs a nickel, how many balloons can you get for 25¢?

Think, "One balloon costs a nickel; 25¢ is worth 5 nickels. So for 25¢ you can get _?_ balloons."

6. If 1 whistle costs a nickel, how many whistles can you get for 15¢?

Think, "One whistle costs a nickel; 15¢ is worth _?_ nickels. So for 15¢ you can get _?_ whistles."

Tell what you think when you solve these problems. Draw pictures of nickels if you need help.

7. If 1 apple costs a nickel, how many apples can you get for 20¢? 35¢? 45¢? 40¢?

8. How many nickels can you get for a quarter?

9. John has saved 21 pennies. How many nickels can he get? Will he have any pennies left over?

10. Peter said, "I'll trade you 35 pennies for 7 nickels." Would that be a fair trade?

189

Be sure you copy all numbers in this test correctly. Work carefully. Check your answers.

Add and check:

1. 446
   374

2. $1.75 + $3.00 + $.69

3. $4 + $2.69 + $.05

4. Susan bought three 10-cent toys. She paid for them with a half dollar. She got two coins in change. What coins were they?

5. Mrs. White buys a gallon of milk every day. Betsy puts the milk into quart bottles to store in the icebox. How many quart bottles does she need for a gallon of milk?

6. This picture of 20 pennies shows that for 20 pennies you can get __?__ nickels.

7. 5¢ + 5¢ + 5¢ + 5¢ + 5¢ + 5¢ = 30¢.
This addition shows that __?__ nickels = 30¢.

8. Which of these does *not* equal 40¢?

- 4 dimes
- 10¢ + 10¢ + 10¢ + 10¢
- 8 nickels
- 1 quarter + 3 nickels
- 2 quarters
- 1 quarter + 1 dime + 1 nickel

9. How many 10-cent balloons can you get for $1.00?

10. There are 347 children in the Wilson School and 468 in the Main Street School. In the two schools there are __?__ children.

Borrowing: changing dimes to cents

John has $2.93. Can you find out without help how much he will have left after he pays $1.65 to have new soles put on his shoes? This is the way John subtracted to find out:

$$\begin{array}{r} \$2.93 \\ -1.65 \\ \hline \end{array}$$

► He wrote the subtraction like this:———→ Then he tried to subtract 5 cents from 3 cents. He couldn't. Why not? What would you have done next?

$$\begin{array}{r} {\scriptstyle 8\ 13} \\ \$2.\cancel{9}\cancel{3} \\ -1.65 \\ \hline \$1.28 \end{array}$$

► He thought, "I'll borrow 1 dime from the 9 dimes and change it into 10 cents. Then the money I have will be 2 dollars, 8 dimes, and 13 cents."

► Then he thought, "5 cents from 13 cents = 8 cents." He wrote the 8 in the cents column.

► He thought, "6 dimes from 8 dimes = 2 dimes." He wrote the 2 in the dimes column.

► Tell what he thought and wrote to finish the subtraction. Check his answer. How much will John have left?

Tell what you think as you subtract and check:

1.	$9.62	$4.83	$5.74	$4.65	$5.86
	8.39	2.78	2.27	.28	5.07

2.	$7.67	$8.98	$9.81	$6.90	$8.82
	3.49	3.79	3.66	5.55	2.44

3.	$7.73	$8.64	$3.95	$8.86	$9.77
	7.49	8.08	.66	.58	.38

4. Tom has $2.35. How much more does he need to buy skates that cost $4.50? a baseball outfit that costs $6.74?

Sue and Doris earn money by selling greeting cards. Sue sold 242 cards. Doris sold 137. Can you find out without help how many more cards Sue sold than Doris?

▶ Write the subtraction like this:→

```
 242  Sue sold
-137  Doris sold
```

▶ Can you subtract 7 ones from 2 ones? Why not? What will you do about it?

```
    3 12
  2 4 2
 -1 3 7
  1 0 5
```

▶ Think, "I'll borrow 1 of the tens from the 4 tens and change it into 10 ones. Then the number of cards Sue sold will be 2 hundreds, 3 tens, and 12 ones."

▶ Then think, "7 ones from 12 ones = 5 ones." Write the 5 in the ones column.

▶ Think, "3 tens from 3 tens = 0 tens." Write the zero in the tens column.

▶ Tell what you think and write to finish the subtraction. Check. How many more cards did Sue sell than Doris?

1. Sue had 270 cards to sell. She has sold 242 cards. How many more has she to sell?

2. Check your answer to Ex. 1 by climbing up the number ladder from 242 to 270. How many rods are there from 242 to 250? from 250 to 270? Then 270 is how much greater than 242?

3. Doris had 150 cards to sell. She has sold 137 cards. How many more has she to sell?

4. Tell what you think as you subtract and check:

763	685	380	490	572	861
− 437	− 276	− 124	− 283	− 356	− 247

192

Problems and practice

1. Carl has saved 75¢. If he spends 49¢ for a knife, how much will he have left?

2. Alice has 50 spelling words for review. She can spell 37 of them. How many words must she study?

3. Jerry saved 34¢ out of his allowance last week and 29¢ this week. How much did he save in the two weeks?

4. How much change should Jane receive from a half dollar if she spends 45¢?

5. Billy is 54 inches tall. Jean is 39 inches tall. How much taller is Billy than Jean?

6. Betty has a dollar. Does she have enough to buy a corn popper for 79¢ and a 15-cent can of corn to pop?

Copy, subtract, and check:

	a	*b*	*c*	*d*	*e*	*f*
7.	$6.66 2.18	$5.92 .55	$9.28 2.19	$6.50 2.35	$7.84 .75	$8.72 .29
8.	273 134	492 347	583 269	385 127	473 224	560 325
9.	$.53 .49	$.67 .59	$.74 .68	83 75	55 48	36 27
10.	347 118	463 148	$5.97 2.69	$4.73 1.42	$5.84 .46	$.62 .56
11.	868 445	952 835	$5.61 1.37	$6.53 .46	$.76 .68	$.59 .36

Pete is to play the part of Christopher Columbus in a play. His costume will cost $3.15. The class has earned $1.72 to pay for it. They want to know how much more they must earn.

$$\begin{array}{r} \$3.15 \\ -1.72 \\ \hline \end{array}$$

▶ They tried to subtract $1.72 from $3.15. They took 2 cents from 5 cents and wrote 3 in the cents column. They tried to subtract 7 dimes from 1 dime, but couldn't. What would you have done?

▶ Borrow one of the 3 dollars. Change it into 10 dimes. Then $3.15 equals 2 dollars, 11 dimes, and 5 cents.

▶ Then subtract this way:

Costume costs ➤ 2 dollars 11 dimes 5 cents = $3.15
They have ⟶ 1 dollar   7 dimes 2 cents = 1.72
They need ⟶ 1 dollar   4 dimes 3 cents = $1.43

▶ Now tell what you think and write to subtract $1.72 from $3.15 as shown in this box. Check the answer by adding.

$$\begin{array}{r} {\scriptstyle 2 \ 11} \\ \$\cancel{3}.\cancel{1}5 \\ -1.72 \\ \hline \$1.43 \end{array}$$

1. $2.36 = 1 dollar, _?_ dimes, and 6 cents.

2. $5.24 = 4 dollars, _?_ dimes, and 4 cents.

Tell what you think as you subtract and check:

3.	$8.57	$5.35	$4.28	966	843
	3.84	2.52	1.43	783	580
	$4.73	$2.83	$2.85	183	263

4.	$8.16	$6.27	$5.16	449	858
	5.80	2.74	3.92	176	378

5.	$6.19	$4.48	$9.39	736	427
	3.77	1.86	3.85	294	380

Borrowing: changing twice

Betty wants to have her picture taken. She has $1.87. How much more money does she need for 6 pictures?

This is the way to subtract $1.87 from $3.50:

▶ Write the subtraction like this: ⟶

▶ Think, "I can't subtract 7 cents from 0 cents. I'll borrow 1 dime from the 5 dimes. 7 cents from 10 cents is _?_ cents."

Where do you write the 3? Where do the 10 and the 4 come from? ⟶

▶ Think, "I can't subtract 8 dimes from 4 dimes. I'll borrow 1 dollar from the 3 dollars. 8 dimes from 14 dimes is _?_ dimes." Where does the 14 dimes come from? Where do you write the 6?

▶ Now tell what you think and write to finish the subtraction. How much money does Betty need? Check.

```
  $3.50
- 1.87
```

```
        14
      2 4 10
   $3.50
  - 1.87
   $1.63
```

Tell what you think as you subtract and check:

1.
$5.40	$4.51	334	510	227	413
1.51	3.78	98	148	149	225
$3.89	$ .73	236	362	78	188

2.
$3.50	$3.62	240	311	357	562
1.99	1.78	173	293	268	95

Can you find any mistakes in these subtractions?

3.
431	310	425	524	763	684
45	167	387	473	675	596
386	143	38	51	188	88

195

1. James wants to buy a wrist watch that costs $9.25. He has saved $7.88. How much more money does he need?

2. Velvet ear muffs cost $.89. Fur ear muffs cost $2.15. Fur ear muffs cost _?_ more than velvet ones.

3. Carl has $2.25. If he pays $1.60 for a knife, how much money will he have left?

4. Peter had $1.25 when he went to the fair. He had $.59 when he came home. He spent _?_ at the fair.

5. A pen and pencil set costs $1.90. The pen alone costs $1.25. Billy said, "The pencil in that set costs _?_."

6. Bill received a reward of $7.50 for finding a lost dog. If he buys a fishing rod for $6.69, how much money will he have left?

In which of these do you need to borrow a ten? a hundred? a ten and a hundred? Copy, subtract, and check.

	a	b	c	d	e	f
7.	725	546	463	475	574	687
	348	159	178	398	287	93
8.	532	446	483	586	462	733
	319	388	235	293	88	259
9.	460	942	743	984	770	965
	186	296	257	799	488	98
10.	345	266	441	963	340	510
	166	85	297	688	76	464
11.	$5.10	$4.67	$6.35	$5.45	$3.68	$9.57
	2.25	1.76	5.45	.55	.90	.08

Put on your thinking cap

▶ Oral review

1. Find the sum of 6, 6, 5, 8.

2. How many days are there in a week? Name them.

3. Does the tenth of this month come on a Friday?

4. Dick has 40¢. With it he can buy _?_ 10-cent candy bars or _?_ 5-cent candy bars.

5. 1 qt. = _?_ pt.   1 yd. = _?_ in.   XII = _?_

6. 1 gal. = _?_ qt.   1 ft. = _?_ in.   1 dollar = _?_ ¢

▶ Written review

1. Write the number that means 3 hundreds, 7 tens, and 4 ones.

2. From 426 subtract 297. Add 247 and 563.

3. Using the figures 8, 2, and 7, write the largest number you can; the smallest.

4. Draw a square. Now draw 1 line to divide the square into triangles. Each triangle is what part of the square?

5. Find the sum of sixty-five and seven. Check.

6. Find the sum of 24 and 55. Check.

7. Carl wants to buy a drum that costs $3.98. He has saved $3.56. How much more does he need? Check.

8. How many minutes is it from quarter after two until quarter of three?

9. A quart of ice cream fills 10 ice-cream cones. How many quarts are needed for 30 cones?

Subtracting money

Mrs. Brown ordered a pair of jeans for Jack. When the boy brought them, he said, "Two dollars and eighteen cents, please."

Mrs. Brown handed the boy a 5-dollar bill.

He said, "I'm sorry. I have no change."

Mrs. Brown said, "Well, come next door with me to Mr. Stone's store."

Mrs. Brown asked Mr. Stone to change the 5-dollar bill. He gave her 5 one-dollar bills. Was she able to pay for the jeans then? Why not?

She said, "Mr. Stone, will you give me 10 dimes for one of these dollar bills, please?" Then she had _?_ one dollar bills and _?_ dimes. Could she pay for the jeans then? Why not?

Finally she asked, "May I bother you again, Mr. Stone? Will you change one of my dimes into pennies, please?"

Then she had → 4 dollars 9 dimes 10 cents
The jeans cost → 2 dollars 1 dime   8 cents
She had left ─→ 2 dollars 8 dimes 2 cents, or $2.82

1. Choose 3 children to act out the story above. Use toy money.

▶ Now tell what you think and write to subtract $2.18 from $5.00 as shown in this box. The $5.00 is changed into _?_ dollars, _?_ dimes, _?_ cents. Why?

$$\begin{array}{r} \overset{4\ \ 9\ 10}{\$\cancel{5}.\cancel{0}\cancel{0}} \\ -2.18 \\ \hline \$2.82 \end{array}$$

▶ How does this subtraction tell Mrs. Brown's story?

2. $6.00 = _5_ dollars, _?_ dimes, _10_ cents

3. $8.00 = _7_ dollars, _9_ dimes, _?_ cents

4. $7.00 = _?_ dollars, _9_ dimes, _10_ cents

Tell what you think when you do these subtractions. Check each answer.

1. $6.00 $9.00 $8.00 $4.00 $7.00 $5.00
    4.45   1.27   5.72   1.56   .39   4.86
    ─────   ─────   ─────   ─────   ─────   ─────
    $1.55 $7.73 $2.28 $2.44 $6.61 $ .14

2. $6.00 $8.00 $2.00 $9.00 $5.00 $7.00
    4.78   2.63   1.75   8.97   3.64   2.28
    ─────   ─────   ─────   ─────   ─────   ─────

3. 700   400   800   500   600   500
    345   276   483   125   75   469
    ────   ────   ────   ────   ────   ────

4. 541   500   712   300   895   704
    206   156   340   198   786   640
    ────   ────   ────   ────   ────   ────

5. 380   534   802   385   700   900
    276   519   275   26   156   482
    ────   ────   ────   ────   ────   ────

6. 601   800   467   502   287   407
    543   69   354   293   87   93
    ────   ────   ────   ────   ────   ────

7. Miss Parks asked June and Roy to find $5.00 − $4.49. This is the way they wrote the example:

JUNE $ 5   ROY $5.00
(Wrong)   4.49   (Right)   4.49
            ─────   ──────
                                     $ .51

Miss Parks was disappointed with the way June did the work. Why?

Copy, find the answers, and check:

8. $8 − $1.75 $4 − $1.53 $.49 + $3.24

9. $6 − $.89 $9.50 + $3 $.10 + $1.85 + $5

10. How much change should you get from a 5-dollar bill if you spend $1.54? if you spend $.94? $1.76? $2.83?

Copy, add, and check:

1.	297	149	203	425	358	546
	200	175	289	263	389	278
	486	638	465	187	174	109

2.	716	27	808	60	9	700
	9	74	87	697	47	398
	65	365	8	58	565	46

3.	$6.10	$4.25	$9.89	$3.75	$8.05	$5.27
	3.39	.72	.47	5.50	.03	6.32
	8.65	7.98	.03	.29	3.69	.04

No pencils, please

1. Is $701 - 690$ about 100, or 10, or 1?

2. Is $6 − $2.98 about $4, or $3, or $2?

3. Is $2 + $3.95 about $5, or $6, or $7?

4. Is the answer to $1.56 + $3.00 between $4 and $5, or between $3 and $4?

5. 9 from $26 = $ __?__ .

6. $18 + $ __?__ $ = 25$.

7. 17 from $25 = $ __?__ .

8. $27 + $ __?__ $ = 30$.

9. $9 + 8 + 7 = $ __?__ .

10. $16 + 8 = $ __?__ .

11. $26 + 7 = $ __?__ .

12. $.25 + $.25 = __?__ .

13. Subtract 40 from 53.

14. $1.00 − $.10 = __?__ .

15. $1.00 − $.01 = __?__ .

16. 5 is 9 less than __?__ .

17. 13 is __?__ more than 8.

18. $50 + 10 + 5 + 4 = $ __?__ .

19. Count by 3's to 30.

20. Count by 4's to 40.

Problem Test 6

1. Jim is saving cereal-box tops to get a baseball glove. He must send 30 tops to get the glove. He has 17 tops. How many more does he need?

2. At Easter Mrs. White hid a dozen colored Easter eggs. The twins hunted for them. Jack found 7. Betsy found the others. Do you know how many she found?

3. Find the cost of an Easter basket for 10¢, an egg for 10¢, a rabbit for 5¢, and paper grass for 8¢.

4. Tom has saved 20 pennies. Draw a picture to show how many nickels he can get for 20 pennies.

5. When the thermometer goes from 48° to 64°, how much does the temperature rise?

6. Jim would like to have some new cars for his electric train. He wants a freight car that costs $1.65 and a flatcar that costs $1.49. How much will the two cars cost?

7. Don bought snowshoes for $4.19. He paid for them with a 5-dollar bill. He got __?__ ¢ change.

8. Tom has a card of thumbtacks. There are 5 tacks in a row. There are 6 rows. Count the tacks by fives. How many thumbtacks are there?

9. How many 10-cent toy trucks can you buy for a half dollar?

10. The Outing Club needs 6 glasses of milk for a picnic lunch. Can they take all the milk they need in a quart thermos bottle?

Write your score on your Problem Test Record.

Add and check:

1.	59	2.	289	3.	$5.50	4.	$6.43
	63		57		2.37		.75
	7		463		4.09		1.08
	44 (129)		371 (200)		1.25 (200)		5.50 (200)

Subtract and check:

5.	690	6.	842	7.	$9.85	8.	$9.00
	354 (192)		379 (195)		6.27 (191)		3.75 (198–199)

Self-Help Test 10

1. Mary has 30¢. How many balloons at a nickel each can she buy? (188–189)

2. Jerry bought a football for $2.98. He gave the clerk a five-dollar bill. How much change should he get? (198)

3. Dick has 62 marbles. If he gives 25 of the marbles to his brother, how many marbles will he have left? (131–135)

4. Jim earned a nickel every day for a week. In all, he earned _?_ ¢. (186–187)

5. Look at your clock. What time is it? (2–3)

6. Which is more, $\frac{1}{2}$ of a pie or $\frac{1}{4}$ of the pie? Draw pictures to prove you are right. (11)

7. Does *3* dollars, *5* dimes, *2* cents = *3* dollars, *4* dimes *12* cents? (191)

8. Jane uses 12 inches of ribbon for a bow. Prove that she can make 3 bows from a yard of ribbon. (25)

Multiplying with fives

Billy belongs to a Cub Pack in the Boy Scouts. The Cubs made three candleholders for their den. They used pieces of log. You can see the holders in the picture. Each holder has places for __?__ candles.

When they had finished making the holders, Billy said, "We'll need 5, 10, 15 candles all together to fill the holders." George said, "That's right. $5 + 5 + 5 = 15$."

Harry said, "Of course we'll need 15 candles. Three 5's are 15."

Saying "5, 10, 15" as Billy did is counting to find three 5's. Saying "$5 + 5 + 5 = 15$" is adding to find three 5's.

Saying "Three 5's are 15" is *multiplying*. Harry did a *multiplication* example. He multiplied 5 by 3.

Which boy used the shortest way to find three 5's?

Here is a picture of some blue stickers that Ben has.

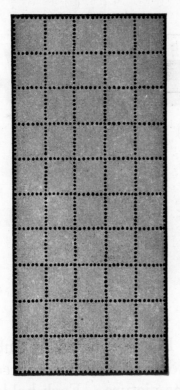

1. How many stickers are there in each row? How many rows?

2. Count the stickers by 5's. Your counting shows that 10 fives are __?__.

3. How many stickers are there in 2 rows? 3? 4? 5? 6? 7? 8? 9? 10?

4. Find the answers in Ex. 3 by adding.

5. Exs. 3 and 4 show that:

2 fives are __?__	6 fives are __?__
3 fives are __?__	7 fives are __?__
4 fives are __?__	8 fives are __?__
5 fives are __?__	9 fives are __?__

6. For 1 nickel you can get __?__ pennies. How many pennies can you get for 2 nickels? 3? 4? 5? 6? 7? 8? 9? 10?

7. John did 3 rows of examples. There were 5 examples in each row. In all, he did __?__ examples. 3 fives are __?__.

8. Mrs. Jones has 6 children. She gave each of them 5 cents. In all, she gave them __?__ cents. 6 fives are __?__.

9. Find the cost of 8 apples at 5¢ each. 8 fives = __?__.

10. What facts have you learned about multiplying 5's?

11. Ten 5's = __?__ four 5's = __?__ two 5's = __?__ eight 5's = __?__

12. Six 5's = __?__ nine 5's = __?__ five 5's = __?__ seven 5's = __?__

Pictures of related multiplication facts

1. Look at this card of buttons. Can you see 3 fives? Can you see 5 threes?

3 fives = _?_; 5 threes = _?_

Do 5 threes equal the same number as 3 fives?

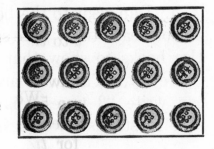

Below are some pictures. Which picture shows each of these groups of facts?

2. 2 fives are 10, and 5 twos are 10.

3. 4 fives are 20, and 5 fours are 20.

4. 5 fives are 25.　　**5.** 6 fives are 30, and 5 sixes are 30.

6. 7 fives are 35, and 5 sevens are 35.

7. 8 fives are 40, and 5 eights are 40.

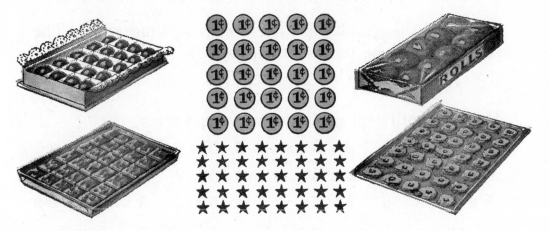

8. Draw a dot picture to show that 9 fives are 45. What other multiplication fact does your picture show?

9. Keep a list in your folder of things you see that show multiplication facts with fives. Tell what facts each shows.

205

1. Dan went to the book closet 3 times. He carried out 5 books each time. We say Dan carried out 3 *times* 5 books. Use books to show that 3 times 5 books is 15 books.

We say, "Three 5's are 15," or "*3 times 5 is 15.*" We can write "3 times 5 is 15" this way: $3 \times 5 = 15$. The sign × stands for *times*. It means to multiply.

2. Tom went to the book closet 5 times. He carried out 3 books each time. In all, he carried out 5 *times* 3 books, or __?__ books. Use books to show that $5 \times 3 = \underline{?}$.

3. Read the multiplication facts below:

$1 \times 5 = 5$	$6 \times 5 = 30$	$5 \times 1 = 5$	$5 \times 6 = 30$
$2 \times 5 = 10$	$7 \times 5 = 35$	$5 \times 2 = 10$	$5 \times 7 = 35$
$3 \times 5 = 15$	$8 \times 5 = 40$	$5 \times 3 = 15$	$5 \times 8 = 40$
$4 \times 5 = 20$	$9 \times 5 = 45$	$5 \times 4 = 20$	$5 \times 9 = 45$
$5 \times 5 = 25$	$10 \times 5 = 50$	$5 \times 5 = 25$	$5 \times 10 = 50$

4. Write these multiplications using the times sign. The first one should be written this way: $7 \times 5 = 35$.

7 fives = 35   2 fives = 10   8 fives = 40   6 fives = 30

Practice until you can say every answer:

5. 7×5 1×5 5×3 8. 5×5 5×8 5×7

6. 5×4 9×5 2×5 9. 5×2 3×5 4×5

7. 5×1 5×6 8×5 10. 6×5 5×4 5×9

11. Alice knows a "twice as many" trick which helps her learn the missing numbers below. Figure out her trick.

$2 \times 5 = 10$, so $4 \times 5 = \underline{20}$ $4 \times 5 = 20$, so $8 \times 5 = \underline{?}$

$3 \times 5 = 15$, so $6 \times 5 = \underline{?}$ $5 \times 5 = 25$, so $10 \times 5 = \underline{?}$

Using multiplication

1. Judy got 4 boxes of gumdrops. There are 5 gumdrops in each box. How many did she get all together?

Think, "There are 5 gumdrops in each box. In 4 boxes there are 4 times 5 gumdrops, or __?__ gumdrops. $4 \times 5 = $ __?__."

2. Ned bought 5 bags of marbles. There are 6 marbles in each bag. How many marbles did he buy all together?

Think, "There are 6 marbles in each bag. In 5 bags there are 5 times 6 marbles, or __?__ marbles. $5 \times 6 = $ __?__."

3. Find the cost of 8 apples at 5¢ each.

Think, "If 1 apple costs 5¢, 8 apples will cost 8 times 5¢, or __?__ ¢. $8 \times 5 = $ __?__."

Tell what you think as you find the answers to these problems:

4. One package of egg dye will color 5 Easter eggs. How many eggs can you color with 5 packages of dye?

5. How many days are there in a week? in 5 weeks?

6. How many feet are there in a yard? in 5 yards?

7. How many pints are there in a quart? in 5 quarts?

8. Find the cost of 7 balloons at 5¢ each.

9. Joe bought 8 five-cent pencils. Tom bought 5 eight-cent pencils. How much money did each boy spend?

10. Molly has a box of caramels. There are 7 rows of caramels. There are 5 caramels in each row. How many caramels are in the box?

11. Make a dot picture to show that five 4-cent cakes cost just as much as four 5-cent cakes.

In the box is a new way to write "2 times 5 is 10."

1. Read the multiplication facts of fives below. Say, "1 times 5 is 5; 2 times 5 is 10"; and so on.

$$\begin{array}{r} 5 \\ \times 2 \\ \hline 10 \end{array}$$

Multiplication Facts of Fives

5	5	5	5	5	5	5	5	5
×1	×2	×3	×4	×5	×6	×7	×8	×9
5	10	15	20	25	30	35	40	45
1	2	3	4	5	6	7	8	9
×5	×5	×5	×5	×5	×5	×5	×5	×5
5	10	15	20	25	30	35	40	45

Practice these until you can say every answer:

2.
5	5	2	5	9	5	5	3	5
×7	×5	×5	×1	×5	×6	×4	×5	×9

3.
4	8	5	6	5	1	5	5	7
×5	×5	×3	×5	×8	×5	×5	×2	×5

4. Copy Exs. 2 and 3 and write the answers.

5. Tell what you think as you find the cost of the following toys. Each toy costs 5¢.

8 kites   5 dolls   7 boats
6 paper caps   4 toy trucks   9 airplanes

6. Start a pack of Help-Yourself Cards in multiplication. Make a card for each multiplication fact in the table above. Practice with your cards until you are sure you know every answer.

$2 \times 5 = 10$
$3 \times 5 = 15$

Coloring eggs

The children in Miss Drake's class are coloring Easter eggs.

1. The children brought 40 hard-boiled eggs to school. One package of coloring will color 5 eggs. They needed to know how many packages of coloring to buy.

Two packages are not enough, because 2×5 is only 10. Three packages are not enough, because 3×5 is only 15.

2. Are 4 packages enough? 5? 6? 7? 8?
What number times 5 equals 40?
How many packages of coloring did they need?

3. Tell the missing numbers in these multiplication examples. Practice until you can give them all.

$$\begin{array}{ccccccccc}
5 & 5 & 5 & 5 & 5 & 5 & 5 & 5 & 5 \\
\times\, ? & \times\, ? & \times\, ? & \times\, ? & \times\, ? & \times\, ? & \times\, ? & \times\, ? & \times\, ? \\
\hline
15 & 30 & 45 & 10 & 25 & 40 & 5 & 20 & 35
\end{array}$$

4. If one package will color 5 eggs, how many packages will you need to color 15 eggs? $\underline{\;?\;} \times 5$ eggs = 15 eggs.

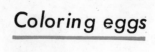

1. Billy was coloring eggs at home. He had 20 eggs to color. He wanted to find out how many packages of coloring to buy. He laid out the eggs by fives, as in the picture.

He thought, "For the first five eggs I'll need 1 package. For the next five I'll need another package. I'll need as many packages as there are fives in 20."

How many fives are there in 20? How many packages of coloring will Billy need for 20 eggs?

2. How many packages would Billy need for 10 eggs? for 15? Draw pictures to show your answers are right.

3. Read the table below this way: "For 5 eggs you need 1 package of coloring. For 10 eggs you need 2 packages"; and so on. Draw dot pictures to prove that the table is right.

Eggs	5	10	15	20	25	30	35	40	45	50
Packages	1	2	3	4	5	6	7	8	9	10

4. How many packages do you need for 15 eggs? for 30 eggs? for 45? 10? 25? 40? 5? 20? 35? 50?

5. Now read the table like this:

5 = _1_ five	20 = _?_ fives	35 = _?_ fives
10 = _2_ fives	25 = _?_ fives	40 = _?_ fives
15 = _?_ fives	30 = _?_ fives	45 = _?_ fives

How many fives in a number?

Mary has 35¢. How many 5-cent balloons can she buy for a class party?

Here are the ways 3 children did this problem:

Harry subtracts

Harry said, "I start with Mary's 35¢ and I buy 5-cent balloons over and over, until I have nothing left." He wrote:———————————➤

Harry took 5¢ out of 35¢ _?_ times. He subtracted 5¢ _?_ times. He found there are _?_ fives in 35. He found Mary could buy _?_ balloons.

Bill draws pictures

Bill said, "My drawing shows that in 35¢ there are 7 groups of 5 pennies. For 35¢ Mary can get _?_ 5-cent balloons."

35¢
− 5¢ ✓
30¢
− 5¢ ✓
25¢
− 5¢ ✓
20¢
− 5¢ ✓
15¢
− 5¢ ✓
10¢
− 5¢ ✓
5¢
− 5¢ ✓
0

Dan uses multiplication

Dan found how many 5-cent balloons Mary could get for 35¢ by thinking: *What number of balloons* × 5¢ = 35¢?

She can get more than 3 balloons; 3 × 5¢ is only 15¢.

She can get more than 5 balloons; 5 × 5¢ is only 25¢.

Dan finally said that Mary could get 7 balloons, because 7 × 5¢ is 35¢. Do you agree?

1. How many balloons did each boy find Mary could buy? Whose way do you like best?

2. Find how many 5's there are in 30 by Harry's way; Bill's way; Dan's way.

How many fives in a number?

1. Miss West's class needs 30 paper cups for a party. The cups come 5 in a package. Try to find out without help how many packages the class should buy.

Roy drew this picture to find out how many packages to buy. First he drew the 30 cups. Now he is drawing a line around each group of 5 cups. How many groups of 5 will he have when he finishes?

2. How many packages of cups are needed? Is the number of packages needed the same as the number of 5's in 30?

When you tell how many 5's there are in 30, you are *dividing*. You are *dividing 30 by 5.*

"30 divided by 5 is 6" is a *division* example. It may be written: *30 ÷ 5 = 6.* The sign ÷ is read *divided by.*

3. Read these division facts. Tell what each one means.

5 ÷ 5 = 1	20 ÷ 5 = 4	35 ÷ 5 = 7
10 ÷ 5 = 2	25 ÷ 5 = 5	40 ÷ 5 = 8
15 ÷ 5 = 3	30 ÷ 5 = 6	45 ÷ 5 = 9

4. "20 ÷ 5 = _?_ " asks, "How many 5's are there in 20?" What question does each of these examples ask?

5 ÷ 5 = _?_	40 ÷ 5 = _?_	20 ÷ 5 = _?_
25 ÷ 5 = _?_	10 ÷ 5 = _?_	30 ÷ 5 = _?_
45 ÷ 5 = _?_	35 ÷ 5 = _?_	15 ÷ 5 = _?_

5. Copy Ex. 4 and write the answers.

Using division

1. How many 5-cent candy bars can you buy for 35¢? Think, "How many groups of 5 cents are there in 35 cents? $35 \div 5 = \underline{\ ?\ }$"

2. Molly can make a bracelet out of 5 paper clips. She has 40 paper clips. How many bracelets can she make?
Think, "How many groups of 5 paper clips are there in 40 paper clips? $40 \div 5 = \underline{\ ?\ }$"

Tell what you think to find each answer. Write each division fact you use. Draw dot pictures if you need to.

3. How many 5-cent toys can you buy for 20¢? 30¢? 15¢? 45¢? 35¢? 40¢?

4. Allowing 5 spools to a doll, how many spool dolls can you make with 15 spools? 20? 10? 35? 40? 45?

5. John can make 1 paper airplane in 5 minutes. How many can he make in 10 minutes? 15 minutes? 35 minutes? Use a clock to prove your answers.

6. Alice made 25 lollipops. If she ties them in bunches of 5 to sell at the school fair, how many bunches will she have?

7. Tom needs 40 little bells for a clown costume. The bells come 5 to a card. How many cards should he buy?

8. Jane needs 15 curlers to curl her hair. The curlers come 5 on a card. How many cards should she buy?

9. How many pies, each cut into 5 equal pieces, would be needed to serve 20 people? Draw a picture to prove that your answer is right.

10. Bill needs 30 doughnuts for a party. They come 5 in a package. How many packages should he buy?

1. These 15 pennies show that:

- Three 5-cent pencils cost _?_ ¢.
- Five 3-cent pencils cost _?_ ¢.
- For 15¢ you can get _?_ 5-cent pencils.
- For 15¢ you can get _?_ 3-cent pencils.
- If you know $3 \times 5 = 15$, then you know $5 \times 3 =$ _?_, $15 \div 5 =$ _?_, $15 \div 3 =$ _?_.

2. These 20 pennies show that:

- Four groups of 5 pennies are _?_ pennies.
- Five groups of 4 pennies are _?_ pennies.
- In 20 pennies there are _?_ groups of 5 pennies.
- In 20 pennies there are _?_ groups of 4 pennies.
- If you know $4 \times 5 = 20$, then you know $5 \times 4 =$ _?_, $20 \div 5 =$ _?_, $20 \div 4 =$ _?_.

3. The pennies in Ex. 2 answer this question: How much will five 4-cent balls cost? Name three other questions the pennies could answer.

4. If you know that $6 \times 5 = 30$, then you know that $5 \times 6 =$ _?_, $30 \div 6 =$ _?_, and $30 \div 5 =$ _?_.

5. If you know that $35 \div 5 = 7$, then you know that $35 \div 7 =$ _?_, $5 \times 7 =$ _?_, and $7 \times 5 =$ _?_.

214

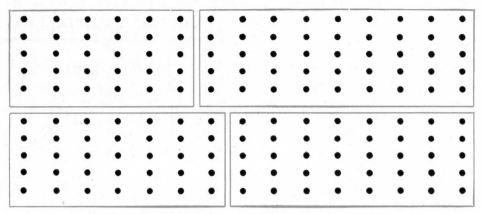

6. Tell 2 multiplication and 2 division facts that each of these dot pictures shows.

7. Name the 3 other members of the family of each of these facts:

$4 \times 5 = 20$	$35 \div 5 = 7$	$10 \div 5 = 2$	$9 \times 5 = 45$
$5 \times 6 = 30$	$15 \div 3 = 5$	$40 \div 8 = 5$	$5 \times 1 = 5$

8. Billy has 40¢. How many 10-cent candy bars can he buy? How many 5-cent candy bars? How many 8-cent candy bars?

9. For 30 cents you can get __?__ 10-cent toys; __?__ 5-cent toys; __?__ 6-cent toys.

10. For 20 cents you can get __?__ 10-cent balls; __?__ 4-cent balls; __?__ 5-cent balls.

11. There are 7 girls in the Outdoor Club. Each girl pays 5 cents a week in dues. They collect __?__ ¢ in dues each week.

There are 5 boys in the Campers Club. Each boy pays 7 cents a week in dues. They collect __?__ ¢ in dues each week.

Does each club have the same number of members? Do the girls pay the same dues as the boys? Do the clubs collect the same amount each week? Explain why.

Penny needs some 5-inch pieces of white yarn to make a tail for a rabbit puppet. How many 5-inch pieces can she cut from a piece of yarn 30 inches long?

Sometimes when we wish to tell how many 5's there are in 30, we write the division this way:➤

$$5\overline{)30} = 6$$

1. Read the division facts of fives below like this:
   How many fives in five? One.
   How many fives in ten? Two; and so on.

Division Facts of Fives

$5\overline{)5}=1$	$5\overline{)10}=2$	$5\overline{)15}=3$	$5\overline{)20}=4$	$5\overline{)25}=5$	$5\overline{)30}=6$	$5\overline{)35}=7$	$5\overline{)40}=8$	$5\overline{)45}=9$
$1\overline{)5}=5$	$2\overline{)10}=5$	$3\overline{)15}=5$	$4\overline{)20}=5$	$5\overline{)25}=5$	$6\overline{)30}=5$	$7\overline{)35}=5$	$8\overline{)40}=5$	$9\overline{)45}=5$

Practice until you can say all the answers:

	a	b	c	d	e	f	g
2.	$5\overline{)40}$	$5\overline{)5}$	$5\overline{)35}$	$2\overline{)10}$	$3\overline{)15}$	$5\overline{)25}$	$5\overline{)20}$
3.	$5\overline{)25}$	$5\overline{)45}$	$5\overline{)10}$	$5\overline{)40}$	$5\overline{)20}$	$5\overline{)15}$	$6\overline{)30}$
4.	$5\overline{)30}$	$8\overline{)40}$	$5\overline{)45}$	$5\overline{)15}$	$9\overline{)45}$	$4\overline{)20}$	$7\overline{)35}$

5. Copy Exs. 2 to 4 and write the answers.

6. How many 5-inch lengths of yarn can you cut from 10 inches? 20 inches? 15 inches? 35? 25? 40? 45?

7. Start a pack of Help-Yourself Cards in division. Make a card for each fact in the table above. Practice with your cards until you know every answer.

Oral practice

1. 1×5
    $20 \div 4$
    5×5

2. $11 - 5$
    $2 + 5$
    $30 \div 6$

3. $15 \div 5$
    $9 - 4$
    5×4

4. 3×5
    $7 - 2$
    $7 + 5$

5. $9 + 5$
    $10 - 5$
    $3 + 5$

6. $12 - 7$
    5×2
    $40 \div 8$

7. $5 + 4$
    $25 \div 5$
    $5 + 5$

8. $45 \div 5$
    $10 \div 2$
    $14 - 5$

9. $35 \div 5$
    8×5
    $13 - 5$

10. 7×5
    $5 + 8$
    $8 - 5$

11. $6 - 5$
    $1 + 5$
    5×6

12. $5 + 6$
    9×5
    $5 \div 1$

Tell whether you add, subtract, multiply, or divide to find each answer below. Then tell the answer.

13. Judy has a nickel. How much more does she need to buy an 8-cent balloon?

14. How many 5-cent balloons can Carl get for 35¢?

15. At 5¢ each, how much will 8 balloons cost?

16. How much will a 5-cent and an 8-cent balloon both cost?

17. How many packages of flower seed at 4¢ a package can Peter buy for 20¢?

18. How many cookies will you get in 5 packages, if there are 6 cookies in a package?

19. Tom has 14¢. If he buys a 5-cent eraser, how much will he have left?

20. At 5¢ each, how much will 9 tickets cost?

21. How many yards are there in 3 feet? in 15 feet?

22. How many gallons are there in 4 quarts? in 20 quarts?

In which of these subtractions do you borrow a ten? a hundred? a ten and a hundred? Copy, subtract, and check.

	a	b	c	d	e	f	g
1.	50 27	90 24	80 43	60 39	70 28	$.40 .19	$.60 .49
2.	82 74	94 87	78 65	83 74	52 47	$.43 .37	$.60 .56
3.	463 39	254 37	388 45	468 83	252 38	$4.70 .98	$5.81 .82
4.	284 78	356 49	340 37	251 46	460 59	$7.83 .76	$6.54 .47
5.	75 57	86 69	68 34	52 37	83 39	$.79 .26	$.82 .36
6.	215 39	413 54	817 28	117 45	216 169	$7.17 .88	$5.10 2.76
7.	400 283	500 476	600 284	700 350	800 227	$9.00 2.35	$3.00 1.98
8.	607 248	407 229	608 248	705 195	802 328	$5.07 2.35	$6.01 2.98
9.	123 113	456 208	789 456	804 628	623 257	$5.35 2.65	$4.03 1.89
10.	689 345	842 769	720 580	321 181	624 587	$5.68 2.59	$6.02 1.28

Review and social applications
Reading and writing four-place
numbers

UNIT
33

Problems and practice

1. Bobby made this bookcase. Would you like to make one like it? You need 3 boards. You need _?_ piles of bricks with 5 bricks in a pile. You need _?_ bricks in all.

2. Five jacks are fastened on a card. How many jacks will Mary get if she buys 6 cards?

3. Al has 5¢. To buy an 8-cent top, he needs _?_ ¢ more.

4. Jane wants an 8-cent candy rabbit and a 5-cent egg. How much money will she need all together?

Say these answers. Then write them on folded paper.

5.	8 +6	5 +1	9 +8	5 ×7	5 −2	5 −5	16 −9	5 +7
6.	14 −5	13 −5	5 ×8	7 ×5	14 −7	5 ×9	5 −4	8 +7
7.	9 ×5	5 ×1	5 −3	5 ×5	15 −6	5 +3	5 +8	5 +0
8.	5 +4	5 ×6	8 +8	12 −9	5 ×3	8 +5	18 −9	5 +6
9.	6 ×5	8 ×5	5 ×2	13 −7	5 +9	5 ×4	5 −0	13 −9

Using addition and subtraction facts

1. Take the addition test on page 110.

2. Take the subtraction test on page 111.

3. Tell what addition facts you should know to do these additions. Then add and check.

32	24	55	86	34	57	93
+ 25	+ 73	+ 64	+ 43	+ 90	+ 82	+ 65

4. Tell what subtraction facts you should know to do these subtractions. Then subtract and check.

86	98	156	165	129	148	137
− 40	− 33	− 73	− 81	− 57	− 66	− 54

5. Jane says she uses the fact 9 + 8 = 17 six times in doing these additions. Prove that she is right.

			29	24
39	394	189	30	63
+ 28	+ 283	+ 288	+ 48	+ 85

6. Peter says he uses the fact 15 − 9 = 6 five times in doing these subtractions. Prove that he is right.

156	245	459	865	487
− 93	− 129	− 196	− 399	− 379

7. Jack had a score of 425 points in a game of darts. Then he won 300 points more, so his score was __?__.

8. The player who gets 500 points first wins in a game of Hi-Ho. Ted has 483 points. He must get __?__ more points to win the game.

Bob has 398 points. He needs __?__ more points to win.

Helping

Mother

1. Susan helps her mother by timing the washing machine. The machine washes the clothes in 7 minutes. Susan is starting it now. Look at the clock. When should she stop?

2. Doris takes her baby brother out for a half-hour ride in his carriage every afternoon. When should she take him home if she takes him out at 20 minutes after 3?

3. Jean helps cook. She needs a quart of water to cook cereal. One morning she could find only a pint measure. How could she measure a quart of water?

4. Don needs a board 33 inches long to fix a broken step. His mother said, "Here is a board 3 feet long." Is that long enough? Will he have to saw off any? If so, how much?

5. Dick washes the breakfast dishes. His mother says he should finish in a half hour. If Dick starts at quarter of eight, when should he finish?

6. Jack goes to the store for his mother. When he buys 4 grapefruit at 5¢ each, how much should he pay? How much change should he get from a quarter?

Thinking about hundreds

Ann

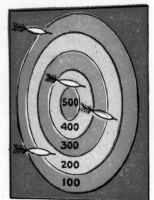

Pete

Ann and Pete are throwing darts. The pictures show how the dart board looked after Ann threw 4 darts; after Pete threw 4 darts.

What is Ann's score? What is Pete's? Who won?

1. Climb up and down the number ladder by 100's to 1,000. Now climb up and down by 50's.

2. What is the sum of 600 + 60 + 6?

What numbers belong in the blank spaces in Exs. 3–7?

3. 468 is __?__ hundreds, __?__ tens, and __?__ ones.

4. 570 is __?__ hundreds, __?__ tens, and __?__ ones.

5. 603 is __?__ hundreds, __?__ tens, and __?__ ones.

6. 650, 660, 670, __?__, __?__, __?__, __?__, __?__, __?__, 740.

7. 200, 225, 250, __?__, __?__, __?__, __?__, __?__, __?__, 425.

8. Which of these is the largest? 400 404 444 440

9. Which of these is the largest? 213 312 321 231

10. In these numbers which 5's mean 5 tens? 5 hundreds?
    456   549   657   751   845

11. Does 297 + 302 equal about 500 or 600? Why?

12. Does 894 − 203 equal about 700 or 600? Why?

13. Does 710 − 489 equal about 300 or 200? Why?

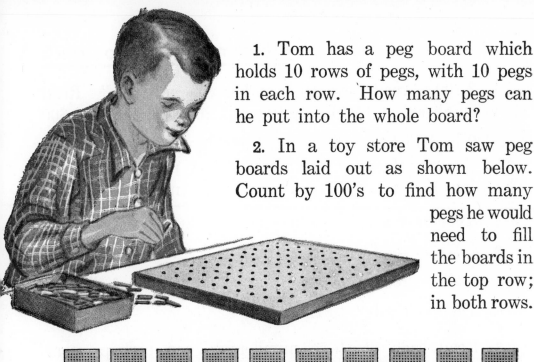

1. Tom has a peg board which holds 10 rows of pegs, with 10 pegs in each row. How many pegs can he put into the whole board?

2. In a toy store Tom saw peg boards laid out as shown below. Count by 100's to find how many pegs he would need to fill the boards in the top row; in both rows.

3. Write the hundreds from 1000 (10 hundred) to 2500 (25 hundred), like this:———————→

| 1000 (10 hundred) |
| 1100 (11 hundred) |
| 1200 (12 hundred) |

Ten hundred is also called *one thousand*. Twenty hundred is called *two thousand*. We usually put a comma after the figure that shows the number of thousands.

4. Write the thousands from 1,000 (1 thousand) to 9,000 (9 thousand), like this:———————→

| 1,000 (1 thousand) |
| 2,000 (2 thousand) |
| 3,000 (3 thousand) |

5. One peg board proves there are ＿?＿ 10's in 100. Ten peg boards prove there are ＿?＿ 100's in 1,000.

1. 2,700 is read "two thousand, seven hundred." Read these numbers: 1,800   1,100   2,200 .   3,400   4,600

2,370 is read "two thousand, three hundred seventy."
The figure before the comma tells how many thousands. The three figures after it tell how many more.

2. 2,653 is read "_?_ thousand, _?_ hundred _?_ _?_."

3. 4,071 is read "_?_ thousand, _?_ _?_."

4. 1,407 is read "_?_ thousand, _?_ hundred _?_."

5. 5,005 is read "_?_ thousand, _?_."

6. Read each of these numbers. Then perhaps your teacher will say them to see if you can write them.

4,769	3,074	5,247	7,981	6,666	5,900
5,600	5,000	1,200	9,099	8,008	4,404

7. The box at the right shows 7,000 + 500 + 80 + 3.   Read the answer.

```
7,000
  500
   80
    3
7,583
```

Write the answer to each addition example below. Then count off three places from the right and put in a comma.   Read each answer.

8. 3,000 + 600 + 70 + 4   11. 8,000 + 60

9. 6,000 + 700 + 60 + 5   12. 9,000 + 5

10. 8,000 + 70 + 3   13. 6,000 + 700 + 4

14. Jim wanted to write in figures: one thousand, one.   He didn't know how, but he put down 1,000 and added 1 to it.   Is his answer one thousand, one?

```
1,000
    1
1,001
```

Addition practice

Write the sums on folded paper. Check each example.

	a	b	c	d	e	f	g	h
1.	6	9	7	4	9	4	6	7
	4	8	3	5	3	7	9	6
	5	7	4	9	2	5	4	8
2.	4	5	3	8	9	6	2	7
	9	4	7	3	7	8	9	8
	3	6	4	9	4	3	7	6
	8	3	8	5	8	5	6	4
3.	89	57	38	27	36	45	93	64
	67	65	49	68	72	79	48	37
4.	43	74	27	48	36	89	56	72
	75	65	86	95	79	58	98	99
	89	38	79	28	67	74	88	68
5.	62	94	61	76	64	74	77	29
	75	76	83	28	79	86	96	70
	80	85	79	35	67	30	83	84
6.	84	6	78	25	76	8	93	50
	5	57	59	94	9	96	9	8
	39	89	86	8	87	9	9	89
	96	74	4	86	8	75	67	76
7.	$.75	$.40	$.63	$.05	$.90	$.12	$.49	$.83
	.50	.10	.95	.74	.32	.79	.05	.20
	.04	.74	.26	.58	.45	.34	.60	.75
	.89	.69	.75	.37	.62	.75	.74	.03

UNIT
34

Uneven division
facts of fives
Finding one fifth

Uneven division facts of fives

Ted found 12 pennies in an old tin box. He wonders how many nickels he can get for them.

Can you tell? Stop and think. Here are the 12 pennies. For each 5 pennies he can get 1 nickel. How many 5's are there? How many pennies will be left over?

1. How many nickels can Ted get for 13 pennies? 14? 15? 16? 17? 18? How many pennies will be left over each time? Draw pictures to show your answers.

2. How many circles are there in each row in this drawing? How many rows are there?

3. How many circles are there in the first 2 rows? How many in 3 rows? in 4? in 5?

4. Count the first 11 circles. How many rows of 5 circles are there in 11 circles? Answer this way: "In 11 circles there are 2 rows of 5 and 1 circle left over."

5. In 12 circles there are ___?___ rows of 5 and ___?___ over.

In 13 there are ___?___ 5's and ___?___ over.
In 14 there are ___?___ 5's and ___?___ over.
In 15 there are ___?___ 5's.
In 16 there are ___?___ 5's and ___?___ over.
In 17 there are ___?___ 5's and ___?___ over.
In 18 there are ___?___ 5's and ___?___ over.
Keep on going up to 50 circles.

1 2 3 4 5
6 7 8 9 10
11 12 13 14 15
16 17 18 19 20
21 22 23 24 25
26 27 28 29 30
31 32 33 34 35
36 37 38 39 40
41 42 43 44 45
46 47 48 49 50

226

Left-overs in division

When Ted found how many 5's there are in 21, he first thought, "How many 5's are there in 20?" He knew there are 4 fives in 20; so in 21 there are 4 fives and 1 over.

This is the way to write "In 21 there are 4 fives and 1 over." ⟶

$$5\overline{)21} \quad \frac{4\ r1}{}$$

The "1 over" is called the *remainder*. The letter *r* stands for remainder.

1. Read the division facts below. Begin, "In 6 there is 1 five and 1 over; in 7 there is 1 five and 2 over." Make a drawing to prove each fact.

Some Uneven Division Facts of Fives

$5\overline{)6}\ \ 1\ r1$	$5\overline{)7}\ \ 1\ r2$	$5\overline{)8}\ \ 1\ r3$	$5\overline{)9}\ \ 1\ r4$	$5\overline{)10}\ \ 2$	$5\overline{)11}\ \ 2\ r1$
$5\overline{)12}\ \ 2\ r2$	$5\overline{)13}\ \ 2\ r3$	$5\overline{)14}\ \ 2\ r4$	$5\overline{)15}\ \ 3$	$5\overline{)16}\ \ 3\ r1$	$5\overline{)17}\ \ 3\ r2$

2. Cover the answers in Ex. 1 and try to say them.

3. When Billy is dividing by 5, he calls these numbers his Dividing-by-Five Helping Numbers. Why?

5   10   15   20   25   30   35   40   45

4. When Billy wants to find how many 5's there are in 19, he thinks, "*15* is my Helping Number. $15 \div 5 = 3$." To find how much is left over, he thinks, "15 from 19 is 4."

$$5\overline{)19} \quad \frac{3\ r4}{}$$

Why did Billy choose 15 for his Helping Number? Why didn't he use 20? 10?

1. Divide 28 by 5 like this:

First think, "My Helping Number is *25*. How many 5's are there in 25?"

Think, "25 ÷ 5 = _?_ ."

Think, "25 from 28 is _?_ ."

Think, "In 28 there are 5 fives and _?_ over."

You can write the division this way:——→

$$\begin{array}{r} 5\ r3 \\ 5\overline{)28} \end{array}$$

2. Divide 34 by 5 like this:

First think, "My Helping Number is *30*. How many 5's are there in 30?"

Think, "30 ÷ 5 = _?_ ."

Think, "30 from 34 is _?_ ."

Think, "In 34 there are _?_ fives and _?_ over."

You can write the division this way:——→

$$\begin{array}{r} 6\ r4 \\ 5\overline{)34} \end{array}$$

3. Billy and Jean wanted to find how many 5's there are in 22.

● Billy *first thought*, "How many 5's are there in 20?" He used 20 for his Helping Number. Did he use the right Helping Number?

$$5\overline{)22}$$

● Jean *first thought*, "How many 5's are there in 15?" She used 15 for her Helping Number.

Jean used the wrong Helping Number. Why is 15 wrong? Can you tell how many 5's there are in 22?

4. What Helping Number would you use in finding how many 5's there are in 16? in 17? in 18? in 19?

5. How many 5-cent apples can you buy for 10¢? for 11¢? 12¢? 13¢? 14¢? 15¢? 16¢?

1. What Helping Number would you use in finding how many 5's there are in 21? 22? 23? 24?

2. What Helping Number would you use in finding how many 5's there are in each of these numbers?

23	12	38	31	15	24	35	37	45	10
28	20	21	14	11	16	25	36	27	47
39	29	13	22	32	34	17	26	19	48
40	46	30	41	33	42	43	18	44	49

3. If you are dividing the numbers in Ex. 2 by 5, tell what subtractions you must do to find the remainders.

4. Divide each of the numbers in Ex. 2 by 5. Write your work like this:——————→

$$5)\overline{23}^{\ 4\,r3}$$

5. How many 5-cent balls can Pete buy with 18¢? How many cents will he have left over?

6. How many bunches of 5 roses can you make from 32 roses? How many roses will be left over?

7. If you use 5 sheets of paper in one booklet, how many booklets can you make from 38 sheets of paper? How many sheets will be left over?

8. Jim knows how to make jumping jacks. He uses 5 spools for each one. He has 28 spools. To find out how many jumping jacks he can make with 28 spools, he did this division:→

$$5)\overline{28}^{\ 5\,r3}$$

Does the remainder of 3 in his division mean he will have 3 spools left over, or 3 jumping jacks left over?

Write the divisions shown by these drawings:

9.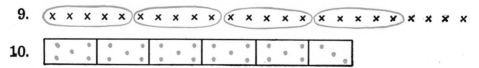

10.

1. Paul has a big ginger cooky. If he shares it equally with Tim, what part of the cooky will each boy get?

2. If 3 boys share the cooky equally, what part of the cooky will each boy get?

3. If 4 boys share the cooky equally, what part of the cooky will each get?

If 5 boys share the cooky equally, each boy will get *one fifth* of the cooky.

One fifth is written $\frac{1}{5}$.

4. If 5 boys share this box of 10 Easter eggs, how many eggs will each boy get?

When you divide the 10 eggs into 5 equal parts, there will be __?__ eggs in each part.

Each boy will get *one fifth* of the 10 eggs.

5. If 5 boys share 25¢ equally, how many cents will each boy get?

6. If 5 girls share a package of 35 flower seeds equally, how many seeds will each one get?

7. There are 40 cards in a game of Fireman. If the cards are dealt out to 5 children, each child will get __?__ cards.

▌**To find $\frac{1}{5}$ of a number, divide the number by 5.**

8. Find $\frac{1}{5}$ of each of these numbers:

10   20   35   40   5   30   15   25   45

Test in multiplying and dividing

Copy and work.

	a	b	c	d	e	f	g
1.	5 × 7	5 × 5	5 × 1	5 × 9	5 × 8	5 × 6	5 × 3
2.	7 × 5	5 × 2	6 × 5	5 × 4	8 × 5	9 × 5	2 × 5
3.	5)42	5)5	5)22	5)23	5)30	5)32	5)11
4.	5)38	5)27	5)10	5)37	5)9	5)25	5)45
5.	5)15	5)12	5)28	5)24	5)17	5)29	5)13
6.	5)40	5)20	5)8	5)14	5)49	5)18	5)48
7.	5)33	5)7	5)35	5)44	5)19	5)47	5)43

	a	b	c	d	e
8.	$45 \div 5$	$35 \div 7$	$10 \div 5$	$30 \div 6$	$5 \div 5$
9.	$15 \div 5$	$20 \div 5$	$40 \div 8$	$25 \div 5$	$30 \div 5$
10.	$\frac{1}{5}$ of 35	$\frac{1}{5}$ of 25	$\frac{1}{5}$ of 10	$\frac{1}{5}$ of 45	$\frac{1}{5}$ of 5
11.	$\frac{1}{5}$ of 40	$\frac{1}{5}$ of 20	$\frac{1}{5}$ of 15	$\frac{1}{5}$ of 35	$\frac{1}{5}$ of 30
12.	5×8	6×5	5×4	9×5	5×3
13.	2×5	5×5	1×5	5×7	10×5

14. Does $5 + 5 + 5 + 5 = 4 \times 5$?

15. Start with 20. Subtract 5 over and over until you have nothing left. Your subtractions show that there are __?__ 5's in 20.

1. George bought 5 cards of fishhooks. There are 3 hooks on each card. How many hooks did he get in all?

2. How many 5-cent false faces can you buy for a quarter?

3. Find the cost of eight 5-cent Christmas cards.

4. John has 48 pennies. How many nickels can he get, and how many pennies will he have left over?

5. How many pieces of string 5 inches long can you cut from a yard of string? Will there be any string left over? How much?

6. What date is New Year's Day? Christmas?

7. Harry wants a scooter that costs $5.50. His mother wants to buy him one that costs $3.95. If his mother gives him the $3.95, how much more must he earn to buy the scooter he wants?

8. Harry paid $1.98 for a fountain pen and 15¢ for a bottle of ink. How much did he spend in all?

9. At a cent apiece, find the cost of 5 lollipops; 6; 7; 8; 9.

10. How much is 4×1? 6×1? 7×1? 8×1?

11. Make up a rule about multiplying 1 by any number; about multiplying any number by 1.

12. How many 1-cent balls can you get for 4¢? 5¢? 7¢?

13. How much is $4 \div 1$? $6 \div 1$? $8 \div 1$? $9 \div 1$?

14. Make up a rule about dividing any number by 1.

15. How much is $4 \div 4$? $5 \div 5$? $6 \div 6$? $7 \div 7$?

16. Make up a rule about dividing any number by itself.

Now is the time to test yourself

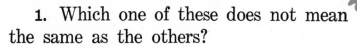

1. Which one of these does not mean the same as the others?

- $5 + 5 + 5 + 5 + 5 + 5$

- 6 fives

- $\begin{array}{r} 5 \\ \times\, 6 \\ \hline \end{array}$

- $6 + 5$

- 6×5

2. Judy bought 3 bunches of lollipops. There were 5 in each bunch. How many lollipops did she get?

3. How many toy airplanes at 5¢ each can Dick buy for 39¢? How much money will he have left?

4. Jerry paid 30¢ for a box of pencils. There were 5 pencils in the box. Ann wants to buy one of the pencils from Jerry. How much should she pay?

5. Write in figures: two thousand, four hundred sixty-one.

6. How much change will you get from $5.00 if you pay $3.69 for new shoes?

7. Tom is reading a book with 315 pages. He has read 147 pages. He has __?__ more pages to read.

8. Polly is filling five Easter baskets. She has 40 jelly beans. How many jelly beans should she put in each basket if she divides the beans equally?

9. Which one of these divisions means the same as the picture?

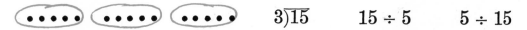

$3\overline{)15}$ $\qquad$ $15 \div 5$ $\qquad$ $5 \div 15$

10. Write the other member of this Number Family:

$9 \times 5 = 45$ $\qquad$ $5 \times 9 = 45$ $\qquad$ $45 \div 9 = 5$

233

Arithmetic in pictures

Jack said that the picture of the egg box below teaches a lot of arithmetic. Make a list of the facts you think it teaches.

Here is Jack's list. Is it like yours?

1. 6 + 6 = 12.
2. Two 6's are 12.
3. 12 − 6 = 6.
4. Six 2's are 12.

5. One half of 12 is 6.
6. One half dozen is 6.
7. In 12 there are two 6's.
8. In 12 there are six 2's.

9. 2 + 2 + 2 + 2 + 2 + 2 = 12.

Make a list of the arithmetic facts each of the other pictures below teaches you.

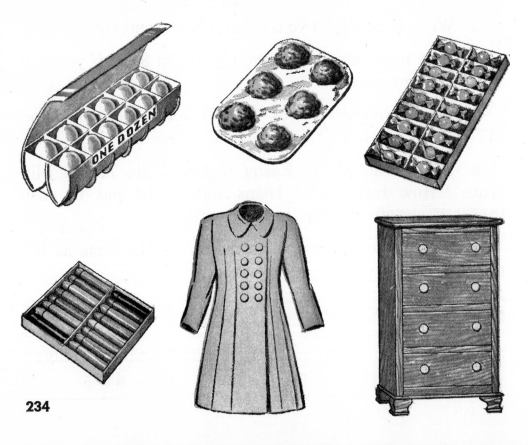

Facts that additions teach you

1. Why are these addition facts called doubles?

1	2	3	4	5	6	7	8	9
+1	+2	+3	+4	+5	+6	+7	+8	+9
2	4	6	8	10	12	14	16	18

2. Jane says the addition facts in Ex. 1 teach these multiplication facts: two 1's are 2; two 2's are 4; two 3's are 6. Name 6 other multiplication facts Ex. 1 teaches.

3. How does Ex. 1 help you answer these questions?

How many 6's in 12?   How many 8's in 16?

How many 7's in 14?   How many 9's in 18?

4. 3 + 3 = _?_; 2 threes are _?_. How many 3's in 6?

5. 2 + 2 + 2 = _?_; 3 twos are _?_. How many 2's in 6?

6. 4 + 4 = _?_; 2 fours are _?_. How many 4's in 8?

7. 2 + 2 + 2 + 2 = _?_; 4 twos are _?_. How many 2's in 8?

8. 5 + 5 = _?_; 2 fives are _?_. How many 5's in 10?

9. 2 + 2 + 2 + 2 + 2 = _?_; 5 twos are _?_.

Which picture helps you answer each of these questions?

10. 6 and 6 are _?_.

11. Two 7's are _?_.

12. How many 2's in 12?

13. How many 7's in 14?

14. Seven 2's are _?_.

15. How many 6's in 12?

16. Two 6's are _?_.

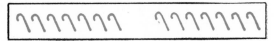

Using twos in cooking

The 18 children in the third grade are going to cook their own lunch in school tomorrow. Each child will have a bowl of soup, a roll, a bottle of milk, and half a grapefruit.

1. One can of soup will make 2 bowls of soup. Can you tell without help how many cans they should buy, so that each of the 18 children can have a bowl of soup?

2. Peter made the drawing in the picture above. First he drew the 18 bowls. Then he drew a can over each group of 2 bowls. Why did he do that?

He found they need to buy _?_ cans of soup. He found there are _?_ twos in 18.

3. Then Miss Bell made this table. Read it this way:

     1 can of soup fills 2 bowls

     2 cans of soup fill 4 bowls; and so on.

Cans of soup	1	2	3	4	5	6	7	8	9
Bowls of soup	2	4	6	8	10	12	14	16	18

4. Each child gets one half of a grapefruit. How many children will 1 grapefruit serve? Draw a picture to show how many grapefruit they should buy for the 18 children.

5. Doris made this drawing and found they should buy _?_ grapefruit. Explain the drawing.

6. Tell what this table means. Tell the missing numbers.

No. of grapefruit	1	2	3	4	5	6	7	8	9
No. of servings	2	4	?	?	10	?	14	?	18

7. How many children are there in your class? How many cans of soup would you need for your class? How many grapefruit?

Draw pictures to show how to find the answers.

Be your own teacher

Some of the pupils in Miss Bell's class figured out the cost of the class lunch. You may do it if you are a *good thinker*. This is a fine chance to *teach yourself* new arithmetic.

They bought 9 cans of soup at 10¢ a can.
They bought 9 grapefruit at 5¢ each.
They bought 18 bottles of milk at 5¢ a bottle.
They bought 18 rolls at 20¢ a dozen.
How much did they spend for the soup? the grapefruit? the milk? the rolls?
How much did they spend all together?

To the Teacher: See Note 6 on page 311.

Using twos in multiplication

1. There are 9 children who live on Elm Street. They want to make tin-can stilts. Do you know how many cans they will need for 9 pairs of stilts?

2. Count the cans by twos. How many are 3 twos? 4 twos? 5 twos? 6 twos? 7 twos? 8 twos? 9 twos?

3. Say, "1 two is 2; 2 twos are 4; 3 twos are 6"; and so on up to "9 twos are 18."

4. Read these facts; 1 times 2 is 2, and so on. Use pebbles or counters to prove each answer.

$1 \times 2 = \underline{\ ?\ }$ $4 \times 2 = \underline{\ ?\ }$ $7 \times 2 = \underline{\ ?\ }$

$2 \times 2 = \underline{\ ?\ }$ $5 \times 2 = \underline{\ ?\ }$ $8 \times 2 = \underline{\ ?\ }$

$3 \times 2 = \underline{\ ?\ }$ $6 \times 2 = \underline{\ ?\ }$ $9 \times 2 = \underline{\ ?\ }$

5. Bobby went to the chicken house 4 times today. He found 2 eggs each time. All together he found 4 times 2 eggs, or $\underline{\ ?\ }$ eggs.

6. To find the cost of 7 candy sticks at 2¢ each, think, "If 1 candy stick costs 2¢, 7 sticks will cost 7 times 2¢, or $\underline{\ ?\ }$ ¢."

7. The picture of the stars below shows that $4 \times 2 = $ _?_ and $2 \times 4 = $ _?_.

8. Which picture shows each of these pairs of multiplication facts?

$\begin{cases} 5 \times 2 \\ 2 \times 5 \end{cases}$
$\begin{cases} 6 \times 2 \\ 2 \times 6 \end{cases}$
$\begin{cases} 7 \times 2 \\ 2 \times 7 \end{cases}$
$\begin{cases} 8 \times 2 \\ 2 \times 8 \end{cases}$
$\begin{cases} 9 \times 2 \\ 2 \times 9 \end{cases}$

9. If $2 \times 8 = 16$, then $8 \times 2 = $ _?_.

10. If $6 \times 2 = 12$, then $2 \times 6 = $ _?_.

Multiply:

11. 4×2	6×5	2×5	2×1	7×5
12. 2×6	9×5	8×2	2×4	2×8
13. 2×2	2×7	2×3	7×2	6×2
14. 9×2	3×2	8×5	5×2	1×2

15. Jerry bought 2 boxes of cookies. There were 8 cookies in each box. In all, he bought 2 times 8 cookies, or _?_ cookies.

16. In a classroom there are 5 rows of desks. There are 6 desks in each row. How many desks are there in all?

17. In Ex. 8 above there are 5 pairs of multiplication facts. How many multiplication facts are there all together in Ex. 8?

1. Read the table below. Say, "1 times 2 is 2; 2 times 2 is 4," and so on.

Multiplication Facts of Twos

$\begin{array}{r}2\\ \times 1\\ \hline 2\end{array}$	$\begin{array}{r}2\\ \times 2\\ \hline 4\end{array}$	$\begin{array}{r}2\\ \times 3\\ \hline 6\end{array}$	$\begin{array}{r}2\\ \times 4\\ \hline 8\end{array}$	$\begin{array}{r}2\\ \times 5\\ \hline 10\end{array}$	$\begin{array}{r}2\\ \times 6\\ \hline 12\end{array}$	$\begin{array}{r}2\\ \times 7\\ \hline 14\end{array}$	$\begin{array}{r}2\\ \times 8\\ \hline 16\end{array}$	$\begin{array}{r}2\\ \times 9\\ \hline 18\end{array}$
$\begin{array}{r}1\\ \times 2\\ \hline 2\end{array}$	$\begin{array}{r}2\\ \times 2\\ \hline 4\end{array}$	$\begin{array}{r}3\\ \times 2\\ \hline 6\end{array}$	$\begin{array}{r}4\\ \times 2\\ \hline 8\end{array}$	$\begin{array}{r}5\\ \times 2\\ \hline 10\end{array}$	$\begin{array}{r}6\\ \times 2\\ \hline 12\end{array}$	$\begin{array}{r}7\\ \times 2\\ \hline 14\end{array}$	$\begin{array}{r}8\\ \times 2\\ \hline 16\end{array}$	$\begin{array}{r}9\\ \times 2\\ \hline 18\end{array}$

2. Practice until you can tell every answer correctly:

$\begin{array}{r}2\\ \times 7\end{array}$	$\begin{array}{r}2\\ \times 5\end{array}$	$\begin{array}{r}6\\ \times 2\end{array}$	$\begin{array}{r}2\\ \times 1\end{array}$	$\begin{array}{r}2\\ \times 8\end{array}$	$\begin{array}{r}7\\ \times 2\end{array}$	$\begin{array}{r}2\\ \times 4\end{array}$	$\begin{array}{r}2\\ \times 2\end{array}$	$\begin{array}{r}1\\ \times 2\end{array}$
$\begin{array}{r}5\\ \times 2\end{array}$	$\begin{array}{r}2\\ \times 3\end{array}$	$\begin{array}{r}4\\ \times 2\end{array}$	$\begin{array}{r}3\\ \times 2\end{array}$	$\begin{array}{r}2\\ \times 6\end{array}$	$\begin{array}{r}8\\ \times 2\end{array}$	$\begin{array}{r}9\\ \times 2\end{array}$	$\begin{array}{r}2\\ \times 9\end{array}$	$\begin{array}{r}2\\ \times 2\end{array}$

3. Copy Ex. 2 and write the answers.

4. Make a Help-Yourself Card for each multiplication fact in the table. Practice with your cards until you know every answer.

5. Mary went to visit her aunt in the city for 2 weeks. 2 weeks = _?_ days.

6. Jean's mother bought 2 gallons of ice cream for a big party. 2 gallons = _?_ quarts.

7. Bobby and Dick are twins. They each made 8 toy cars. In all, they made _?_ cars.

Problems you might meet

Tell what you think as you solve each problem:

1. Find the cost of five 2-cent erasers.

Think, "If one eraser costs 2¢, five erasers will cost 5 times 2¢, or ___?___ cents."

2. Find the cost of two 5-cent erasers.

3. A peanut contains two nuts. How many nuts will you have if you break open five peanuts?

4. Eight quarts of milk equal ___?___ pints of milk.

5. Drinking straws often come in packages of 2. How many straws are there in 7 packages? 8 packages?

6. Find the cost of two 3-cent stamps.

7. Jean wants to hang 3 pairs of socks on the line to dry. She needs a clothespin for each sock. How many clothespins will she need all together?

8. If two children use one seesaw, how many children can play on four seesaws?

9. Mary found the cost of six 2-cent whistles in this way:

$$2¢ + 2¢ + 2¢ + 2¢ + 2¢ + 2¢ = 12¢$$

Jack found the cost of six 2-cent whistles in this way:

$$6 \times 2¢ = 12¢$$

Which way do you like better?

10. Bobby bought 2 bags of pretzels. There were 9 pretzels in each bag. How many pretzels did he get in all?

11. It takes 8 pairs of children to do the Leapfrog Dance. How many children are needed for the dance?

Put on your thinking cap

▶ Oral review

1. Read these numbers: 5,600   8,704   1,175

2. When the thermometer goes from 57° to 45°, the air becomes __?__ degrees cooler.

3. At what time do you go home from school?

4. Add 8 to each of these numbers.   Add 9.

34   76   53   61   87   75   19

5. Read these prices: $.54 $9.02 $.04 $10.10

6. Tell what coins you could get in change from a half dollar after spending 35¢.

7. What is ⅕ of 25? 35? 15? 45?

8. At 5¢ each, find the cost of 8 balls; 7 balls; 9; 6.

9. Count by 5's to 50; by 3's to 30; by 2's to 20.

10. Divide each of these numbers by 5:

16   27   38   41   23   12   46

11. Could you dip the water out of a barrel more quickly with a quart measure or with a gallon measure?

12. If you laid out 37 pennies in rows of 10, you would have __?__ rows of 10 pennies, and __?__ extra pennies.

13. Which of these are rectangles?

a dime   a dollar bill   a stamp

14. Tom has a new bicycle. He is letting his friends take 5-minute rides on it. How many boys will get a ride in a half hour? Use a clock to prove your answer.

Put on your thinking cap

▶ **Written review**

1. Write in figures: three dollars and thirty-two cents.

2. Ann has three boxes of crayons. There are five crayons in each box. How many crayons has she in all?

3. How many 8-cent toys can you get for 40¢?

4. A pony ride costs 5¢. Jane has 47¢. She has enough to pay for rides for __?__ children. She will have __?__ ¢ left.

5. Find the cost of seven 2-cent pencils.

6. Billy bought a pair of white rats for $.75 and a cage for $2.98. How much did he spend in all?

7. Licorice shoestrings are 5¢ a package. How many packages can you get for 17¢? How many cents will you have left over?

8. James had 52 newspapers to sell last evening. He sold all that he could. Then he counted the ones that were left. He had 14. How many papers had he sold?

9. Write the date for today.

	a	*b*	*c*	*d*	*e*
10.	400 − 275	575 − 489	363 − 154	$4.56 − .69	$4.95 − 2.77
11.	963 − 287	846 − 772	604 − 597	$5.00 − 2.87	$6.00 − .70
12.	$4.65 8.23 4.45 + 5.67	$6.84 3.05 .76 + 4.83	$2.56 4.38 5.73 + .07	$4.25 6.38 5.46 + 8.24	$3.46 8.32 .96 + 5.87

1. Add and check.   Use folded paper.

174	70	34	37	204	43	102	205
32	109	126	78	508	304	208	308
107	37	78	63	38	206	409	204
206	775	189	159	119	107	103	106

2. Can you subtract and check these in three minutes?

| 87 | 99 | 76 | 66 | 55 | 92 | 83 | 79 |
| 38 | 28 | 47 | 52 | 41 | 25 | 38 | 34 |

Do not use a pencil.

	a	*b*	*c*	*d*
3.	$47 + 10$	$47 - 20$	$47 - 21$	$47 + 32$
4.	$47 - 10$	$47 + 20$	$47 + 21$	$47 - 32$
5.	$85 + 10$	$85 + 20$	$85 + 31$	$85 + 42$
6.	$85 - 10$	$85 - 20$	$85 - 31$	$85 - 42$

7. Does $496 + 302 =$ about 700 or 800?   Why?

8. Does $501 + 410 =$ about 900 or 1000?   Why?

9. Does $6.98 + 2.00 =$ about $8.00 or $9.00?   Why?

10. Does $795 - 204 =$ about 500 or 600?   Why?

11. Does $812 - 608 =$ about 200 or 300?   Why?

12. Does $9.03 - $2.95 =$ about $7.00 or $6.00?   Why?

13. $9 + 8 = $ _?_; $19 + 8 = $ _?_; $29 + 8 = $ _?_; $39 + 8 = $ _?_

14. $6 + 9 = $ _?_; $16 + 9 = $ _?_; $26 + 9 = $ _?_; $36 + 9 = $ _?_

15. $5.00 = 4$ dollars, _?_ dimes, 10 cents.

16. $95 = 9$ tens 5 ones $= 8$ tens _?_ ones.

Even and uneven
division facts of twos.
Finding one half

UNIT
37

How many twos in a number?

How many 2-cent tickets to the class circus can Ann get for 8¢? Explain these ways 3 children did the problem.

Bill draws pictures

Bill wrote: ➤

(1¢) (1¢)   (1¢) (1¢)   (1¢) (1¢)   (1¢) (1¢)

| 1 ticket | | 1 ticket | | 1 ticket | | 1 ticket |

Bill said, "My drawing shows Ann can get four 2-cent tickets for 8¢."

Peter subtracts

Peter wrote:————————————————————➤

$$\begin{array}{r} 8¢ \\ -2¢ ✓ \\ \hline 6¢ \\ -2¢ ✓ \\ \hline 4¢ \\ -2¢ ✓ \\ \hline 2¢ \\ -2¢ ✓ \\ \hline 0¢ \end{array}$$

Peter said,
"Ann buys 1 ticket; she has 6¢ left.
Ann buys a second ticket; she has 4¢ left.
Ann buys a third ticket; she has 2¢ left.
Ann buys a fourth ticket; she has 0¢ left.

"After Ann buys 4 tickets, she will not have any money left. So she can buy only 4 tickets."

Jane divides

Jane wrote: $8¢ \div 2¢ = 4$

Jane said, "One ticket costs 2¢. For 8¢ Ann can get as many tickets as there are 2's in 8. To find how many 2's there are in 8, I divide 8 by 2. $8 \div 2 = 4$.

"Ann can get 4 tickets. I'll prove I'm right. $4 \times 2¢ = 8¢$."

1. Use Bill's way, Peter's way, and Jane's way to find:

    $10¢ \div 2¢$ $6¢ \div 2¢$ $12¢ \div 2¢$

2. Whose way is shortest to write?

245

1. The third-grade pupils expect 18 children to come to their circus. They will seat the children on boxes. Two children can sit on each box.

Dick is drawing this picture to help him find out how many boxes to get:

First he drew the 18 children. Now he is drawing a box for each group of 2 children. How many boxes will he have when he has finished? Is the number of boxes needed the same as the number of 2's in 18?

2. Look at Dick's picture. How many boxes would be needed for 6 children? 12 children? 10? 14? 16?

3. Each child must pay 2¢ to come to the circus. Ann has a dime. She can pay for _?_ children. How many groups of 2 pennies are there in 10 pennies? Draw a picture.

4. Use toy pennies to show how many 2-cent tickets Ann can buy for 18¢; 8¢; 2¢; 6¢; 12¢; 14¢; 16¢.

5. Read this table:——————➤

In	2 there is	1	two
In	4 there are	2	twos
In	6 there are	3	twos
In	8 there are	4	twos
In	10 there are	5	twos
In	12 there are	6	twos
In	14 there are	7	twos
In	16 there are	8	twos
In	18 there are	9	twos
In	20 there are	10	twos

6. $8 \div 2$ $6 \div 2$ $12 \div 2$

7. $10 \div 2$ $2 \div 2$ $16 \div 2$

8. $14 \div 2$ $20 \div 2$ $18 \div 2$

1. Martha has 10 pennies. How many 5-cent balls can she buy? How many 2-cent balls can she buy?

2. In 10 there are __?__ 5's. $10 \div 5 =$ __?__
   In 10 there are __?__ 2's. $10 \div 2 =$ __?__

The dot pictures will help you tell the missing numbers:

3. In 8 there are __?__ 2's. $8 \div 2 =$ __?__
   In 8 there are __?__ 4's. $8 \div 4 =$ __?__

4. In 16 there are __?__ 2's. $16 \div 2 =$ __?__
   In 16 there are __?__ 8's. $16 \div 8 =$ __?__

5. In 14 there are __?__ 2's. $14 \div 2 =$ __?__
   In 14 there are __?__ 7's. $14 \div 7 =$ __?__

6. In 18 there are __?__ 2's. $18 \div 2 =$ __?__
   In 18 there are __?__ 9's. $18 \div 9 =$ __?__

7. $3 + 3 = 6$ shows there are __?__ 3's in 6. $6 \div 3 =$ __?__

8. $2 + 2 + 2 = 6$ shows __?__ 2's in 6. $6 \div 2 =$ __?__

9. $6 + 6 = 12$ shows there are __?__ 6's in 12. $12 \div 6 =$ __?__

10. What does $2 + 2 + 2 + 2 + 2 + 2$ teach you?

11. $10 \div 2$ $12 \div 6$ $6 \div 2$ $8 \div 4$

12. $14 \div 7$ $8 \div 2$ $18 \div 9$ $16 \div 8$

13. $16 \div 2$ $2 \div 2$ $10 \div 5$ $4 \div 2$

14. $6 \div 3$ $12 \div 2$ $14 \div 2$ $18 \div 2$

1. Read the division facts of twos like this:

How many twos are there in two? One.
How many twos are there in four? Two; and so on.

Division Facts of Twos

$$\overset{1}{2\overline{)2}} \quad \overset{2}{2\overline{)4}} \quad \overset{3}{2\overline{)6}} \quad \overset{4}{2\overline{)8}} \quad \overset{5}{2\overline{)10}} \quad \overset{6}{2\overline{)12}} \quad \overset{7}{2\overline{)14}} \quad \overset{8}{2\overline{)16}} \quad \overset{9}{2\overline{)18}}$$

$$\overset{2}{1\overline{)2}} \quad \overset{2}{2\overline{)4}} \quad \overset{2}{3\overline{)6}} \quad \overset{2}{4\overline{)8}} \quad \overset{2}{5\overline{)10}} \quad \overset{2}{6\overline{)12}} \quad \overset{2}{7\overline{)14}} \quad \overset{2}{8\overline{)16}} \quad \overset{2}{9\overline{)18}}$$

2. Practice these until you can say every answer:

$2\overline{)16}$ $3\overline{)6}$ $2\overline{)14}$ $2\overline{)4}$ $2\overline{)6}$ $4\overline{)8}$ $2\overline{)2}$ $7\overline{)14}$ $2\overline{)10}$

$5\overline{)10}$ $8\overline{)16}$ $2\overline{)8}$ $9\overline{)18}$ $1\overline{)2}$ $2\overline{)12}$ $2\overline{)18}$ $2\overline{)4}$ $6\overline{)12}$

3. Copy the divisions in Ex. 2 and write the answers.

4. You know that $8 \times 2 = 16$. Then $16 \div 2 = \underline{\ ?\ }$

5. You know that $7 \times 2 = 14$. Then $14 \div 2 = \underline{\ ?\ }$

6. You know that $9 \times 2 = 18$. Then $18 \div 2 = \underline{\ ?\ }$

These four facts belong to a Number Family:

$$6 \times 2 = 12 \qquad 2 \times 6 = 12 \qquad 12 \div 2 = 6 \qquad 12 \div 6 = 2$$

Tell the other members of the family of each of these:

7. $4 \times 2 = 8$ $\qquad 6 \div 3 = 2 \qquad 2 \times 5 = 10 \qquad 16 \div 8 = 2$

8. $2 \times 7 = 14 \qquad 12 \div 2 = 6 \qquad 18 \div 2 = 9 \qquad 2 \times 2 = 4$

9. Make Help-Yourself Cards for the facts in the table above. Practice until you can say every answer.

Uneven division facts of twos

Rose is making some leapfrog beanbags like the one in the picture. She uses buttons for eyes. She needs 2 buttons for each frog. She has 13 buttons. She wonders how many frogs she can make. Can you tell?

Can she make as many as 7? How many buttons will she need for 7 frogs? Has she enough buttons?

She laid out the 13 buttons by 2's like this:

She can see that in 13 buttons there are six 2's and 1 button left over. She decided she could make 6 frogs and have one button left. Is that right?

This picture shows that:

In 3 there is 1 two and 1 over.

In 4 there are 2 twos.

In 5 there are 2 twos and 1 over.

In 6 there are 3 twos.

In 7 there are 3 twos and 1 over.

Uneven division facts of twos

1. Tell how many twos there are in each number from 8 to 20. Begin this way: "In 8 there are 4 twos; in 9 there are 4 twos and 1 left over"; and so on.

2. When Betsy is dividing by 2, she calls these numbers her Dividing-by-Two Helping Numbers. Why?

| 2 | 4 | 6 | 8 | 10 | 12 | 14 | 16 | 18 | 20 |

3. When Betsy finds how many 2's there are in 11, she must *first think*, "How many 2's are there in 10?" *10* is her Helping Number. 10 can be divided by 2 without a remainder.

$$\begin{array}{r} 5\ r1 \\ 2\overline{)11} \end{array}$$

Then she thinks, "There are five 2's in 10."
To find how much is left over, she thinks, "10 from 11 is 1."

4. Read the divisions below. Begin: "In 3 there is one 2 and 1 over; in 5 there are two 2's and 1 over."

Uneven Division Facts of Twos

$$\begin{array}{r} 1\ r1 \\ 2\overline{)3} \end{array} \qquad \begin{array}{r} 2\ r1 \\ 2\overline{)5} \end{array} \qquad \begin{array}{r} 3\ r1 \\ 2\overline{)7} \end{array} \qquad \begin{array}{r} 4r1 \\ 2\overline{)9} \end{array} \qquad \begin{array}{r} 5\ r1 \\ 2\overline{)11} \end{array}$$

$$\begin{array}{r} 6\ r1 \\ 2\overline{)13} \end{array} \qquad \begin{array}{r} 7\ r1 \\ 2\overline{)15} \end{array} \qquad \begin{array}{r} 8\ r1 \\ 2\overline{)17} \end{array} \qquad \begin{array}{r} 9\ r1 \\ 2\overline{)19} \end{array}$$

Betsy knows that 2, 4, 6, 8, 10, and so on are *even numbers*. She knows also that 1, 3, 5, 7, 9, and so on are *odd numbers*. Say all the even numbers to 20; all the odd numbers to 21.

Betsy learned that in finding the number of 2's in an even number there is never anything left over. She learned that in finding the number of 2's in an odd number there is always 1 left over.

5. What Helping Number would you use in finding how many 2's there are in each of these numbers?

   9   13   17   5   11   19   3   15   7

6. If you are dividing the numbers in Ex. 5 by 2, tell what subtractions you do to find the remainders.

7. Practice doing these examples until you can say every answer correctly:

$2\overline{)5}$ $2\overline{)7}$ $2\overline{)9}$ $2\overline{)11}$ $2\overline{)13}$ $2\overline{)15}$ $2\overline{)17}$ $2\overline{)19}$

8. Copy the divisions in Ex. 7 and write the answers.

9. Divide each of these numbers by 2:

   13   7   19   5   11   17   3   9   15

10. Dick has a nickel. How many 2-cent pencils can he buy? How many cents will he have left over?

11. 11 stockings are _?_ pairs and _?_ stocking.

12. Jane has 15 jacks. When she is "for twos," she can pick up 2 jacks _?_ times, and then _?_ jack.

13. If you lay out 17 pennies in piles of 2, you will have _?_ piles of 2 pennies, and _?_ extra penny.

Tell the answers:

14. $13 \div 2$ $9 \div 5$ $19 \div 2$ $11 \div 5$ $13 \div 5$

15. $17 \div 2$ $19 \div 5$ $7 \div 2$ $9 \div 2$ $17 \div 5$

16. What division facts do these drawings show?

Jack said, "May we divide into 2 teams to play dodge ball?"

"Yes, you may," said Miss Bell. "There are 12 of you present today. How many of you will there be on each team?"

Jack said, "One half of 12 children is 6 children. There will be 6 of us on each team."

1. Put your hand over half of the 12 children shown here. You can see __?__ children. You covered __?__ children. $\frac{1}{2}$ of 12 = __?__.

2. Here are 14 balls. Cover one half of the 14 balls. Now you can see __?__ balls. You have covered __?__ balls. $\frac{1}{2}$ of 14 = __?__.

3. Billy said, "I can look at these 10 gumdrops one way and see that $\frac{1}{2}$ of 10 = 5.

"I can look at the box another way and see that there are five 2's in 10; so $10 \div 2 = 5$."

Tell the way Billy looks at the gumdrops to see that $\frac{1}{2}$ of 10 = 5; to see that $10 \div 2 = 5$.

4. Does $\frac{1}{2}$ of 10 equal the same number as $10 \div 2$?

5. How do you look at these caramels to see that $\frac{1}{2}$ of 8 = 4? to see that $8 \div 2 = 4$?

6. Does $\frac{1}{2}$ of 8 equal the same number as $8 \div 2$?

Tell the missing numbers:

1. $\begin{cases} \frac{1}{2} \text{ of } 2 = 1 \\ 2 \div \underline{\ ?\ } = 1 \end{cases}$
4. $\begin{cases} \frac{1}{2} \text{ of } 8 = 4 \\ 8 \div \underline{\ ?\ } = 4 \end{cases}$
7. $\begin{cases} \frac{1}{2} \text{ of } 14 = 7 \\ 14 \div \underline{\ ?\ } = 7 \end{cases}$

2. $\begin{cases} \frac{1}{2} \text{ of } 4 = 2 \\ 4 \div \underline{\ ?\ } = 2 \end{cases}$
5. $\begin{cases} \frac{1}{2} \text{ of } 10 = 5 \\ 10 \div \underline{\ ?\ } = 5 \end{cases}$
8. $\begin{cases} \frac{1}{2} \text{ of } 16 = 8 \\ 16 \div \underline{\ ?\ } = 8 \end{cases}$

3. $\begin{cases} \frac{1}{2} \text{ of } 6 = 3 \\ 6 \div \underline{\ ?\ } = 3 \end{cases}$
6. $\begin{cases} \frac{1}{2} \text{ of } 12 = 6 \\ 12 \div \underline{\ ?\ } = 6 \end{cases}$
9. $\begin{cases} \frac{1}{2} \text{ of } 18 = 9 \\ 18 \div \underline{\ ?\ } = 9 \end{cases}$

10. What is half of each of these numbers? Practice until you know every answer.

12   6   18   4   10   16   2   8   14   20

11. One half of Betsy's 6 chicks are yellow. One half are black. So Betsy has __?__ yellow and __?__ black chicks. $\frac{1}{2}$ of 6 = __?__; 6 ÷ 2 = __?__. Draw a picture.

12. Carl wants $\frac{1}{2}$ pound of feed for his chicks. At 16¢ a pound, what will $\frac{1}{2}$ pound cost? $\frac{1}{2}$ of 16 = __?__. 16 ÷ 2 = __?__.

13. Jack has 18 marbles. He wants to share them equally with Tom. How many should he give Tom? How many should he keep? $\frac{1}{2}$ of 18 = __?__. 18 ÷ 2 = __?__.

▍To find $\frac{1}{2}$ of a number, divide the number by 2.

14. If 14 children divide into 2 equal teams, how many children will there be on each team?

15. Bill went to a "Half-Price Sale." At the sale a 10-cent ball sold for $\frac{1}{2}$ of 10¢, or __?__¢.

16. There are 12 eggs in a dozen. How many eggs are there in a half dozen?

17. A gallon pail is half full of milk. How many quarts of milk are in the pail?

Oral problems

1. Joe saw these airplanes. How many planes are there in each group? in the 3 groups?

2. Sam went to the store to buy 2-cent cookies. He had a dime. He wondered how many cookies he ought to get for a dime. He asked himself, "How many 2's are there in 10?" How many cookies should he get?

3. How many 2-cent cookies could you buy for 6¢? for 10¢? for 14¢? for 8¢? 12¢? 18¢? 16¢? 20¢?

4. When Bob's father takes Bob on the train, he pays only half fare for him. When his father's ticket costs 20¢, Bob's costs _?_. What is the cost of a half fare when the full fare is 8¢? 14¢? 18¢? 12¢? 16¢? 10¢?

5. Jim was standing in line for a drink at the fountain. There were 4 children in front of him and 3 behind him. There were _?_ in line, counting Jim.

6. Miss Smith said, "Half of you children go to the other fountain." The three children behind Jim went. (See Ex. 5.) Should he have gone, too?

7. Name all the numbers from 1 to 20 which have no remainder when divided by 2. Name all the numbers from 1 to 20 which have a remainder when divided by 2.

Problem Test 7

1. How much will 9 paper hats cost at 5¢ each?

2. Mrs. White bought a box of caramels. There were 16 caramels in it. She gave them to the twins to share equally. How many caramels should each get?

3. How many bookmarks, 5 inches long, can be cut from a yard of ribbon? How much ribbon will be left?

4. Mary paid 10¢ for a thimble, 29¢ for scissors, 5¢ for needles, and 15¢ for a zipper. How much did she spend in all?

5. Miss Smith bought a box of flower bulbs. There were 90 bulbs in it. She planted 65 bulbs. She said Billy might have the others for the school garden. Do you know how many bulbs Billy got?

6. How much change would you get from a 5-dollar bill after buying a bathing suit for $2.49?

7. Find the cost of a bathing suit at $2.79, bathing slippers at $.49, and a bathing cap for $.39.

8. Tony can get a tennis racket at the Fun Shop for $3.25, or one at the Sport Center for $2.89. How much can he save if he buys at the Sport Center?

9. Sally and her mother are canning strawberries. They have their gallon kettle half full of cooked berries. How many quart jars will they need?

10. How many clothespins will Marie need to hang up 7 pairs of socks, if she uses a clothespin for each sock?

Write your score on your Problem Test Record.

Self-Help Test 11

1. 347
   65
   289
   174 (200)

2. $9 + 5 + 5 + 7$ (120–122)

3. $3.84 + $6.75 (158)

4. $9 + $.36 + $4.86 (164)

5. $3.84 − $2.70 (152)

6. $8 − $4.64 (198–199)

7. $9 − $.25 (198–199)

Subtract and check:

8. 179
   93 (100)

9. 96
   37 (131–135)

10. 983
    316 (192)

11. 652
    278 (195)

12. $9.00
    4.67 (198)

Self-Help Test 12

1. At the store Sue can buy gumdrops by the package. There are 5 gumdrops in 1 package. She wants 20 gumdrops. How many packages should she buy? (216)

2. Write the sum of $3000 + 400 + 20 + 7$. (223–224)

3. Does $9 + 9 = 18$ prove that $2 \times 9 = 18$? (235)

4. Carl says that $2 + 2 + 2 + 2 + 2 + 2 = 12$ shows that there are 2 sixes in 12. Is he right? (235)

5. How many 2-cent balloons can you get for 15¢? How much will you have left over? (249–251)

6. Draw 2 chocolate bars the same size. Show that $\frac{1}{2}$ of a bar is more than $\frac{1}{3}$ of a bar. (11)

7. How many 5-cent whistles can you buy for 49¢? How much will you have left over? (226–228)

8. Jean practices her music 45 minutes each day. She has practiced 15 minutes today. How much longer must she practice? (47–48)

Using addition

1. Dan wants to buy a key chain for $.98, a knife for $1.39, and a whistle for $.35. How much will the chain, knife, and whistle cost?

2. Ann wants to buy a pair of roller skates for $3.98 and a hockey stick for $1.19. How much will the skates and stick cost?

3. Before doing the additions below, take the test on page 110.

Write the sums on folded paper. Check carefully.

	a	b	c	d	e	f	g
4.	79	57	98	17	36	645	493
	67	75	49	68	82	179	248
5.	43	74	27	78	56	289	156
	95	95	76	95	79	158	498
	89	38	79	28	67	374	288
6.	62	94	51	76	64	574	177
	95	96	83	68	79	86	696
	80	85	79	35	67	230	83
7.	74	7	78	25	66	508	93
	5	57	69	94	9	96	899
	39	89	86	9	87	89	9
	96	74	4	86	8	275	167
8.	$.85	$.04	$.36	$.05	$.90	$3.12	$2.49
	.50	.10	.95	.47	.32	1.79	5.05
	.04	.47	.62	.58	.45	2.34	.60
	.89	.69	.75	.73	.60	4.75	6.74

1. George has $5.00. How much will he have left if he buys a cowboy hat for $2.98?

2. Tom has $.79. He wants to buy a red reflector for the mudguard of his bike. It costs $1.25. How much more money does he need?

3. Jane has 113 names in her birthday book. Betty has 97. How many more does Jane have than Betty?

4. Before doing the subtractions below, take the test on page 111.

Subtract. Use folded paper. Check.

	a	b	c	d	e	f
5.	84 63	46 18	462 187	473 289	572 287	887 93
6.	90 23	47 39	874 357	507 186	462 185	984 275
7.	56 48	47 38	598 279	684 439	750 284	506 237
8.	65 29	23 18	560 283	358 195	653 649	802 463
9.	194 46	540 87	700 87	800 197	600 345	500 287
10.	$2.03 .68	$3.84 .97	$4.63 1.74	$6.00 1.74	$7.00 .96	$8.50 1.87

11. PUZZLE. Dan subtracted a number from 500. His answer was 263. What number did he subtract?

Yes or no

Read each question. Then write on your paper the number of the question and the answer "Yes" or "No."

1. Does $16 \div 2 = 8$?

2. Does $9 \times 2 = 2 \times 9$?

3. Does $14 \div 2 = \frac{1}{2}$ of 14?

4. Does $0 + 8 = 8$?

5. Does $6 + 6 = 2 \times 6$?

6. Is 20 an odd number?

7. Can odd numbers be divided evenly by 2?

8. Is 1,000 the same as 10 hundreds?

9. Is 587 nearer to 600 than to 500?

10. Is one thousand sixty written like this: 1,006?

11. Do you add to find how much more Jim weighs than Judy?

12. Are there 36 inches in a yard?

13. If a foot of wire is cut in the middle, is each piece 6 inches long?

14. In 15 are there seven 2's and 1 left over?

15. To check subtraction, do you add the answer to the number that is subtracted?

16. Does $\$7.00 = 6$ dollars, 9 dimes, and 10 cents?

17. Is 9786 less than 9876?

18. If $7 + 9 = 16$, does $16 - 9 = 7$?

Are the answers to these examples correct?

19.
$$
\begin{array}{r}
765 \\
48 \\
70 \\
4 \\
\hline
887
\end{array}
$$

20.
$$
2\overline{)19} \quad 8 \text{ r}1
$$

21.
$$
\begin{array}{r}
\$9.00 \\
- 7.37 \\
\hline
\$2.63
\end{array}
$$

22.
$$
\begin{array}{r}
\$56.09 \\
.90 \\
.03 \\
40.00 \\
\hline
\$97.00
\end{array}
$$

1. Add 5 to each of the numbers below:

92   43   56   78   89   54   67   45

2. Add 6 to each number in Ex. 1. Add 7; 8; 9; 10.

3. Subtract 5 from each number in Ex. 1. Subtract 6; subtract 7; 8; 9; 10.

4. $324 = 300 + 20 +$?

5. $324 = 304 +$?

6. $324 = 124 +$?

7. $324 = 200 +$?

8. $324 = 320 +$?

9. $324 = 100 + 200 +$?

10. $537 = 530 +$?

11. $537 = 500 +$?

12. $537 = 300 + 200 +$?

13. $537 = 500 + 30 +$?

14. $537 = 507 +$?

15. $537 = 137 +$?

16. Add 20 to each of the numbers in Ex. 1.

17. Add 21 to each number in Ex. 1. Add this way: first add the 20, then add the 1.

18. Add 22 to each number in Ex. 1; add 23; add 30; add 31; add 34; add 40; add 42; add 45.

19. Subtract 20 from each number in Ex. 1.

20. Subtract 21 from each number in Ex. 1. Subtract this way: first subtract 20, and then subtract 1.

21. Subtract 22 from each number in Ex. 1; subtract 30; subtract 31; 32; 40; 42.

Can you figure out these missing numbers?

22. $803 +$? $= 853$

23. $550 -$? $= 500$

24. $700 +$? $+ 5 = 785$

25. ? $- 70 = 302$

Multiplying two-place
numbers with and
without carrying

UNIT
39

Multiplying two-place numbers

1. Dick wants to buy 4 batteries for his flashlight. They cost 12¢ each. First try to find out *without help* how much the 4 batteries will cost. Then study these three ways of finding the cost of 4 batteries.

Adding to find the cost of 4 batteries:

1 battery costs $.12
1 battery costs $.12
1 battery costs $.12
1 battery costs $.12
$.48 ← By adding you find that
4 batteries cost $.48.

Using coins to find the cost of 4 batteries:

Use toy coins (dimes and cents) to show that if one battery costs 12¢ (1 dime and 2 cents), then 4 batteries will cost 4 dimes and 8 cents, or 48¢.

Multiplying to find the cost of 4 batteries:

▶ If 1 battery costs $.12, then 4 batteries cost 4 times $.12:———————————————→

$$\begin{array}{r} \$.12 \\ \times 4 \\ \hline \$.48 \end{array}$$

▶ Think, "4 times 2 cents is 8 cents." Write the 8 in the cents column.

▶ Think, "4 times 1 dime is 4 dimes." Write the 4 in the dimes column. Write the dollar sign and cents point.

▶ The multiplication shows that 4 batteries cost 4 dimes and 8 cents, or $.48.

2. Most children prefer to *multiply* to find the answer to a problem like the one above. Why?

3. Find the cost of 3 batteries at $.12 each by adding; by using coins; by multiplying. Are the answers the same?

4. Multiply. Check to see if the answers are sensible.

$.22	$.33	$.43	$.24	$.22	$.44
× 4	× 2	× 2	× 2	× 3	× 2

5. Nancy needs some name tapes to sew on her clothes for camp. She can get 3 dozen name tapes for $1.00. Find without help how many name tapes there are in 3 dozen.

Study these 2 ways of finding how many tapes there are in 3 dozen. Which way do you like better?

Adding to find how many tapes in 3 dozen:

Number of tapes in 1 dozen = 12
Number of tapes in 1 dozen = 12
Number of tapes in 1 dozen = 12
By adding you find the number of tapes in 3 dozen = 36

Multiplying to find how many tapes in 3 dozen:

▶ If there are 12 tapes in 1 dozen, then in 3 dozen there are 3 times 12 tapes:——————————————▶

$$\begin{array}{r} 12 \\ \times 3 \\ \hline 36 \end{array}$$

▶ Think, "3 times 2 ones are 6 ones." Write the 6 in the ones column.

▶ Think, "3 times 1 ten is 3 tens." Write the 3 in the tens column.

▶ The multiplication shows that 3 dozen are _?_.

6. Multiply to find how many there are in 2 doz.; in 4 doz.

7.

34	44	22	24	22	33
× 2	× 2	× 3	× 2	× 4	× 2

8. See if your answers in Ex. 7 are sensible. In the first one think, "34 is *more than* 3 tens. 2 × 3 tens = 6 tens, or 60. My answer should be *more than* 60." Is it?

Multiplying zeros

Miss Bell's class had these multiplications to do:

40	10	20	20	20	10	30	10
×2	×4	×2	×3	×4	×5	×2	×3

Tom's way

Tom said, "I do these multiplications in my head. In the first one I see that $40 = 4$ tens; so 2×4 tens $= 8$ tens, or 80." Tell how Tom did the other examples.

Frank's way

Frank said, "I write the examples this way:⟶
I think 2×0 ones $= 0$ ones. I write the 0 in ones place. I think 2×4 tens is 8 tens. I write the 8 in tens place. My answer is 80."

$$\begin{array}{r} 40 \\ \times 2 \\ \hline 80 \end{array}$$

1. Grace asked, "How do you know that $2 \times 0 = 0$, Frank?"

Frank said, "Look at these additions. The first shows that 2 zeros are zero."

$$\begin{array}{r} 0 \\ +0 \\ \hline 0 \end{array} \qquad \begin{array}{r} 0 \\ 0 \\ +0 \\ \hline 0 \end{array} \qquad \begin{array}{r} 0 \\ 0 \\ 0 \\ +0 \\ \hline 0 \end{array}$$

What multiplication facts do Frank's other additions show?

2. Write an addition that proves that 5 zeros are zero.

3. How much is any number times zero?

4. Copy the multiplications at the top of the page. Multiply, using Frank's way.

5. Molly said, "Tom's way of multiplying is good when you do those multiplications mentally. Frank's way is good when you do them as written work."

Go back and see how Tom and Frank multiplied. Do you agree with Molly?

Do these multiplications mentally. Then copy them and do them as written work.

1.
$$\begin{array}{ccccccccc} 10 & 10 & 10 & 10 & 10 & 10 & 10 & 10 & 10 \\ \times 1 & \times 2 & \times 3 & \times 4 & \times 5 & \times 6 & \times 7 & \times 8 & \times 9 \end{array}$$

2.
$$\begin{array}{cccccc} 31 & 14 & 12 & 40 & 13 & 20 \\ \times 2 & \times 2 & \times 3 & \times 2 & \times 2 & \times 2 \end{array}$$

3.
$$\begin{array}{cccccc} \$.12 & \$.20 & \$.11 & \$.41 & \$.21 & \$.30 \\ \times 4 & \times 3 & \times 6 & \times 2 & \times 3 & \times 2 \end{array}$$

4. Joe wants to buy 6 jars of paint (blue, green, red, black, white, yellow). The jars cost $.21 each. Try to find without help how much the 6 jars will cost.

To find the cost of 6 jars at $.21 each, you find 6 times $.21:————————————————→

$$\begin{array}{r} \$ .21 \\ \times 6 \\ \hline \$1.26 \end{array}$$

▶ Think, "6 times 1 cent is 6 cents." Write the 6 in the cents column.

▶ Think, "6 times 2 dimes is 12 dimes; but 12 dimes = 10 dimes and 2 dimes = 1 dollar and 2 dimes." Write 2 in the dimes column. Write 1 in the dollars column.

▶ Don't forget to write the dollar sign and cents point.

▶ The multiplication shows that 6 jars of paint at $.21 each will cost __?__. Use toy money to prove this multiplication.

5. Do an addition to prove the multiplication in Ex. 4.

6. To find the cost of 7 jars of paint at $.21 a jar, Joe wrote: ——→ Explain his work. Show two other ways to find the cost of 7 jars.

6 jars cost	$1.26
1 jar costs	$ .21
7 jars cost	$1.47

Multiplication practice

1. Find the cost of 5 yards of ribbon at $.31 a yard; at $.51 a yard; at $.71 a yard.

2. John needs 7 feet of rubber cord for his chemistry set. The cord costs $.21 a yard. How much will 7 feet cost?

3. Cover the answers to this row of examples. Multiply. Then see if your answers are correct.

$ .71	$.12	$ .81	$.20	$ .50	$ .51	$ .52
× 5	× 2	× 2	× 3	× 6	× 8	× 4
$3.55	$.24	$1.62	$.60	$3.00	$4.08	$2.08

Multiply. Check by using toy money.

4. $.80	$.21	$.50	$.20	$.60	$.91	$.51
× 5	× 6	× 8	× 7	× 5	× 2	× 9

5. $.52	$.91	$.50	$.81	$.41	$.22	$.71
× 3	× 5	× 5	× 5	× 2	× 3	× 5

6. Teddy knows there are 52 weeks in a year. He says he can find out how many weeks there are in 3 years by finding 3 × 52. Can you?

▶ There are 52 weeks in 1 year, so in 3 years there are 3 times 52 weeks:⟶

$$\begin{array}{r} 52 \\ \times 3 \\ \hline 156 \end{array}$$

▶ To find 3 times 52, think, "3 times 2 ones are 6 ones." Where do you write the 6?

▶ Think, "3 times 5 tens are _?_ tens; but 15 tens = 10 tens and 5 tens = 1 hundred and 5 tens." In which column do you write the 5? the 1?

▶ The multiplication shows there are _?_ weeks in 3 years.

7. 91	70	21	52	92	83	81
× 5	× 5	× 7	× 4	× 2	× 2	× 5

Multiplying with carrying

For a class picnic Jean is to buy 6 packages of rolls at $.12 a package. First try to find out *without help* how much the 6 packages will cost. Then study these 3 ways of finding the cost of 6 packages of rolls.

Adding to find the cost of 6 packages of rolls:

1 package costs $.12
1 package costs $.12
1 package costs $.12
1 package costs $.12
1 package costs $.12
1 package costs $.12

By adding, you find 6 packages cost $.72

Using coins to find the cost of 6 packages of rolls:

Use toy coins (dimes and cents) to show that if 1 package costs 12¢ (1 dime and 2 cents), then 6 packages will cost 6 dimes and 12 cents, or 7 dimes and 2 cents, or 72¢.

Multiplying to find the cost of 6 packages of rolls:

▶If 1 package costs $.12, then 6 packages cost 6 times $.12:——————————————————→

```
$.12
   6
$.72
```

▶Think, "6 times 2 cents is 12 cents; but 12 cents = 1 dime and 2 cents." Write the 2 in the cents column. (*Carry* 1 dime to dimes column.)

▶Think, "6 times 1 dime is 6 dimes, plus the 1 dime to carry is 7 dimes." Where do you write the 7?

▶6 packages of rolls at 12¢ a package cost   ? .

Is the cost of the rolls the same when you find it by adding as when you find it by multiplying? Which way is shorter?

1. The following multiplications are done correctly. Explain each one. Then copy them without the answers and multiply. Look to see if your answers are right.

$.15	$.12	$ .25	$ .52	$ .25	15	22	55
× 6	× 5	× 4	× 7	× 8	× 3	× 9	× 8
$.90	$.60	$1.00	$3.64	$2.00	45	198	440

Multiply. Check by using toy money.

2.

$.22	$.25	$.52	$.21	$.21	$.52	$.15	$.12
× 5	× 9	× 4	× 9	× 8	× 5	× 5	× 4

3.

$.25	$.13	$.12	$.22	$.52	$.25	$.51	$.52
× 8	× 5	× 6	× 6	× 6	× 5	× 4	× 8

4.

12	15	51	19	26	15	57	12
× 3	× 2	× 5	× 5	× 5	× 4	× 2	× 7

5.

51	12	15	27	22	51	15	51
× 2	× 5	× 8	× 5	× 2	× 9	× 7	× 3

6. Do Exs. 2 and 3 mentally. To do the first example in Ex. 2, Jean thought, "$.22 = 2 dimes and 2 cents. 5×2 dimes = 10 dimes, or 1 dollar. 5×2 cents = 10 cents. My answer is one dollar and ten cents."

To do the next one in Ex. 2, Tom thought, "25¢ = 1 quarter. 4 quarters = $1.00; 8 quarters = $2.00; 9 quarters = $2.25; so $9 \times \$.25 = \$2.25$."

7. The school is going to plant 5 rows of pansy plants. There will be a dozen plants in each row. How many plants are needed?

8. Judy has 3 packs of drawing paper. There are 25 sheets in each pack. How many sheets of paper has she?

267

1. Take the tests on pages 110 and 111 today.

Add and check:

2.	79	3.	289	4.	$4.10	5.	$5.62
	63		46		1.12		2.84
	23		543		2.25		9.73
	53		271		4.39		4.87

Subtract and check:

6.	380	7.	407	8.	$8.95	9.	$4.00
	254		178		6.78		2.76

10. A half dollar is worth 1 quarter, 1 dime, and _?_ nickels.

11. A dollar is worth 3 quarters and _?_ nickels.

12. A dollar is worth 2 quarters and _?_ dimes.

13. A yard = _?_ feet; a foot = _?_ inches.

14. A quart = _?_ pints; a gallon = _?_ quarts.

15. What is the largest three-figure number you can write with the figures 7, 5, and 9? the smallest number?

16. There are 5 school days in a week. How many school days are there in 2 weeks? 5 weeks? 9 weeks?

17. Susan needs a new hat and coat. If the hat costs $2.98 and the coat $9.98, what will be the total cost?

18. Judy bought shoes for $3.95, socks for $.19, and gloves for $.59. How much did she pay in all?

19. Tom gathered a gallon of maple syrup. He wants to put it in pint jars. How many pint jars will he need? You may have to draw a picture of this problem.

Dividing larger numbers

Ralph and Nancy want to share these caramels.

There are _?_ boxes; _?_ caramels in each box; _?_ caramels in all.

Ralph said, "We each get $\frac{1}{2}$ of 4 boxes, or _?_ boxes. That is _?_ caramels."

Nancy said, "Yes, we each get $\frac{1}{2}$ of 40 caramels, or _?_ caramels."

1. $\frac{1}{2}$ of 4 tens = _?_ tens; $\frac{1}{2}$ of 40 = _?_. So $40 \div 2 =$ _?_.

2. $\frac{1}{2}$ of 6 tens = _?_ tens; $\frac{1}{2}$ of 60 = _?_. So $60 \div 2 =$ _?_.

3. $\frac{1}{2}$ of 8 tens = _?_ tens; $\frac{1}{2}$ of 80 = _?_. So $80 \div 2 =$ _?_.

4. $\frac{1}{2}$ of 10 tens = _?_ tens; $\frac{1}{2}$ of 100 = _?_. So $100 \div 2 =$ _?_.

5. $\frac{1}{2}$ of 12 tens = _?_ tens; $\frac{1}{2}$ of 120 = _?_. So $120 \div 2 =$ _?_.

6. $\frac{1}{2}$ of 14 tens = _?_ tens; $\frac{1}{2}$ of 140 = _?_. So $140 \div 2 =$ _?_.

Bob and Barbara want to share these gumdrops. There are _?_ full boxes; _?_ gumdrops in each full box; _?_ gumdrops in 4 full boxes; 6 extra gumdrops; _?_ gumdrops in all.

First they shared the full boxes. Then each had $\frac{1}{2}$ of 40 gumdrops, or _?_ gumdrops.

Next they shared the 6 separate gumdrops. $\frac{1}{2}$ of 6 gumdrops is _?_ gumdrops. Then each had 20 gumdrops + 3 gumdrops, or _?_ gumdrops.

$\frac{1}{2}$ of 40 is _?_; $\frac{1}{2}$ of 6 is _?_; $\frac{1}{2}$ of 46 is _?_.

1. To find $\frac{1}{2}$ of 64, think, "$\frac{1}{2}$ of 60 = __?__; $\frac{1}{2}$ of 4 = __?__; $\frac{1}{2}$ of 64 = 30 + 2, or __?__."

2. If you know that $\frac{1}{2}$ of 64 is 32, then 64 ÷ 2 = __?__.

3. To find $\frac{1}{2}$ of 86, think, "$\frac{1}{2}$ of 80 = __?__; $\frac{1}{2}$ of 6 = __?__; $\frac{1}{2}$ of 86 = 40 + 3, or __?__."

4. If you know that $\frac{1}{2}$ of 86 = 43, then 86 ÷ 2 = __?__.

5. To find $\frac{1}{2}$ of 106, think, "$\frac{1}{2}$ of 100 = __?__; $\frac{1}{2}$ of 6 = __?__; $\frac{1}{2}$ of 106 = 50 + 3, or __?__."

6. If you know that $\frac{1}{2}$ of 106 = 53, then 106 ÷ 2 = __?__.

7. To find $\frac{1}{2}$ of 128, think, "$\frac{1}{2}$ of 120 = __?__; $\frac{1}{2}$ of 8 = __?__; $\frac{1}{2}$ of 128 = 60 + 4, or __?__."

8. If you know that $\frac{1}{2}$ of 128 = 64, then 128 ÷ 2 = __?__.

Remember, no pencils. Tell what you think to find:

9. $\frac{1}{2}$ of 48 $\frac{1}{2}$ of 86 $\frac{1}{2}$ of 68 $\frac{1}{2}$ of 82

10. $\frac{1}{2}$ of 108 $\frac{1}{2}$ of 142 $\frac{1}{2}$ of 124 $\frac{1}{2}$ of 166

11. $\frac{1}{2}$ of 188 $\frac{1}{2}$ of 164 $\frac{1}{2}$ of 148 $\frac{1}{2}$ of 128

12. $\frac{1}{2}$ of 126 $\frac{1}{2}$ of 104 $\frac{1}{2}$ of 168 $\frac{1}{2}$ of 146

13. If $\frac{1}{2}$ of 48 is 24, then 48 ÷ 2 = __?__.

14. If $\frac{1}{2}$ of 64 is __?__, then 64 ÷ 2 = __?__.

15. If $\frac{1}{2}$ of 108 is __?__, then 108 ÷ 2 = __?__.

16. If 2 boys share 88 stamps equally, each will get __?__ stamps.

17. If 2 girls share 48 paper dolls equally, each girl will get __?__ dolls.

Three ways to do a division

Tom and Ellen gathered 48 sea shells, which they want to share equally. How many shells should each take?

Tell what you think when you find ½ of 48.

Peter solved the problem this way:

½ of 40 is 20; ½ of 8 is 4. So ½ of 48 is 20 + 4, or __?__ .

Jane solved the problem this way:

48 is 4 tens and 8 ones.

½ of 4 tens is 2 tens; ½ of 8 ones is 4 ones. So ½ of 48 is 2 tens and 4 ones, or __?__ .

Bill solved the problem this way:

▶He wrote the example like this:———————➤ $2\overline{)48}$

▶He thought, "2 in 4, 2 times," and wrote the 2 above the 4.

$$\begin{array}{r} 24 \\ 2\overline{)48} \end{array}$$

▶Then he thought, "2 in 8, 4 times," and wrote the 4 above the 8.

▶Then he said, "My work shows that 48 ÷ 2 = 24; or that ½ of 48 is 24. Tom and Ellen should each take 24 shells."

1. Copy these examples without the answers and divide as Bill did. When you finish each one, look to see if your answer is right and if it is written in the right place.

23	41	22	21	21	43
$2\overline{)46}$	$2\overline{)82}$	$3\overline{)66}$	$4\overline{)84}$	$3\overline{)63}$	$2\overline{)86}$

2. How many songbooks will be needed for 64 children, if 2 children share each book?

3. If one grapefruit serves 2 persons, how many grapefruit are needed for 28 persons?

271

How many piles of pennies, with 2 pennies in a pile, can you make with 128 pennies?

Tom solved the problem this way:

128 = 12 tens and 8 ones; 12 tens ÷ 2 = 6 tens; 8 ones ÷ 2 = 4 ones. So 128 ÷ 2 = 6 tens and 4 ones, or 64. 128 pennies make 64 piles of pennies, with 2 pennies in each pile.

Jean solved the problem this way:

▶ She wrote the division like this: ⟶ $2\overline{)128}$

▶ She thought, "2 in 12, 6 times." She wrote 6 as shown in the box.

▶ She thought, "2 in 8, 4 times." She wrote 4 as shown in the box.

$$\begin{array}{r} 64 \\ 2\overline{)128} \end{array}$$

▶ She said, "My work shows that 128 ÷ 2 is 64. 128 pennies make 64 piles of pennies with 2 pennies in each pile."

Copy these divisions. Divide as Jean did. Then check each answer by Tom's method of dividing.

1. $2\overline{)146}$ $2\overline{)108}$ $2\overline{)124}$ $2\overline{)162}$ $2\overline{)86}$ $2\overline{)148}$

2. $2\overline{)64}$ $2\overline{)186}$ $2\overline{)164}$ $2\overline{)102}$ $2\overline{)48}$ $2\overline{)184}$

3. $2\overline{)168}$ $2\overline{)142}$ $2\overline{)128}$ $2\overline{)82}$ $2\overline{)42}$ $2\overline{)104}$

4. Find $\frac{1}{2}$ of 188; of 166; of 144; of 84; of 182; of 22.

5. Billy and Tom bought a bag of 146 jelly beans. How many will each boy get if they share them equally?

6. Jack is helping a florist plant 164 tulip bulbs in pots. They put 2 bulbs in each pot. They will need _?_ pots.

Dividing zero

1. How many peanuts will Dick and Sue each get if they share equally 12 peanuts? 10 peanuts? 8? 6? 4? 2? 0?

2. Dick says Ex. 1 uses these divisions. Do you agree?

$$\overset{6}{2)\overline{12}} \qquad \overset{5}{2)\overline{10}} \qquad \overset{4}{2)\overline{8}} \qquad \overset{3}{2)\overline{6}} \qquad \overset{2}{2)\overline{4}} \qquad \overset{1}{2)\overline{2}} \qquad \overset{0}{2)\overline{0}}$$

3. Sue says Exs. 1 and 2 show that *zero divided by 2 is zero.* Prove that Sue is right.

4. How many peanuts will each of 5 boys get if they share equally 20 peanuts? 15 peanuts? 10? 5? 0?

5. What divisions do you use in Ex. 4?

6. Does Ex. 4 show that *zero divided by 5 is zero?*

7. Make a rule for dividing zero by 3; by 4; by 6.

Copy and divide. The first row is done to help you. Check each answer to see if it is sensible.

8. $\overset{40}{2)\overline{80}} \qquad \overset{30}{5)\overline{150}} \qquad \overset{50}{5)\overline{250}} \qquad \overset{80}{2)\overline{160}} \qquad \overset{40}{5)\overline{200}} \qquad \overset{60}{5)\overline{300}}$

9. $5)\overline{350} \qquad 4)\overline{40} \qquad 5)\overline{450} \qquad 2)\overline{180} \qquad 5)\overline{50} \qquad 5)\overline{400}$

10. $3)\overline{150} \qquad 6)\overline{120} \qquad 2)\overline{120} \qquad 7)\overline{140} \qquad 2)\overline{140} \qquad 8)\overline{160}$

11. Five girls bought a bag of 105 jelly beans. If the girls share them equally, how many beans will each girl get?

12. Miss Bell asked Tom, Jerry, and Jim to set out 60 pansy plants in the school garden. If the boys share the work equally, how many pansy plants will each boy set out?

Bob and Dick want to share 47 marbles equally.

▶ Bob said, "½ of 40 marbles is 20 marbles; ½ of 7 marbles is 3 marbles with 1 marble left over. So ½ of 47 marbles is 23 marbles and 1 marble left over. We'll each take 23 marbles. Let's give Ted the 1 marble that's left over."

▶ To find how many marbles each should take, Dick divided 47 by 2 like this:——▶

$$\begin{array}{r} 23\text{ r1} \\ 2\overline{)47} \end{array}$$

Explain his division. It shows that each boy should take _?_ marbles. There is _?_ marble left over.

Copy and divide. See if each answer is sensible.

	a	b	c	d	e	f
1.	42 r1 2)85	54 r1 2)109	71 r1 2)143	31 r1 5)156	64 r1 2)129	91 r2 5)457
2.	5)256	5)405	5)306	2)167	5)358	2)185
3.	2)43	2)25	2)149	5)57	2)123	5)355
4.	2)45	5)107	2)183	2)87	2)105	2)125
5.	5)158	2)86	5)456	2)69	5)406	2)189
6.	5)209	2)67	5)307	2)187	5)259	2)128
7.	2)163	5)409	2)147	5)308	2)107	5)207

Now is the time to test yourself

Copy the numbers correctly in this test. Work carefully. Check your answers.

1. 21
    × 8

2. 25
    × 9

3. $.28
    × 5

4. 2)86   5. 5)355   6. 2)87

7. Caramels cost 64¢ a pound. How much should Nancy pay for a half pound of them?

8. Here are 4 ways to write what this box of candies shows:

- 7 + 7 = 14
- 2 sevens are 14
- 14 ÷ 2 = 7
- 7 × 2 = 14

Write what it shows in 3 other ways.

9. How many 2-cent plants can you buy with 45¢? Will you have any money left? If so, how much?

10. Find the cost of eight games at $.52 each.

Just for fun

Find the sum of the numbers in each row of this square.

Find the sum of the numbers in each column.

Find the sum of the numbers on the red arrow; on the black arrow.

Are all your sums the same? If so, this is a magic square.

Sensible answers

1. How much change will you get from $1.00 if you spend 49¢ for a pocket knife? This is the way Jim solved the problem: ⟶

Wrong
$1.00
−.49
$ .61

Bobby looked at Jim's work and said, "Your answer isn't sensible. 49¢ is about 50¢. 50¢ from $1.00 leaves 50¢. Your change should be *about* 50¢. Your answer is 61¢. That's too much."

What should Jim's answer be?

Whenever you solve a problem, you should always look at the answer to see if it is sensible. This is called *estimating your answer*. Estimating will help you get correct answers.

2. Ann found the cost of 4 books at 51¢ each: ➤

Wrong
$ .51
4
$204

Is her answer sensible? Think, "51¢ is about 50¢. 2 books at 50¢ each would cost $1.00; so 4 books would cost $2.00. The answer should be *about* $2.00."

What mistake did Ann make when she wrote her answer? Would she have made that mistake if she had estimated her answer?

3. Judy found the cost of a 98-cent game, a 2-dollar book, and a 49-cent puzzle: ⟶

Wrong
$ .98
2.00
.49
$2.47

Is her answer sensible? Think, "98¢ is about $1.00. $1.00 and $2.00 are $3.00. $3.00 and $.49 are $3.49. The answer should be *about* $3.49."

What mistake did Judy make in her addition?

4. Estimate the cost of 3 pairs of socks at 49¢ a pair.

Estimating answers

At the end of each of the following problems there are three answers. None of the answers is exactly correct, but one is almost correct.

Tell which answer is almost correct and tell why you think so. Then work each problem to see whether you chose the answer that is nearest to being right.

1. Dotty would like to give each of 4 friends a bar of pink soap. The soap costs 19¢ a bar. Will 4 bars cost about $.50, $.80, or $2.00?

2. Eric wants a raincoat that costs $3.98 and a pair of rubbers that costs $1.50. Will both of them cost about $4.00, $5.00, or $5.50?

3. Andy and Billy found 162 nuts. They divided them equally. Did each get about 80 nuts, 60 nuts, or 90 nuts?

4. Becky has $9.96. If she buys a doll carriage for $7.98, will she have left about $3.00, $2.00, or $1.00?

5. Susan's father gave her 84¢ and sent her to the post office for 2-cent stamps. Can she get about 40 or 60 or 30 stamps?

6. If you buy a 49-cent ball and give the clerk a dollar, will your change be about 40¢, 60¢, or 50¢?

7. If you buy a 28-cent game and give the clerk a half dollar, will your change be about 20¢, 30¢, or 40¢?

8. If you spend 68¢ and give the clerk a dollar, will your change be about 40¢, 20¢, or 30¢?

9. If one yard of gingham costs $.22, will 5 yards cost about $2.00, $1.00, or $1.50?

1. Add and check:

a	b	c	d	e	f	g
3	4	5	$4.04	7	3	45
6	8	6	.94	538	21	450
7	5	7	.05	0	4	540
9	7	8	.01	82	87	405
8	6	5	.66	467	584	504

2. Subtract and check:

a	b	c	d	e	f
784	408	349	400	307	633
692	278	76	146	49	150

3. Do each of these multiplication examples, and then add 2 to each answer. In the first example, think, "6 fives are 30, and 2 are 32."

5	7	5	9	5	2	6	2	5	3
6	5	8	5	5	8	2	9	1	5

4. Do each of the above multiplication examples again, adding 3 to each answer; adding 4 to each answer.

5. Multiply; then check by going over your work:

25	52	28	22	11	21	52	29
2	9	2	5	5	5	8	5

6. Divide:

5)8   2)17   5)18   5)17   2)17   2)13   5)27

7. Count by 5's to 50, beginning "5, 10, 15," and so on.

278

Be your own teacher

Good thinkers like to figure out things for themselves. They *teach themselves* how to solve hard problems. See how many ways the class can find to do each problem.

1. Mary wants to serve ½ of a cantaloupe to each of 7 persons. How many cantaloupes should she buy?

2. Jane has 1½ pounds of popcorn, to be shared equally by 3 children. What part of a pound will each get?

3. George has saved 230 pennies. How many quarters can he get for them? How many pennies will be left over?

4. Sue's father bought 13 gallons of gasoline for 25 cents a gallon. He offered to buy her an ice-cream cone if she could figure out the cost of the gasoline. She won the ice-cream cone. Could you have won it?

5. Grace bought 2½ yards of gingham for a new dress. The gingham cost 40 cents a yard. Her mother gave her a dollar. How much change, if any, did she get?

6. Bob buys meat for his dog. It costs 40¢ a pound. How much money does he need for ¼ pound? for ¾ pound?

7. Tom is going to cut a 10-foot pole into stakes each 2½ feet long. How many of the stakes can he get? You will need to draw a picture to help you see this.

8. Thirty-five pupils spent $5.60 for a picnic. Bill had to figure out each pupil's share of the cost.

He thought, "If each one pays 10 cents, I'll collect $3.50; if each one pays 5 cents more, I'll collect __?__"; and so on. Finish Bill's work.

To the Teacher: See Note 6 on page 311.

UNIT

42

Multiplying dollars and cents
Multiplying three-place numbers,
including zeros

Multiplying dollars and cents

1. Billy needs new tires for his bicycle. Can you find out without help how much a pair of Standard Tires will cost at the tire sale? Look at the picture below.

To find the cost of 2 Standard Tires at $3.12 each, you find 2 times $3.12:————————————————→

$$\begin{array}{r} \$3.12 \\ \times 2 \\ \hline \$6.24 \end{array}$$

▶ Think, "2 times 2 cents is _?_ cents." Where do you write the 4?

▶ Think, "2 times 1 dime is _?_ dimes." Where do you write the 2?

▶ Think, "2 times 3 dollars is _?_ dollars." Where do you write the 6?

▶ Write the dollar sign and cents point. The multiplication shows that 2 Standard Tires will cost _?_.

Copy and multiply:

2. $\begin{array}{r} \$1.23 \\ \times 2 \\ \hline \end{array}$ $\qquad$ $\begin{array}{r} \$4.32 \\ \times 2 \\ \hline \end{array}$ $\qquad$ $\begin{array}{r} \$3.24 \\ \times 2 \\ \hline \end{array}$ $\qquad$ $\begin{array}{r} \$1.34 \\ \times 2 \\ \hline \end{array}$ $\qquad$ $\begin{array}{r} \$2.11 \\ \times 2 \\ \hline \end{array}$ $\qquad$ $\begin{array}{r} \$4.33 \\ \times 2 \\ \hline \end{array}$

3. Find the cost of 2 bicycle handle-bar grips at $1.23 each.

Bicycle Tire Sale

Standard Tires $ 3.12 each
Improved Tires $ 3.49 each
Long-Wear Tires $ 3.92 each
Very Best Tires $ 4.69 each

4. To find the cost of 2 Improved Tires at $3.49 each, you find 2 times $3.49:————→

$$\begin{array}{r} \$3.49 \\ \times 2 \\ \hline \$6.98 \end{array}$$

▶Think, "2 times 9 cents is 18 cents; but 18 cents = 1 dime and 8 cents." Write 8 in the cents column. (Don't forget the 1 dime to carry to the dimes column.)

▶Think, "2 times 4 dimes is 8 dimes, plus the 1 dime to carry is _?_ dimes." Where do you write the 9?

▶Tell how to finish the multiplication. It shows that 2 Improved Tires will cost _?_.

Copy and multiply:

5. $\begin{array}{r}\$1.12\\ \times 5\\ \hline\end{array}$ $\begin{array}{r}\$3.48\\ \times 2\\ \hline\end{array}$ $\begin{array}{r}\$2.37\\ \times 2\\ \hline\end{array}$ $\begin{array}{r}\$1.45\\ \times 2\\ \hline\end{array}$ $\begin{array}{r}\$2.16\\ \times 2\\ \hline\end{array}$ $\begin{array}{r}\$4.19\\ \times 2\\ \hline\end{array}$

6. $\begin{array}{r}\$2.15\\ \times 3\\ \hline\end{array}$ $\begin{array}{r}\$1.15\\ \times 4\\ \hline\end{array}$ $\begin{array}{r}\$1.12\\ \times 8\\ \hline\end{array}$ $\begin{array}{r}\$1.14\\ \times 5\\ \hline\end{array}$ $\begin{array}{r}\$1.13\\ \times 5\\ \hline\end{array}$ $\begin{array}{r}\$4.39\\ \times 2\\ \hline\end{array}$

7. Find the cost of a pair of new bicycle pedals at $2.15 each; at $2.35 each.

8. How much will 2 bicycle pumps cost at $1.49 each?

9. A red plastic, streamlined bicycle headlight costs $1.38. A horn to match is the same price. How much money will Doris need for the light and horn?

10. Both Roy and his brother want wire baskets to put on the handle bars of their bicycles. The baskets cost $1.37 each. How much will the two baskets cost?

11. Both Fred and Don need new chains for their bicycles. The chains cost $1.29 each. How much will two chains cost?

12. Bicycle coaster brakes cost $4.25 each. How much will two brakes cost?

1. To find the cost of 2 Long-Wear Bicycle Tires at $3.92 each, you find 2 times $3.92:———————————→

▶Think, "2 times 2 cents is _?_ cents." Where do you write the 4?

$$\begin{array}{r} \$3.92 \\ \times 2 \\ \hline \$7.84 \end{array}$$

▶Think, "2 times 9 dimes is _?_ dimes; but 18 dimes is 1 dollar and 8 dimes." Write the 8 in the dimes column. (Don't forget the 1 dollar to carry to the dollars column.)

▶Think, "2 times 3 dollars is _?_ dollars, plus the 1 dollar to carry is 7 dollars." Tell how to finish the multiplication. It shows that 2 Long-Wear Tires cost _?_.

2.
$1.64	$4.73	$1.51	$3.82	$2.91	$4.83
× 2	× 2	× 5	× 2	× 2	× 2

3. To find the cost of 2 Very Best Tires at $4.69 each, you find 2 times $4.69:———————————→

▶Think, "2 times 9 cents is 18 cents; but 18 cents = 1 dime and 8 cents." Where do you write the 8?

$$\begin{array}{r} \$4.69 \\ \times 2 \\ \hline \$9.38 \end{array}$$

▶Think, "2 times 6 dimes is 12 dimes, plus 1 dime to carry is 13 dimes. But 13 dimes = 1 dollar and 3 dimes." Where do you write the 3?

▶Think, "2 times 4 dollars is _?_ dollars, plus 1 dollar to carry is _?_ dollars." Tell how to finish the multiplication. It shows that 2 Very Best Tires cost _?_.

4. Copy without answers and multiply. Then check.

$5.25	$5.25	$2.15	$2.52	122	252
4	5	7	6	8	6
$21.00	$26.25	$15.05	$15.12	976	1512

Multiply:

1. $2.65 × 2 $1.67 × 5 $3.98 × 2 $1.87 × 5 $1.55 × 4 $1.55 × 3

2. $2.55 9 $9.15 5 $1.52 6 $2.57 5 $5.25 8 $2.55 6

3. $2.54 5 $2.55 3 $5.52 8 $5.22 3 $5.26 5 $5.22 9

4. 528 2   251 2   524 5   559 5   515 5   522 7

Work each problem below. Then check your answer by estimating to see if it is sensible.

5. How much will 5 books cost at $.72 each?

6. Find the cost of 8 dolls at $2.25 each.

7. What will the nine suits for a boys' baseball team cost if one suit costs $5.22?

8. Miss Smith has 7 nephews. She plans to buy them each a sailboat. The sailboats cost $2.55 each. How much will all the boats cost?

9. Both Betsy and Jack want tennis rackets that cost $3.85 each. How much will two rackets cost?

10. Find the cost of a half-dozen hats at $1.15 each.

11. If Mr. King buys each of his 3 boys a sweater for $3.85, how much will the 3 sweaters cost?

12. The fare from Upton to Dover is $1.25. How much will it cost four Scouts to go from Upton to Dover?

13. Find the cost of two pairs of sandals at $2.75 a pair.

1. 3×2 ones = _?_ ones; 3×2 = _?_
   3×2 tens = _?_ tens; 3×20 = _?_
   3×2 hundreds = _?_ hundreds; 3×200 = _?_

2.

2	20	200	4	40	400
$\times 3$	$\times 3$	$\times 3$	$\times 2$	$\times 2$	$\times 2$

Explain the multiplication examples that are done. Then do the others. Read your answers.

3.

	a	b	c	d	e	f	g
	20	20	20	20	$.20	$.20	$.20
	3	4	7	5	8	6	9
	60	80	140				

4.

200	300	500	300	$5.00	$5.00	$2.00
2	5	5	2	4	2	5

5. What is the cost of 8 toy airplanes at 10¢ each?

6. Judy bought a box of candy for 80¢. There are 2 pounds in it. She paid _?_¢ a pound for the candy.

7. Jerry is reading a book of 120 pages. He has read 60 pages. Has he read half the book?

8. Ann bought 4 packages of napkins. There were 100 napkins in each package. She bought _?_ napkins.

9. Nancy paid 50¢ for a package containing 5 handkerchiefs. How much did each handkerchief cost?

10. How many sheets of writing paper are needed to give 2 sheets of paper to each of 20 children?

11. If there are 500 paper napkins in one package, how many are there in 3 packages?

Multiplying zeros

1. Mary needed to find 2 times 201. She thought, "2 × 200 is 400; 2 × 1 is 2. So 2 times 201 is 400 + 2, or _?_."

2. To find 3 × 105, think, "3 × 100 is _?_; 3 × 5 is _?_; so 3 × 105 is 300 + 15, or _?_."

Tell what you think to find:

3. 3 × 102   2 × 203   4 × 201   2 × 303   2 × 206

4. 2 × 308   5 × 105   5 × 109   6 × 102   7 × 105

5. Nancy found 2 × 201 this way:————————→

$$\begin{array}{r} 201 \\ \times\,2 \\ \hline 402 \end{array}$$

▶ She thought, "2 × 1 = 2." She wrote the 2 in the ones place.

▶ She thought, "2 × 0 tens = 0 tens." She wrote the 0 in the tens place.

▶ She thought, "2 × 2 hundreds = 4 hundreds." She wrote 4 in the hundreds place. 2 × 201 = _?_.

$$\begin{array}{r} 105 \\ \times\,3 \\ \hline 315 \end{array}$$

6. To find 3 × 105, think, "3 × 5 = _?_." Write the 5 in ones place and carry the 1 ten.

▶ "3 × 0 tens = _?_ tens. But I have 1 ten to carry; 0 + 1 to carry = 1." Write the 1 in tens place.

▶ "3 × 1 hundred = _?_ hundred." Write the 3 in the hundreds place. So 3 × 105 = _?_.

Multiply. Check to see if each answer is sensible.

7.
102	201	502	201	$3.02	$2.08	$5.03
3	4	3	3	5	5	5

8.
201	102	505	502	$5.01	$2.06	$2.05
7	2	2	4	2	5	3

285

Getting ready to multiply threes

Ted said the pan of gingerbread boys below teaches him these facts:

1. 6 threes are 18
2. 3 sixes are 18
3. $6 + 6 + 6 = 18$
4. $3 + 3 + 3 + 3 + 3 + 3 = 18$
5. In 18 there are 3 sixes.
6. In 18 there are 6 threes.

Make a list of the things each of the other pictures below teaches you.

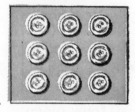 

7. Write an addition which shows there are 3 sevens in 21. Write an addition which shows there are 7 threes in 21.

8. If you know that 3 fives are 15, you also know that 5 threes are __?__.

9. Draw a picture to show that 4 threes are twice as many as 2 threes.

10. Are 8 threes twice as many as 4 threes?

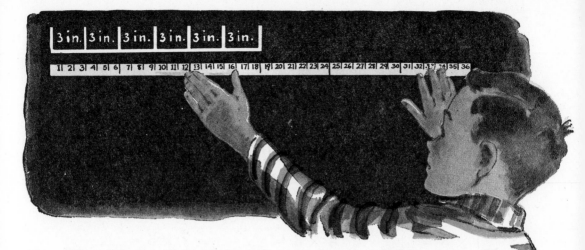

The Adams School is going to have a field meet. Six of the children in Miss Bell's room are on the Red Team. Six are on the Blue Team.

Each child on the Red Team will wear a red ribbon badge 3 inches long. The Blue Team will wear blue badges. How would you find out how much red ribbon to buy? how much blue ribbon?

1. Jane is to buy the red ribbon.

Jane said, "For each badge we need 3 inches. I'll put down six 3's in a column and add. That will give me the number of inches of red ribbon we need for 6 badges."

How many inches will Jane find are needed?

$$\begin{array}{r} 3 \\ 3 \\ 3 \\ 3 \\ 3 \\ 3 \\ \hline \end{array}$$

2. Look at Peter's work on the blackboard. How is he finding out how much ribbon is needed for 6 badges, each 3 inches long? What will his answer be?

3. Dick is to buy the blue ribbon. He said, "I'll multiply to find six 3's. That's the shortest way. $6 \times 3 = 18$." Is Dick right?

$$\begin{array}{r} 3 \\ \times 6 \\ \hline 18 \end{array}$$

4. Count by 3's from 3 to 30.

Multiplication facts of threes

1. In the picture below, how many balloons are there in 1 bunch? 2 bunches? 3? 4? 5? 6? 7? 8? 9? 10?

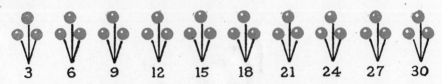

3   6   9   12   15   18   21   24   27   30

2. Use the balloons to find these missing numbers:

$1 \times 3 = \underline{\ ?\ }$ $4 \times 3 = \underline{\ ?\ }$ $7 \times 3 = \underline{\ ?\ }$

$2 \times 3 = \underline{\ ?\ }$ $5 \times 3 = \underline{\ ?\ }$ $8 \times 3 = \underline{\ ?\ }$

$3 \times 3 = \underline{\ ?\ }$ $6 \times 3 = \underline{\ ?\ }$ $9 \times 3 = \underline{\ ?\ }$

3. The picture of stars below shows that $4 \times 3 = 12$ and $3 \times 4 = 12$. Tell 2 multiplication facts that each of the other pictures shows.

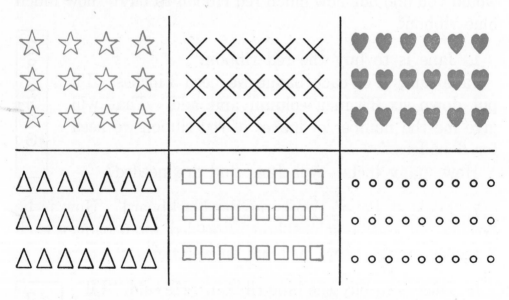

4. $8 + 8 + 8 = 24$ shows that 3 eights are $\underline{\ ?\ }$.

5. Write an addition which shows that $4 \times 3 = 12$. Write an addition which shows that $3 \times 4 = 12$.

6. Read the multiplication facts of threes. Say, "1 times 3 is 3; 2 times 3 is 6"; and so on.

Multiplication Facts of Threes

3 ×1 3	3 ×2 6	3 ×3 9	3 ×4 12	3 ×5 15	3 ×6 18	3 ×7 21	3 ×8 24	3 ×9 27
1 ×3 3	2 ×3 6	3 ×3 9	4 ×3 12	5 ×3 15	6 ×3 18	7 ×3 21	8 ×3 24	9 ×3 27

7. Practice these multiplication facts of threes until you can give every answer correctly:

3 × 8	5 × 3	3 × 2	3 × 6	3 × 9	3 × 3	4 × 3	7 × 3
2 × 3	3 × 5	1 × 3	8 × 3	6 × 3	3 × 4	9 × 3	3 × 7

8. Say each answer in Ex. 7. Then, after you say the answer, add 1 to it.

9. Copy Ex. 7 and write the answers. Then use addition to prove your answers.

10. At 3¢ each, find the cost of 2 balloons; 8 balloons; 5 balloons; 6; 9; 3; 4; 7.

11.

$$\underline{?} \times 3 = 15 \qquad \underline{?} \times 3 = 12 \qquad \underline{?} \times 3 = 18$$
$$\underline{?} \times 3 = 24 \qquad \underline{?} \times 3 = 21 \qquad \underline{?} \times 3 = 27$$
$$\underline{?} \times 3 = 6 \qquad \underline{?} \times 3 = 3 \qquad \underline{?} \times 3 = 9$$

12. Find the cost of eight 3-cent stamps.

13. Make and study Help-Yourself Cards for threes.

1. If a quart of ice cream serves 8 persons, how many persons can be served from 3 quarts?

2. How many children are needed to form 3 teams with 9 children on a team?

3. If 1 bench seats 3 persons, how many persons can sit on 3 benches? 6? 9? 8? 7?

Multiply. Check each answer by seeing if it is sensible.

4.	304	127	154	203	$2.35	$3.84
	5	3	2	3	4	3

5.	495	809	516	203	$6.27	$2.35
	3	5	3	6	3	7

6.	105	738	150	840	$7.80	$9.59
	8	3	9	3	2	3

7.	160	153	270	608	$3.81	$2.35
	3	4	3	5	3	6

8.	103	492	213	503	$3.03	$6.14
	7	3	8	3	9	3

9. At $2.35 a pair, find the cost of 3 pairs of sandals; of 6 pairs; 7; 8; 9.

10. At $1.23 a pair, find the cost of 3 pairs of bathing slippers; of 6 pairs; 7; 8; 9.

11. Use addition to find the cost of 3 pairs of shorts at $1.49 a pair.

12. Now use multiplication to do Ex. 11. Do you get the same answer you got by adding?

Put on your thinking cap

▶ Oral review

Tell the missing numbers:

1. 1 week = _?_ days
2. 1 year = _?_ months
3. 1 hour = _?_ minutes
4. VIII = _?_
5. 1 quarter = _?_ nickels
6. 1 dollar = _?_ dimes
7. 1 pint = _?_ glasses
8. 1 quart = _?_ pints

9. 1 gallon = _?_ quarts
10. 1 yard = _?_ inches
11. 1 yard = _?_ feet
12. 1 foot = _?_ inches
13. 1 dozen = _?_ things
14. 1 pair = _?_ things
15. 80 = _?_ tens
16. 3500 = _?_ hundreds

17. If you can get a set of six arrows for $5.98, would you estimate the cost of one arrow to be about $1.50, or $1.00?

18. Read these numbers: 705   892   1,225   1,476

19. How many sides has a square? a triangle?

20. A pint equals what part of a quart?

▶ Written review

1. $\begin{array}{r} 12 \\ \times\,3 \\ \hline \end{array}$

2. $\begin{array}{r} 35 \\ \times\,8 \\ \hline \end{array}$

3. $\begin{array}{r} \$.25 \\ \times\,7 \\ \hline \end{array}$

4. $\begin{array}{r} \$2.15 \\ \times\,6 \\ \hline \end{array}$

5. $2\overline{)48}$

6. $5\overline{)48}$

7. $2\overline{)129}$

8. $5\overline{)257}$

9. $8.62 + $5

10. $8 − $2.46

11. ½ of 18 = _?_

12. Don's uncle sent a box of 6 dozen oranges from Florida. How many oranges was that?

13. ⅕ of 45 = _?_

14. 4 + 7 + 5 + 8 = _?_

291

UNIT
44

Even and uneven
division facts of threes
Finding one third of a
number

Using threes in division

1. Ted has 18¢. Try to find out *without help* how many 3-cent apples he can buy.

Here are 18 dots to show the 18¢. Ted is drawing a line around each group of 3 dots. When he has finished, the drawing will show that you can divide 18 cents into __?__ groups of 3 cents. There are __?__ 3's in 18.

Ted can get __?__ 3-cent apples for 18¢.

2. How do these subtractions prove that there are 6 threes in 18? ————————→

3. __?__ × 3 = 15   __?__ × 3 = 12   __?__ × 3 = 18
   __?__ × 3 = 24   __?__ × 3 = 21   __?__ × 3 = 27
   __?__ × 3 = 6   __?__ × 3 = 3   __?__ × 3 = 9

$$18$$
$$-3\checkmark$$
$$15$$
$$-3\checkmark$$
$$12$$
$$-3\checkmark$$
$$9$$
$$-3\checkmark$$
$$6$$
$$-3\checkmark$$
$$3$$
$$-3\checkmark$$
$$0$$

4. $8 \times 3 = 24$, so $24 \div 3 =$ __?__.

5. $6 \times 3 = 18$, so $18 \div 3 =$ __?__.

6. $9 \times 3 = 27$, so $27 \div 3 =$ __?__.

7. $7 \times 3 = 21$, so $21 \div 3 =$ __?__.

8. $3 + 3 + 3 + 3 + 3 + 3 = 18$ shows that there are __?__ 3's in 18.

The dot picture below shows these 4 facts:

$7 \times 3 = 21$ $21 \div 7 = 3$
$3 \times 7 = 21$ $21 \div 3 = 7$

9. What 4 facts does each dot picture below show?

10. Read the division facts below like this: "In 3 there is 1 three; in 6 there are 2 threes"; and so on.

11. Now read the facts this way: "How many threes in 3? One. How many threes in 6? Two."

Division Facts of Threes

$$3\overline{)3}^{\,1} \quad 3\overline{)6}^{\,2} \quad 3\overline{)9}^{\,3} \quad 3\overline{)12}^{\,4} \quad 3\overline{)15}^{\,5} \quad 3\overline{)18}^{\,6} \quad 3\overline{)21}^{\,7} \quad 3\overline{)24}^{\,8} \quad 3\overline{)27}^{\,9}$$

$$1\overline{)3}^{\,3} \quad 2\overline{)6}^{\,3} \quad 3\overline{)9}^{\,3} \quad 4\overline{)12}^{\,3} \quad 5\overline{)15}^{\,3} \quad 6\overline{)18}^{\,3} \quad 7\overline{)21}^{\,3} \quad 8\overline{)24}^{\,3} \quad 9\overline{)27}^{\,3}$$

12. Say the answers. Use a drawing if you need help.

$3\overline{)3} \quad 5\overline{)15} \quad 3\overline{)6} \quad 3\overline{)21} \quad 3\overline{)9} \quad 7\overline{)21} \quad 3\overline{)12} \quad 3\overline{)27} \quad 4\overline{)12}$

$3\overline{)9} \quad 3\overline{)18} \quad 8\overline{)24} \quad 1\overline{)3} \quad 3\overline{)24} \quad 9\overline{)27} \quad 2\overline{)6} \quad 6\overline{)18} \quad 3\overline{)15}$

13. Copy the examples in Ex. 12 and write the answers.

14. Roy uses 3 buttons for wheels on each of his model airplanes. He has 12 buttons. He has enough wheels for _?_ planes. Think, "He uses 3 buttons on 1 plane; so he can make as many planes as there are 3's in 12. $12 \div 3 = $ _?_ ".

15. How many yards are there in 3 ft.? in 6 ft.? in 9 ft.? in 24 ft.? 12? 27? 15? 18? 21? Use a yardstick to prove your answers are right.

16. At 3¢ each, how many balloons can Ann buy for 15¢? for 12¢? for 18¢? 27¢? 24¢? 21¢? 6¢? 9¢? 3¢?

17. Ann needs 15 hair curlers. The curlers come 3 on a card. How many cards of curlers should Ann buy?

18. Make and study Help-Yourself Cards.

Finding one third of a number

Bob bought a bag of peanuts. He wants to share them equally with Jack and Jerry. How many peanuts should each boy get? There are 24 peanuts in the bag.

He said, "If I had an apple to share equally among the three of us, I'd cut it into *three equal parts*. Each part would be *one third* of the apple.

"I can't cut a bag of peanuts into three equal pieces, but I can divide the peanuts into three equal piles."

1. Deal out 24 peanuts into three equal piles. You may use small pieces of paper if you have no peanuts. How many are in each pile?

2. Deal out 21 cards into 3 equal piles. How many are in each pile? $\frac{1}{3}$ of 21 = _?_; 21 ÷ 3 = _?_.

3. Deal out 18 cards into 3 equal piles. How many are in each pile? $\frac{1}{3}$ of 18 = _?_; 18 ÷ 3 = _?_.

4. Deal out 9 cards into 3 equal piles. How many are in each pile? $\frac{1}{3}$ of 9 = _?_; 9 ÷ 3 = _?_.

5. Find $\frac{1}{3}$ of 6 peanuts; of 15 peanuts; of 12; of 18; of 27; 24; 21; 9; 3.

6. Find $\frac{1}{3}$ of 27; of 18; of 9; 21; 12; 3; 24; 15.

7. If 3 girls share 18 gumdrops equally, how many gumdrops will each girl get?

8. If 3 boys share 24 rubber bands equally, how many bands will each boy get?

9. If 2 boys share 18 cents equally, each boy will get _?_ ¢. But if 3 boys share 18¢ equally, each boy will get only _?_ ¢.

10. To find $\frac{1}{3}$ of a number, divide the number by _?_.

294

Oral problems

1. If you have a dime, how many three-cent stamps can you buy and how much change will you get? Draw a picture.

2. Find the cost of 6 three-cent stamps; of 7; 8; 10.

3. Sally needs 18 buttons for a dress. The buttons are sold 6 on a card. How many cards of buttons does she need?

4. How many feet are there in a yard? in 2 yards? in 5 yards? 9? Use a yardstick to prove your answers.

5. How many yards are there in 27 feet? in 21 feet?

6. If 4 children share a dozen cookies, how many cookies will each child get?

7. If 2 children share a dozen cookies, how many cookies will each child get?

8. Mary paid 15¢ for a set of 5 drawing pencils. She knows how much she paid for each pencil. Do you?

9. Jane has 14 slices of bread. If she uses 2 slices of bread for 1 sandwich, how many sandwiches can she make for a class picnic?

10. The 20 children in Miss Bell's class wanted to divide into 3 equal groups for a game.
John said, "We can't do it."
Betty said, "We can, if Miss Bell plays with us."
What did John and Betty mean?

11. How many safety matchboxes would you need to make 3 of these doll bureaus?

Ann and Jean like to play jacks. One day Ann said, "Jean, did you ever think that when we play jacks we keep dividing over and over again?"

"Yes," answered Jean. "I'm 'for threes.' Look! In our 10 jacks I can pick up 3 jacks 3 times and then the 1 jack that is left over."

How many times could the girls pick up 3 jacks if they had 8 jacks? 9 jacks? 11 jacks? 12? 13? 14? 15? How many jacks would be left over each time?

Look at the next drawing and say, "Three in 6, 2 times; three in 7, 2 times and 1 over"; and so on.

1. Name all the numbers from 3 to 30 that can be divided by 3 without a remainder. Name all that can be divided with a remainder.

2. Name your Dividing-by-Three Helping Numbers.

3. What Helping Number would you use in finding how many 3's there are in each of these numbers?

13	8	19	4	14	5	11	23	20
7	28	26	10	22	16	29	25	17

4. In dividing the numbers in Ex. 3, tell what subtractions you must do to find the remainders.

5. Divide each of the numbers in Ex. 3 by 3. Say the answers first.
Then write the divisions like this:——————➔

$$\begin{array}{r} 4\ \text{r1} \\ 3\overline{)13} \end{array}$$

6. How many 3-cent stamps can you buy for a nickel? for a dime? for a quarter? How many cents will you have left each time?

Oral practice

Use your head — not your pencil — on these problems.

1. Multiply 5 by each of the numbers below; then multiply 2 by each number below; then 3; then 1.

    8   5   9   2   7   6   4   3   1

2. Divide each of the numbers below by 2; by 3; by 5.

    9   12   16   11   14   19   13   10   15

3. Add 7 to each of the numbers below; add 8; add 9.

   34   56   12   78   23   19   45   67   21

4. Subtract 6 from each of the numbers below; subtract 5; subtract 4.

   22   53   19   31   75   40   64   23   41

5. If 1 bench will seat 3 persons, how many persons can sit on 7 benches? 8 benches? 6? 9? 5?

6. Tom has 35 books to carry to the office for Miss Bell. If he carries 7 books at a time, how many trips will he have to make?

7. Ann can get 2 candy kisses for a cent. How many can she get for 2¢? for 4¢? 5¢? 7¢? 8¢? 9¢?

Toothbrush	$.15
Pencil	$.05
Crayon	$.10
Notebook	$.12
Thread	$.10
Needles	$.08
Thimble	$.10
Toothpaste	$.20
Rag doll	$.25
Toy airplane	$.10
Ball	$.15

Junior Red Cross problems

Miss Bell's class is packing a Junior Red Cross box.

1. Ann has a quarter. Choose 3 things she could buy that add up to 25¢ or less.

2. Peter bought a ball, notebook, and toothbrush to put in a Red Cross box. How much did those things cost?

3. Choose 4 things you would like to send in a box. How much would they cost?

4. If you had 35¢, what things could you buy for a box?

5. What problems has your class had with Red Cross boxes?

Dividing larger numbers

1. Roy, Bob, and Terry have offered to help Miss Bell stamp some new books with the school seal. There are 96 books to be stamped. Can you tell how many books each should stamp if they share the work equally?

Roy said, "96 books is 90 books and 6 books. $\frac{1}{3}$ of 90 is the same as $\frac{1}{3}$ of 9 tens, or 3 tens. That's 30. $\frac{1}{3}$ of 6 is 2. So $\frac{1}{3}$ of 96 is 30 + 2, or 32. We should each stamp 32 books." $96 \div 3 =$ _?_

2. To find $\frac{1}{3}$ of 123, think, "123 is 120 + 3. $\frac{1}{3}$ of 120 is the same as $\frac{1}{3}$ of 12 tens. $\frac{1}{3}$ of 12 tens is 4 tens, or _?_. $\frac{1}{3}$ of 3 is _?_. So $\frac{1}{3}$ of 123 is 40 + 1, or _?_. $123 \div 3 =$ _?_."

Tell what you think when you find:

3. $\frac{1}{3}$ of 69 $\frac{1}{3}$ of 150 $\frac{1}{3}$ of 180 $\frac{1}{3}$ of 240

4. $\frac{1}{3}$ of 36 $\frac{1}{3}$ of 156 $\frac{1}{3}$ of 189 $\frac{1}{3}$ of 243

Copy and divide. When you finish each division, tell what you think to see if the answer is sensible.

5. $3\overline{)156}$ $3\overline{)39}$ $3\overline{)213}$ $9\overline{)270}$ $3\overline{)129}$ $2\overline{)186}$

6. $4\overline{)248}$ $3\overline{)157}$ $3\overline{)63}$ $3\overline{)215}$ $3\overline{)188}$ $3\overline{)277}$

7. $3\overline{)37}$ $3\overline{)127}$ $3\overline{)64}$ $3\overline{)94}$ $8\overline{)240}$ $5\overline{)157}$

8. $7\overline{)218}$ $3\overline{)187}$ $3\overline{)245}$ $5\overline{)357}$ $3\overline{)125}$ $3\overline{)98}$

9. Molly bought a package of flower seeds. There are 96 seeds in the package. If 3 children share the seeds equally, how many seeds will each get?

10. Jane baked 63 cookies to sell. If she packs the cookies in bags, 3 cookies to a bag, how many bags will she need?

Use folded paper when you do these examples:

	a	b	c	d	e
1.	531 287 614 +513	208 24 765 +498	1 52 689 +735	45 316 25 +843	674 2 35 +918
2.	735 98 +324	969 48 +903	89 362 + 84	888 78 +690	66 508 +870
3.	609 −430	394 −185	967 −705	567 −298	842 −300
4.	500 −387	658 − 49	970 −709	807 −699	650 −586
5.	$.26 × 5	$.35 × 5	$.53 × 9	$3.51 × 8	$2.55 × 4
6.	$3.57 × 3	$3.32 × 6	$3.23 × 5	$2.39 × 3	$1.38 × 3
7.	$3.35 × 7	$3.15 × 6	$5.23 × 5	$2.35 × 4	$5.33 × 3

Copy and divide:

8.	3)96	3)98	2)165	3)276	3)247
9.	5)259	6)186	7)217	2)186	3)274
10.	3)185	2)149	8)248	4)128	5)355

Test on multiplication facts

Write the answers to these multiplication examples on folded paper. If you make a mistake in any row, practice the whole row until you can do it without a mistake.

1.
$$\begin{array}{c}2\\ \underline{1}\end{array} \qquad \begin{array}{c}3\\ \underline{3}\end{array} \qquad \begin{array}{c}5\\ \underline{7}\end{array} \qquad \begin{array}{c}3\\ \underline{5}\end{array} \qquad \begin{array}{c}5\\ \underline{5}\end{array} \qquad \begin{array}{c}5\\ \underline{8}\end{array}$$

2.
$$\begin{array}{c}1\\ \underline{2}\end{array} \qquad \begin{array}{c}4\\ \underline{3}\end{array} \qquad \begin{array}{c}8\\ \underline{5}\end{array} \qquad \begin{array}{c}6\\ \underline{2}\end{array} \qquad \begin{array}{c}7\\ \underline{5}\end{array} \qquad \begin{array}{c}2\\ \underline{2}\end{array}$$

3.
$$\begin{array}{c}3\\ \underline{1}\end{array} \qquad \begin{array}{c}3\\ \underline{4}\end{array} \qquad \begin{array}{c}3\\ \underline{7}\end{array} \qquad \begin{array}{c}3\\ \underline{6}\end{array} \qquad \begin{array}{c}3\\ \underline{2}\end{array} \qquad \begin{array}{c}1\\ \underline{1}\end{array}$$

4.
$$\begin{array}{c}1\\ \underline{3}\end{array} \qquad \begin{array}{c}5\\ \underline{3}\end{array} \qquad \begin{array}{c}2\\ \underline{3}\end{array} \qquad \begin{array}{c}7\\ \underline{3}\end{array} \qquad \begin{array}{c}5\\ \underline{4}\end{array} \qquad \begin{array}{c}4\\ \underline{1}\end{array}$$

5.
$$\begin{array}{c}4\\ \underline{5}\end{array} \qquad \begin{array}{c}1\\ \underline{4}\end{array} \qquad \begin{array}{c}6\\ \underline{3}\end{array} \qquad \begin{array}{c}1\\ \underline{8}\end{array} \qquad \begin{array}{c}5\\ \underline{9}\end{array} \qquad \begin{array}{c}2\\ \underline{6}\end{array}$$

6.
$$\begin{array}{c}8\\ \underline{3}\end{array} \qquad \begin{array}{c}4\\ \underline{2}\end{array} \qquad \begin{array}{c}6\\ \underline{5}\end{array} \qquad \begin{array}{c}5\\ \underline{1}\end{array} \qquad \begin{array}{c}8\\ \underline{1}\end{array} \qquad \begin{array}{c}9\\ \underline{2}\end{array}$$

7.
$$\begin{array}{c}9\\ \underline{5}\end{array} \qquad \begin{array}{c}7\\ \underline{2}\end{array} \qquad \begin{array}{c}3\\ \underline{8}\end{array} \qquad \begin{array}{c}2\\ \underline{4}\end{array} \qquad \begin{array}{c}1\\ \underline{7}\end{array} \qquad \begin{array}{c}1\\ \underline{5}\end{array}$$

8.
$$\begin{array}{c}1\\ \underline{9}\end{array} \qquad \begin{array}{c}2\\ \underline{9}\end{array} \qquad \begin{array}{c}1\\ \underline{6}\end{array} \qquad \begin{array}{c}2\\ \underline{7}\end{array} \qquad \begin{array}{c}5\\ \underline{2}\end{array} \qquad \begin{array}{c}2\\ \underline{8}\end{array}$$

9.
$$\begin{array}{c}9\\ \underline{1}\end{array} \qquad \begin{array}{c}5\\ \underline{6}\end{array} \qquad \begin{array}{c}3\\ \underline{9}\end{array} \qquad \begin{array}{c}8\\ \underline{2}\end{array} \qquad \begin{array}{c}9\\ \underline{3}\end{array} \qquad \begin{array}{c}2\\ \underline{5}\end{array}$$

Write the answers to these examples on folded paper. If you make a mistake in any row, practice the whole row until you can do it without a mistake.

1. $3\overline{)3}$ $2\overline{)2}$ $4\overline{)20}$ $1\overline{)4}$ $5\overline{)45}$ $1\overline{)9}$

2. $2\overline{)12}$ $3\overline{)24}$ $2\overline{)4}$ $6\overline{)30}$ $3\overline{)27}$ $5\overline{)40}$

3. $1\overline{)8}$ $4\overline{)8}$ $3\overline{)9}$ $2\overline{)6}$ $5\overline{)10}$ $2\overline{)10}$

4. $1\overline{)7}$ $5\overline{)30}$ $2\overline{)8}$ $1\overline{)6}$ $3\overline{)15}$ $9\overline{)27}$

5. $5\overline{)20}$ $7\overline{)7}$ $1\overline{)5}$ $5\overline{)25}$ $7\overline{)35}$ $2\overline{)18}$

6. $4\overline{)12}$ $7\overline{)14}$ $5\overline{)5}$ $8\overline{)40}$ $3\overline{)21}$ $3\overline{)18}$

7. $6\overline{)6}$ $2\overline{)14}$ $8\overline{)16}$ $5\overline{)35}$ $9\overline{)45}$ $7\overline{)21}$

8. $8\overline{)24}$ $2\overline{)16}$ $9\overline{)18}$ $3\overline{)6}$ $3\overline{)12}$ $6\overline{)18}$

9. $6\overline{)12}$ $5\overline{)15}$ $1\overline{)2}$ $9\overline{)9}$ $1\overline{)3}$ $1\overline{)1}$

Problems without numbers

1. Jane knows how much money she has in her bank and how much she earned by running errands. To find how much money she has all together, she should _?_ (add, subtract, multiply, divide).

2. Bill knows how many rows of seats there are in his classroom. He knows the number of seats in each row. He can find the number of seats in the room by _?_ (adding, subtracting, multiplying, dividing).

3. Dick and Jack want to share some cookies equally. To find how many cookies each should have, they should _?_.

4. Betsy mailed invitations to her birthday party. She knows how many stamps she used and how much each stamp cost. To find the cost of all the stamps, she should _?_.

5. Tom knows how much money he has. He knows how much roller skates cost. To find how much more he needs to buy the skates, he should _?_.

6. Cora knows the price of one dozen eggs. To find how much she should pay for $\frac{1}{2}$ dozen eggs, she should _?_.

7. Jack knows how many pages there are in his book. He knows how many pages he has read. To find how many more pages he must read, he should _?_.

8. Molly knows how many cookies she needs for a party. She knows how many cookies there are in one package. To find how many packages to buy, she should _?_.

9. Ted knows how much one flashlight battery costs. He knows how many batteries he needs for his flashlight. Tell what you think to find the cost of the batteries.

1. Miss Wall's class needs 5 packages of paper plates for a picnic. Each package costs 10¢. To find how much all the plates will cost, Jean thought, "One package of plates will cost 10¢. Five packages will cost 5 times 10¢, or _?_¢."

2. Tell what Jean would think in finding how much 8 packages of paper cups would cost at 5¢ a package.

3. Tell what Jean would think in finding how much the paper plates and paper cups would cost together.

4. Tell what you would think in finding how many "hot dog" rolls there are in two dozen.

5. Mary has 35¢. She wants to treat her friends to 5-cent ice-cream cones. To find how many cones she can buy, she thinks, "I can buy 1 cone for each 5¢ in the 35¢; so I can buy as many cones as there are 5's in 35, or _?_ cones."

6. Tell what you would think in finding how many 3-cent apples you could buy for 15¢.

7. The baker has chocolate cakes for 40¢ each. To find how much she should pay for half a cake, Nancy thought, "The whole cake costs 40¢. One half of the cake would cost only $\frac{1}{2}$ of 40¢, or _?_¢."

8. Five boys bought a bag of peanuts. There were 30 peanuts in the bag. Tell what you would think in finding out how many peanuts each boy should have.

9. Make up a problem for each of these. Ask a classmate to solve the problem. $18 \div 3$ 3×25 $\$1.00 - \$.35$

10. Tell about problems you had at home when you needed to add; to subtract; to multiply; to divide.

Pounds and ounces

1. Bob has a new pup. He is weighing it on his mother's kitchen scales. How many pounds does it weigh?

2. Bob weighs his dog every week. He can weigh it on these scales until it grows to weigh __?__ pounds.

3. Where does the arrow point when there is one pound on the scales? when there are 3 pounds? 4 pounds? ½ pound? 5 pounds?

4. Jane is weighing her smallest doll. It weighs *one ounce*. Where does the arrow point when 2 ounces are on the scales? 3 ounces? 4 ounces? 6? 8?

5. Count the small black marks on the scales to find how many ounces there are in ½ pound.

6. If you know there are 8 ounces in ½ lb., how many ounces are there in a whole pound?

 *16 ounces (oz.) = 1 pound (lb.)*

7. What does oz. stand for? lb.?

8. Find the cost of ½ lb. of candy at 60¢ a lb.; at 80¢ a lb.

1. How much will six 3-cent stamps cost?

2. Don caught 39 tadpoles. He said ⅓ of them turned into frogs. How many turned into frogs?

3. Sally found 17 four-leaf clovers in the front yard last year. She found 9 there this year. How many did she find in all?

4. Find the cost of caps for the nine members of a baseball team at $.35 each.

5. A city license for Jane's dog costs $1.50. A collar for the dog costs $1.59. How much does Jane have to pay for both license and collar?

6. Jane, Dick, and Don each gave the organ-grinder's monkey a nickel. How much did they give in all?

7. How much will play shoes for the 4 children in Dick's family cost at $3.25 a pair?

8. When Jane got her kitten it weighed only 13 ounces. Now it weighs a pound. It has gained __?__ ounces.

9. Sally can get a box of 3 sticks of chalk for one cent. How many cents' worth of chalk will she need to buy if she wants to have 24 sticks of chalk? Draw a picture of this problem.

10. Carl got a Build-Your-Own Airplane Kit. The kit cost $4.98. From the kit Carl made 5 planes. Would you estimate that each plane cost Carl about $.50, about $1.00, or about $2.00?

Write your score on your Problem Test Record.

Add and check:

1.	29	2.	629	3.	175	4.	$5.05
	64		485 (162–163)		309		7.96
	70				46		.89
	85 (129)				862 (200)		3.40 (200)

Subtract and check:

5.	43	6.	952	7.	$8.37	8.	$9.00
	29 (131–135)		898 (195)		5.89 (195)		2.62 (198–199)

Multiply:

9.	22	10.	31	11.	52	12.	$.40
	4 (262)		9 (265)		8 (266–267)		5 (284)

13.	286	14.	$3.92	15.	602	16.	205
	3 (282)		2 (282)		3 (285)		6 (285)

Divide:

1. $3\overline{)69}$ (298) 2. $2\overline{)187}$ (274) 3. $3\overline{)97}$ (298) 4. $5\overline{)350}$ (273)

5. What will be the date a year from today? (117)

6. A sign at the beach said, "Temperature of water today, 78°." Bobby looked at the thermometer hanging on the wall of the bathhouse. It read 82°. He said, "The water is _?_ degrees cooler today than the air." (131–135)

7. How many lollipops are 6 dozen lollipops? (266–267)

Work carefully.   Check your answers.

1. $2.35
    × 6   *Bubby*

2. 802
    × 3

3. 506
    × 3

4. 2)68

5. 3)278

6. ⅓ of 246 = __?__

7. Bobby needs 15 feet of rope to tie his rowboat to the wharf.   If he buys a piece of rope marked "Length, 5 yards," will it be long enough?

8. Nan's mother sent her to buy a pound of cheese at the store.   The cheese was cut in pieces and wrapped in wax paper.   The weight of each piece was marked on it.

Nan didn't find a piece marked 1 lb., but she found one marked 17 oz. and one marked 20 oz.   Which should she buy?

9. Three boys plan to share the cost of painting a hut. How much should each boy pay if the paint costs 69¢?

10. Judy bought a box of Pup Crackers for Trixie.   There are 3 layers of crackers in the box.   There are 16 crackers in each layer.   How many crackers are there in the box?

Just for fun

● Take one look and tell the answer: $5 \times 3 \times 2 \times 1 \times 0 =$ __?__.

● John says, "I can write 6 three-figure numbers with the figures 1, 2, and 3, and not use the same figure twice in any number."   Can you?

● Mary needs to measure out 2 quarts of milk. She has no quart measure, but she found this measuring tin which holds a gallon.   How can she use it to measure out the milk she needs?

308

The addition facts with answers

1 1 — 2	2 1 — 3	3 1 — 4	4 1 — 5	5 1 — 6	6 1 — 7	7 1 — 8	8 1 — 9	9 1 — 10
1 2 — 3	2 2 — 4	3 2 — 5	4 2 — 6	5 2 — 7	6 2 — 8	7 2 — 9	8 2 — 10	9 2 — 11
1 3 — 4	2 3 — 5	3 3 — 6	4 3 — 7	5 3 — 8	6 3 — 9	7 3 — 10	8 3 — 11	9 3 — 12
1 4 — 5	2 4 — 6	3 4 — 7	4 4 — 8	5 4 — 9	6 4 — 10	7 4 — 11	8 4 — 12	9 4 — 13
1 5 — 6	2 5 — 7	3 5 — 8	4 5 — 9	5 5 — 10	6 5 — 11	7 5 — 12	8 5 — 13	9 5 — 14
1 6 — 7	2 6 — 8	3 6 — 9	4 6 — 10	5 6 — 11	6 6 — 12	7 6 — 13	8 6 — 14	9 6 — 15
1 7 — 8	2 7 — 9	3 7 — 10	4 7 — 11	5 7 — 12	6 7 — 13	7 7 — 14	8 7 — 15	9 7 — 16
1 8 — 9	2 8 — 10	3 8 — 11	4 8 — 12	5 8 — 13	6 8 — 14	7 8 — 15	8 8 — 16	9 8 — 17
1 9 — 10	2 9 — 11	3 9 — 12	4 9 — 13	5 9 — 14	6 9 — 15	7 9 — 16	8 9 — 17	9 9 — 18

The subtraction facts with answers

2 1 ― 1	3 1 ― 2	4 1 ― 3	5 1 ― 4	6 1 ― 5	7 1 ― 6	8 1 ― 7	9 1 ― 8	10 1 ― 9
3 2 ― 1	4 2 ― 2	5 2 ― 3	6 2 ― 4	7 2 ― 5	8 2 ― 6	9 2 ― 7	10 2 ― 8	11 2 ― 9
4 3 ― 1	5 3 ― 2	6 3 ― 3	7 3 ― 4	8 3 ― 5	9 3 ― 6	10 3 ― 7	11 3 ― 8	12 3 ― 9
5 4 ― 1	6 4 ― 2	7 4 ― 3	8 4 ― 4	9 4 ― 5	10 4 ― 6	11 4 ― 7	12 4 ― 8	13 4 ― 9
6 5 ― 1	7 5 ― 2	8 5 ― 3	9 5 ― 4	10 5 ― 5	11 5 ― 6	12 5 ― 7	13 5 ― 8	14 5 ― 9
7 6 ― 1	8 6 ― 2	9 6 ― 3	10 6 ― 4	11 6 ― 5	12 6 ― 6	13 6 ― 7	14 6 ― 8	15 6 ― 9
8 7 ― 1	9 7 ― 2	10 7 ― 3	11 7 ― 4	12 7 ― 5	13 7 ― 6	14 7 ― 7	15 7 ― 8	16 7 ― 9
9 8 ― 1	10 8 ― 2	11 8 ― 3	12 8 ― 4	13 8 ― 5	14 8 ― 6	15 8 ― 7	16 8 ― 8	17 8 ― 9
10 9 ― 1	11 9 ― 2	12 9 ― 3	13 9 ― 4	14 9 ― 5	15 9 ― 6	16 9 ― 7	17 9 ― 8	18 9 ― 9

To the teacher

This series is planned to develop progressively the important concepts, relationships, and computational skills needed in arithmetic. In doing this, the books of the series organize the learning into a meaningful system of related ideas; they make maximum use of children's needs for number; and they provide the practice, self-diagnosis, and remedial work required to make learning permanent. The books are the outcome of years of research and classroom experience.

For the textbook for each grade there is available a *Teacher's Guide*. The *Guide* contains suggestions for making the learning of arithmetic meaningful and interesting. It provides helps for utilizing the textbook material most effectively. It also gives a concise statement of the authors' philosophy and psychology of teaching the subject.

NOTE 1 (*Page 14*). Have each child cut out a slip of paper 5 inches long and $2\frac{1}{2}$ inches wide. Then have him place it over the slip shown covering the bead frame in the drawing on page 15, and trace the top line. This will show him how to cut out the upper left corner of the slip. When the corner piece is cut out, his slip is ready for use.

NOTE 2 (*Page 20*). In using the numbered circles to find the sum of 6 and 3, for example, have the pupil put his finger on circle 6, and count forward 3 more circles. This gives him a convenient visual method of discovering addition facts.

NOTE 3 (*Page 23*). Sets of Help-Yourself Cards in the four fundamentals, called *Modern-School Individual Number Cards*, may be purchased from World Book Company.

NOTE 4 (*Pages 30 and 31*). On these pages the pupil is introduced to a simple technique of discovering the answers to subtraction facts. He uses a group of circles to represent the minuend. He covers the group that is being taken away, and discovers by counting the "number remaining." On page 33 he uses this same technique to discover by counting "how many more are needed." On page 35 he again uses the same technique to find the "difference between two numbers." This one technique, applied to each of these three concepts of subtraction is economical, concrete, and meaningful.

NOTE 5 (*Page 38*). If the pupils use a sheet of colored paper for their Problem Test Record, they will be able to find it easily in their folder when they wish to record their test score.

NOTE 6 (*Pages 77–237–279*). These "Be Your Own Teacher" pages are included as challenges to superior pupils. The solutions require ingenuity and understanding of the number system, rather than recall of learnings previously presented and practiced. Pupils who work on the problems should be given a chance to explain to each other the various methods they used in obtaining their answers. *The teacher should never tell the pupils how to do these problems, introduce conventional methods of solution, or assign the problems for homework.*

Games with numbers
   addition, 54, 98, 107, 109, 222
   counting, 40–41
   division, 296
   Just for fun, 37, 39, 154, 275, **308**
   riddles, 39, 113, 308
   subtraction, 107, 109
Geometric figures, 10
Grouping and regrouping tens and ones, 126–130, 131–136

Halves, 11–12, 252–253, 269–272
Helping Numbers, 227–229, 250–251, 296
Help-Yourself Cards, how to make, 23

Individual differences, provisions for
   addition, 22, 76, 80, 91, 92, 94, 102, 105, 106, 108, 110
   Be your own teacher, 77, 237, 279
   division, 216, 231, 248, 293, 302
   Help-Yourself Cards, 22, 23, 37, 76, 80, 91, 92, 94, 102, 105, 106, 108, 110, 111, 208, 216, 240, 248, 289, 293
   multiplication, 208, 240, 289, 301
   problem solving, 77, 182–183, 237, 239
   Problem Test Record, 38
   Self-Help Tests, 59, 115, 147, 177, 202, 256, 307
   subtraction, 37, 76, 80, 91, 92, 94, 102, 105, 106, 108, 111

Just for fun, 37, 39, 154, 275, 308

Length, measures of, 24–25
Liquid measures, 28–29, 178–179

Measurement
   dozen, 79
   estimating, 171
   inch, foot, yard, 25
   length, 24–25, 34
   liquid, 28–29, 178–179
   ounce, pound, 305
   pint, quart, gallon, 28–29, 178–179
   temperature, 62–63, 145
   time, 2–3, 26–27, 82–83
   weight, 305
Mental arithmetic, 120, 138–139, 141, 171, 244, 262, 263, 264, 267, 270, 271, 272, 276–277, 283, 285, 299, 304
Minus sign, 30
Money
   adding, 18, 43–45, 55–56, 61, 64–65, 75, 126–127, 130, 148, 151, 156, 158, 160, 163–164, 169
   cents point, 73

Money — *Continued*
   change, 64, 173, 175–176
   coins, 4, 8, 18, 61, 64, 75, 90, **151**
   multiplying, 261–262, 264–267, 280–283
   reading, 4, 73, 86
   subtracting, 30, 33, 43, 47, 50–51, 64, 75, 90, 93, 101, 131–132, 136, 152, 160, 169, 175–176, 191, 193, 194–196, 198–199
   using dimes, 172–176
   using nickels, 186–189
   writing, 73, 86, 151, 169
Months, names of, 26–27
Multiplication
   explanation of, 203–204, 206, 208, 261–267, 280–282, 285, 286–288
   facts: of fives, 204–208; of twos, 238–241; of threes, 286–290
   money, 261–262, 264–267, 280–283
   practice, 217, 278, 297
   readiness for, 124, 168, 172–173, 186–187, 234–235
   sign, 206
   two-place numbers, 261–267
   with carrying, 266–267
   without carrying, 261–265
   zero, 263–264, 284–285

Now is the time to test yourself, 39, 67, 125, 154, 190, 233, 275, 308
Number chart, 7, 16, 42
Numbers
   even and odd, 250
   meaning of: two-place, 14–18; zero, 54; three-place, 69–72, 184, 222; four-place, 223–224
   reading, 16–17, 20, 70, 72–73, 184, 224
   Roman, 66
   writing, 18, 69–70, 72, 73, 184, 223–224

Odd numbers, 250–251

Place value, 14–18, 54, 69–72, 184, 222, 223–224
Plus sign, 19
Practice pages, 22, 37, 81, 92, 122, 135, 142, 161, 193, 200, 217, 218, 225, 244, 260, 270, 278, 297
Problems, 36, 77, 103, 150, 166, 182, 193, 217, 241, 254, 279, 295, 304
Problem-solving helps, 34–35, 36, 118, 138–139, 141, 143, 150, 168, 171, 182–183, 207, 213, 217, 241, 249, 276–277, 303, 304

In Appreciation

The authors are indebted to numerous teachers and elementary school pupils, and to Miss Ruth I. Baldwin. They also wish to thank Miss Monica M. Hoye for her valuable criticisms and helpful suggestions.